C-1298   CAREER EXAMINATION SERIES

This is your
PASSBOOK for...

Groundskeeper

Test Preparation Study Guide
Questions & Answers

COPYRIGHT NOTICE

This book is SOLELY intended for, is sold ONLY to, and its use is RESTRICTED to individual, bona fide applicants or candidates who qualify by virtue of having seriously filed applications for appropriate license, certificate, professional and/or promotional advancement, higher school matriculation, scholarship, or other legitimate requirements of education and/or governmental authorities.

This book is NOT intended for use, class instruction, tutoring, training, duplication, copying, reprinting, excerption, or adaptation, etc., by:

1) Other publishers
2) Proprietors and/or Instructors of "Coaching" and/or Preparatory Courses
3) Personnel and/or Training Divisions of commercial, industrial, and governmental organizations
4) Schools, colleges, or universities and/or their departments and staffs, including teachers and other personnel
5) Testing Agencies or Bureaus
6) Study groups which seek by the purchase of a single volume to copy and/or duplicate and/or adapt this material for use by the group as a whole without having purchased individual volumes for each of the members of the group
7) Et al.

Such persons would be in violation of appropriate Federal and State statutes.

PROVISION OF LICENSING AGREEMENTS – Recognized educational, commercial, industrial, and governmental institutions and organizations, and others legitimately engaged in educational pursuits, including training, testing, and measurement activities, may address request for a licensing agreement to the copyright owners, who will determine whether, and under what conditions, including fees and charges, the materials in this book may be used them. In other words, a licensing facility exists for the legitimate use of the material in this book on other than an individual basis. However, it is asseverated and affirmed here that the material in this book CANNOT be used without the receipt of the express permission of such a licensing agreement from the Publishers. Inquiries re licensing should be addressed to the company, attention rights and permissions department.

All rights reserved, including the right of reproduction in whole or in part, in any form or by any means, electronic or mechanical, including photocopying, recording, or by any information storage and retrieval system, without permission in writing from the Publisher.

Copyright © 2024 by
National Learning Corporation

212 Michael Drive, Syosset, NY 11791
(516) 921-8888 • www.passbooks.com
E-mail: info@passbooks.com

PUBLISHED IN THE UNITED STATES OF AMERICA

PASSBOOK® SERIES

THE *PASSBOOK® SERIES* has been created to prepare applicants and candidates for the ultimate academic battlefield – the examination room.

At some time in our lives, each and every one of us may be required to take an examination – for validation, matriculation, admission, qualification, registration, certification, or licensure.

Based on the assumption that every applicant or candidate has met the basic formal educational standards, has taken the required number of courses, and read the necessary texts, the *PASSBOOK® SERIES* furnishes the one special preparation which may assure passing with confidence, instead of failing with insecurity. Examination questions – together with answers – are furnished as the basic vehicle for study so that the mysteries of the examination and its compounding difficulties may be eliminated or diminished by a sure method.

This book is meant to help you pass your examination provided that you qualify and are serious in your objective.

The entire field is reviewed through the huge store of content information which is succinctly presented through a provocative and challenging approach – the question-and-answer method.

A climate of success is established by furnishing the correct answers at the end of each test.

You soon learn to recognize types of questions, forms of questions, and patterns of questioning. You may even begin to anticipate expected outcomes.

You perceive that many questions are repeated or adapted so that you can gain acute insights, which may enable you to score many sure points.

You learn how to confront new questions, or types of questions, and to attack them confidently and work out the correct answers.

You note objectives and emphases, and recognize pitfalls and dangers, so that you may make positive educational adjustments.

Moreover, you are kept fully informed in relation to new concepts, methods, practices, and directions in the field.

You discover that you are actually taking the examination all the time: you are preparing for the examination by "taking" an examination, not by reading extraneous and/or supererogatory textbooks.

In short, this PASSBOOK®, used directedly, should be an important factor in helping you to pass your test.

GROUNDSKEEPER

DUTIES
Maintains, fertilizes and seeds lawns; mows, trims and rakes grass and athletic areas; responsible for snow removal, sanding and salting activities for all walks, driveways and parking areas; supervises the proper use of recreational facilities; performs related duties.

SUBJECT OF EXAMINATION
The written test will be designed to test for knowledge, skills, and or abilities in such areas as:
1. Grounds maintenance including turf, trees and shrubs;
2. Installation and maintenance of recreation areas including playing fields;
3. Tools and equipment and their uses; and
4. Preparing written material.

HOW TO TAKE A TEST

I. YOU MUST PASS AN EXAMINATION

A. WHAT EVERY CANDIDATE SHOULD KNOW

Examination applicants often ask us for help in preparing for the written test. What can I study in advance? What kinds of questions will be asked? How will the test be given? How will the papers be graded?

As an applicant for a civil service examination, you may be wondering about some of these things. Our purpose here is to suggest effective methods of advance study and to describe civil service examinations.

Your chances for success on this examination can be increased if you know how to prepare. Those "pre-examination jitters" can be reduced if you know what to expect. You can even experience an adventure in good citizenship if you know why civil service exams are given.

B. WHY ARE CIVIL SERVICE EXAMINATIONS GIVEN?

Civil service examinations are important to you in two ways. As a citizen, you want public jobs filled by employees who know how to do their work. As a job seeker, you want a fair chance to compete for that job on an equal footing with other candidates. The best-known means of accomplishing this two-fold goal is the competitive examination.

Exams are widely publicized throughout the nation. They may be administered for jobs in federal, state, city, municipal, town or village governments or agencies.

Any citizen may apply, with some limitations, such as the age or residence of applicants. Your experience and education may be reviewed to see whether you meet the requirements for the particular examination. When these requirements exist, they are reasonable and applied consistently to all applicants. Thus, a competitive examination may cause you some uneasiness now, but it is your privilege and safeguard.

C. HOW ARE CIVIL SERVICE EXAMS DEVELOPED?

Examinations are carefully written by trained technicians who are specialists in the field known as "psychological measurement," in consultation with recognized authorities in the field of work that the test will cover. These experts recommend the subject matter areas or skills to be tested; only those knowledges or skills important to your success on the job are included. The most reliable books and source materials available are used as references. Together, the experts and technicians judge the difficulty level of the questions.

Test technicians know how to phrase questions so that the problem is clearly stated. Their ethics do not permit "trick" or "catch" questions. Questions may have been tried out on sample groups, or subjected to statistical analysis, to determine their usefulness.

Written tests are often used in combination with performance tests, ratings of training and experience, and oral interviews. All of these measures combine to form the best-known means of finding the right person for the right job.

II. HOW TO PASS THE WRITTEN TEST

A. NATURE OF THE EXAMINATION

To prepare intelligently for civil service examinations, you should know how they differ from school examinations you have taken. In school you were assigned certain definite pages to read or subjects to cover. The examination questions were quite detailed and usually emphasized memory. Civil service exams, on the other hand, try to discover your present ability to perform the duties of a position, plus your potentiality to learn these duties. In other words, a civil service exam attempts to predict how successful you will be. Questions cover such a broad area that they cannot be as minute and detailed as school exam questions.

In the public service similar kinds of work, or positions, are grouped together in one "class." This process is known as *position-classification*. All the positions in a class are paid according to the salary range for that class. One class title covers all of these positions, and they are all tested by the same examination.

B. FOUR BASIC STEPS

1) Study the announcement

How, then, can you know what subjects to study? Our best answer is: "Learn as much as possible about the class of positions for which you've applied." The exam will test the knowledge, skills and abilities needed to do the work.

Your most valuable source of information about the position you want is the official exam announcement. This announcement lists the training and experience qualifications. Check these standards and apply only if you come reasonably close to meeting them.

The brief description of the position in the examination announcement offers some clues to the subjects which will be tested. Think about the job itself. Review the duties in your mind. Can you perform them, or are there some in which you are rusty? Fill in the blank spots in your preparation.

Many jurisdictions preview the written test in the exam announcement by including a section called "Knowledge and Abilities Required," "Scope of the Examination," or some similar heading. Here you will find out specifically what fields will be tested.

2) Review your own background

Once you learn in general what the position is all about, and what you need to know to do the work, ask yourself which subjects you already know fairly well and which need improvement. You may wonder whether to concentrate on improving your strong areas or on building some background in your fields of weakness. When the announcement has specified "some knowledge" or "considerable knowledge," or has used adjectives like "beginning principles of…" or "advanced … methods," you can get a clue as to the number and difficulty of questions to be asked in any given field. More questions, and hence broader coverage, would be included for those subjects which are more important in the work. Now weigh your strengths and weaknesses against the job requirements and prepare accordingly.

3) Determine the level of the position

Another way to tell how intensively you should prepare is to understand the level of the job for which you are applying. Is it the entering level? In other words, is this the position in which beginners in a field of work are hired? Or is it an intermediate or advanced level? Sometimes this is indicated by such words as "Junior" or "Senior" in the class title. Other jurisdictions use Roman numerals to designate the level – Clerk I, Clerk II, for example. The word "Supervisor" sometimes appears in the title. If the level is not indicated by the title, check the description of duties. Will you be working under very close supervision, or will you have responsibility for independent decisions in this work?

4) Choose appropriate study materials

Now that you know the subjects to be examined and the relative amount of each subject to be covered, you can choose suitable study materials. For beginning level jobs, or even advanced ones, if you have a pronounced weakness in some aspect of your training, read a modern, standard textbook in that field. Be sure it is up to date and has general coverage. Such books are normally available at your library, and the librarian will be glad to help you locate one. For entry-level positions, questions of appropriate difficulty are chosen – neither highly advanced questions, nor those too simple. Such questions require careful thought but not advanced training.

If the position for which you are applying is technical or advanced, you will read more advanced, specialized material. If you are already familiar with the basic principles of your field, elementary textbooks would waste your time. Concentrate on advanced textbooks and technical periodicals. Think through the concepts and review difficult problems in your field.

These are all general sources. You can get more ideas on your own initiative, following these leads. For example, training manuals and publications of the government agency which employs workers in your field can be useful, particularly for technical and professional positions. A letter or visit to the government department involved may result in more specific study suggestions, and certainly will provide you with a more definite idea of the exact nature of the position you are seeking.

III. KINDS OF TESTS

Tests are used for purposes other than measuring knowledge and ability to perform specified duties. For some positions, it is equally important to test ability to make adjustments to new situations or to profit from training. In others, basic mental abilities not dependent on information are essential. Questions which test these things may not appear as pertinent to the duties of the position as those which test for knowledge and information. Yet they are often highly important parts of a fair examination. For very general questions, it is almost impossible to help you direct your study efforts. What we can do is to point out some of the more common of these general abilities needed in public service positions and describe some typical questions.

1) General information

Broad, general information has been found useful for predicting job success in some kinds of work. This is tested in a variety of ways, from vocabulary lists to questions about current events. Basic background in some field of work, such as sociology or economics, may be sampled in a group of questions. Often these are principles which have become familiar to most persons through exposure rather than through formal training. It is difficult to advise you how to study for these questions; being alert to the world around you is our best suggestion.

2) Verbal ability

An example of an ability needed in many positions is verbal or language ability. Verbal ability is, in brief, the ability to use and understand words. Vocabulary and grammar tests are typical measures of this ability. Reading comprehension or paragraph interpretation questions are common in many kinds of civil service tests. You are given a paragraph of written material and asked to find its central meaning.

3) Numerical ability

Number skills can be tested by the familiar arithmetic problem, by checking paired lists of numbers to see which are alike and which are different, or by interpreting charts and graphs. In the latter test, a graph may be printed in the test booklet which you are asked to use as the basis for answering questions.

4) Observation

A popular test for law-enforcement positions is the observation test. A picture is shown to you for several minutes, then taken away. Questions about the picture test your ability to observe both details and larger elements.

5) Following directions

In many positions in the public service, the employee must be able to carry out written instructions dependably and accurately. You may be given a chart with several columns, each column listing a variety of information. The questions require you to carry out directions involving the information given in the chart.

6) Skills and aptitudes

Performance tests effectively measure some manual skills and aptitudes. When the skill is one in which you are trained, such as typing or shorthand, you can practice. These tests are often very much like those given in business school or high school courses. For many of the other skills and aptitudes, however, no short-time preparation can be made. Skills and abilities natural to you or that you have developed throughout your lifetime are being tested.

Many of the general questions just described provide all the data needed to answer the questions and ask you to use your reasoning ability to find the answers. Your best preparation for these tests, as well as for tests of facts and ideas, is to be at your physical and mental best. You, no doubt, have your own methods of getting into an exam-taking mood and keeping "in shape." The next section lists some ideas on this subject.

IV. KINDS OF QUESTIONS

Only rarely is the "essay" question, which you answer in narrative form, used in civil service tests. Civil service tests are usually of the short-answer type. Full instructions for answering these questions will be given to you at the examination. But in case this is your first experience with short-answer questions and separate answer sheets, here is what you need to know:

1) Multiple-choice Questions

Most popular of the short-answer questions is the "multiple choice" or "best answer" question. It can be used, for example, to test for factual knowledge, ability to solve problems or judgment in meeting situations found at work.

A multiple-choice question is normally one of three types—
- It can begin with an incomplete statement followed by several possible endings. You are to find the one ending which *best* completes the statement, although some of the others may not be entirely wrong.
- It can also be a complete statement in the form of a question which is answered by choosing one of the statements listed.

- It can be in the form of a problem – again you select the best answer.

Here is an example of a multiple-choice question with a discussion which should give you some clues as to the method for choosing the right answer:

When an employee has a complaint about his assignment, the action which will *best* help him overcome his difficulty is to
- A. discuss his difficulty with his coworkers
- B. take the problem to the head of the organization
- C. take the problem to the person who gave him the assignment
- D. say nothing to anyone about his complaint

In answering this question, you should study each of the choices to find which is best. Consider choice "A" – Certainly an employee may discuss his complaint with fellow employees, but no change or improvement can result, and the complaint remains unresolved. Choice "B" is a poor choice since the head of the organization probably does not know what assignment you have been given, and taking your problem to him is known as "going over the head" of the supervisor. The supervisor, or person who made the assignment, is the person who can clarify it or correct any injustice. Choice "C" is, therefore, correct. To say nothing, as in choice "D," is unwise. Supervisors have and interest in knowing the problems employees are facing, and the employee is seeking a solution to his problem.

2) True/False Questions

The "true/false" or "right/wrong" form of question is sometimes used. Here a complete statement is given. Your job is to decide whether the statement is right or wrong.

SAMPLE: A roaming cell-phone call to a nearby city costs less than a non-roaming call to a distant city.

This statement is wrong, or false, since roaming calls are more expensive.

This is not a complete list of all possible question forms, although most of the others are variations of these common types. You will always get complete directions for answering questions. Be sure you understand *how* to mark your answers – ask questions until you do.

V. RECORDING YOUR ANSWERS

Computer terminals are used more and more today for many different kinds of exams.
For an examination with very few applicants, you may be told to record your answers in the test booklet itself. Separate answer sheets are much more common. If this separate answer sheet is to be scored by machine – and this is often the case – it is highly important that you mark your answers correctly in order to get credit.
An electronic scoring machine is often used in civil service offices because of the speed with which papers can be scored. Machine-scored answer sheets must be marked with a pencil, which will be given to you. This pencil has a high graphite content which responds to the electronic scoring machine. As a matter of fact, stray dots may register as answers, so do not let your pencil rest on the answer sheet while you are pondering the correct answer. Also, if your pencil lead breaks or is otherwise defective, ask for another.

Since the answer sheet will be dropped in a slot in the scoring machine, be careful not to bend the corners or get the paper crumpled.

The answer sheet normally has five vertical columns of numbers, with 30 numbers to a column. These numbers correspond to the question numbers in your test booklet. After each number, going across the page are four or five pairs of dotted lines. These short dotted lines have small letters or numbers above them. The first two pairs may also have a "T" or "F" above the letters. This indicates that the first two pairs only are to be used if the questions are of the true-false type. If the questions are multiple choice, disregard the "T" and "F" and pay attention only to the small letters or numbers.

Answer your questions in the manner of the sample that follows:

32. The largest city in the United States is
    A. Washington, D.C.
    B. New York City
    C. Chicago
    D. Detroit
    E. San Francisco

1) Choose the answer you think is best. (New York City is the largest, so "B" is correct.)
2) Find the row of dotted lines numbered the same as the question you are answering. (Find row number 32)
3) Find the pair of dotted lines corresponding to the answer. (Find the pair of lines under the mark "B.")
4) Make a solid black mark between the dotted lines.

VI. BEFORE THE TEST

Common sense will help you find procedures to follow to get ready for an examination. Too many of us, however, overlook these sensible measures. Indeed, nervousness and fatigue have been found to be the most serious reasons why applicants fail to do their best on civil service tests. Here is a list of reminders:

- Begin your preparation early – Don't wait until the last minute to go scurrying around for books and materials or to find out what the position is all about.
- Prepare continuously – An hour a night for a week is better than an all-night cram session. This has been definitely established. What is more, a night a week for a month will return better dividends than crowding your study into a shorter period of time.
- Locate the place of the exam – You have been sent a notice telling you when and where to report for the examination. If the location is in a different town or otherwise unfamiliar to you, it would be well to inquire the best route and learn something about the building.
- Relax the night before the test – Allow your mind to rest. Do not study at all that night. Plan some mild recreation or diversion; then go to bed early and get a good night's sleep.
- Get up early enough to make a leisurely trip to the place for the test – This way unforeseen events, traffic snarls, unfamiliar buildings, etc. will not upset you.
- Dress comfortably – A written test is not a fashion show. You will be known by number and not by name, so wear something comfortable.

- Leave excess paraphernalia at home – Shopping bags and odd bundles will get in your way. You need bring only the items mentioned in the official notice you received; usually everything you need is provided. Do not bring reference books to the exam. They will only confuse those last minutes and be taken away from you when in the test room.
- Arrive somewhat ahead of time – If because of transportation schedules you must get there very early, bring a newspaper or magazine to take your mind off yourself while waiting.
- Locate the examination room – When you have found the proper room, you will be directed to the seat or part of the room where you will sit. Sometimes you are given a sheet of instructions to read while you are waiting. Do not fill out any forms until you are told to do so; just read them and be prepared.
- Relax and prepare to listen to the instructions
- If you have any physical problem that may keep you from doing your best, be sure to tell the test administrator. If you are sick or in poor health, you really cannot do your best on the exam. You can come back and take the test some other time.

VII. AT THE TEST

The day of the test is here and you have the test booklet in your hand. The temptation to get going is very strong. Caution! There is more to success than knowing the right answers. You must know how to identify your papers and understand variations in the type of short-answer question used in this particular examination. Follow these suggestions for maximum results from your efforts:

1) Cooperate with the monitor

The test administrator has a duty to create a situation in which you can be as much at ease as possible. He will give instructions, tell you when to begin, check to see that you are marking your answer sheet correctly, and so on. He is not there to guard you, although he will see that your competitors do not take unfair advantage. He wants to help you do your best.

2) Listen to all instructions

Don't jump the gun! Wait until you understand all directions. In most civil service tests you get more time than you need to answer the questions. So don't be in a hurry. Read each word of instructions until you clearly understand the meaning. Study the examples, listen to all announcements and follow directions. Ask questions if you do not understand what to do.

3) Identify your papers

Civil service exams are usually identified by number only. You will be assigned a number; you must not put your name on your test papers. Be sure to copy your number correctly. Since more than one exam may be given, copy your exact examination title.

4) Plan your time

Unless you are told that a test is a "speed" or "rate of work" test, speed itself is usually not important. Time enough to answer all the questions will be provided, but this does not mean that you have all day. An overall time limit has been set. Divide the total time (in minutes) by the number of questions to determine the approximate time you have for each question.

5) Do not linger over difficult questions

If you come across a difficult question, mark it with a paper clip (useful to have along) and come back to it when you have been through the booklet. One caution if you do this – be sure to skip a number on your answer sheet as well. Check often to be sure that you have not lost your place and that you are marking in the row numbered the same as the question you are answering.

6) Read the questions

Be sure you know what the question asks! Many capable people are unsuccessful because they failed to *read* the questions correctly.

7) Answer all questions

Unless you have been instructed that a penalty will be deducted for incorrect answers, it is better to guess than to omit a question.

8) Speed tests

It is often better NOT to guess on speed tests. It has been found that on timed tests people are tempted to spend the last few seconds before time is called in marking answers at random – without even reading them – in the hope of picking up a few extra points. To discourage this practice, the instructions may warn you that your score will be "corrected" for guessing. That is, a penalty will be applied. The incorrect answers will be deducted from the correct ones, or some other penalty formula will be used.

9) Review your answers

If you finish before time is called, go back to the questions you guessed or omitted to give them further thought. Review other answers if you have time.

10) Return your test materials

If you are ready to leave before others have finished or time is called, take ALL your materials to the monitor and leave quietly. Never take any test material with you. The monitor can discover whose papers are not complete, and taking a test booklet may be grounds for disqualification.

VIII. EXAMINATION TECHNIQUES

1) Read the general instructions carefully. These are usually printed on the first page of the exam booklet. As a rule, these instructions refer to the timing of the examination; the fact that you should not start work until the signal and must stop work at a signal, etc. If there are any *special* instructions, such as a choice of questions to be answered, make sure that you note this instruction carefully.

2) When you are ready to start work on the examination, that is as soon as the signal has been given, read the instructions to each question booklet, underline any key words or phrases, such as *least, best, outline, describe* and the like. In this way you will tend to answer as requested rather than discover on reviewing your paper that you *listed without describing*, that you selected the *worst* choice rather than the *best* choice, etc.

3) If the examination is of the objective or multiple-choice type – that is, each question will also give a series of possible answers: A, B, C or D, and you are called upon to select the best answer and write the letter next to that answer on your answer paper – it is advisable to start answering each question in turn. There may be anywhere from 50 to 100 such questions in the three or four hours allotted and you can see how much time would be taken if you read through all the questions before beginning to answer any. Furthermore, if you come across a question or group of questions which you know would be difficult to answer, it would undoubtedly affect your handling of all the other questions.

4) If the examination is of the essay type and contains but a few questions, it is a moot point as to whether you should read all the questions before starting to answer any one. Of course, if you are given a choice – say five out of seven and the like – then it is essential to read all the questions so you can eliminate the two that are most difficult. If, however, you are asked to answer all the questions, there may be danger in trying to answer the easiest one first because you may find that you will spend too much time on it. The best technique is to answer the first question, then proceed to the second, etc.

5) Time your answers. Before the exam begins, write down the time it started, then add the time allowed for the examination and write down the time it must be completed, then divide the time available somewhat as follows:
   - If 3-1/2 hours are allowed, that would be 210 minutes. If you have 80 objective-type questions, that would be an average of 2-1/2 minutes per question. Allow yourself no more than 2 minutes per question, or a total of 160 minutes, which will permit about 50 minutes to review.
   - If for the time allotment of 210 minutes there are 7 essay questions to answer, that would average about 30 minutes a question. Give yourself only 25 minutes per question so that you have about 35 minutes to review.

6) The most important instruction is to *read each question* and make sure you know what is wanted. The second most important instruction is to *time yourself properly* so that you answer every question. The third most important instruction is to *answer every question*. Guess if you have to but include something for each question. Remember that you will receive no credit for a blank and will probably receive some credit if you write something in answer to an essay question. If you guess a letter – say "B" for a multiple-choice question – you may have guessed right. If you leave a blank as an answer to a multiple-choice question, the examiners may respect your feelings but it will not add a point to your score. Some exams may penalize you for wrong answers, so in such cases *only*, you may not want to guess unless you have some basis for your answer.

7) Suggestions
   a. Objective-type questions
      1. Examine the question booklet for proper sequence of pages and questions
      2. Read all instructions carefully
      3. Skip any question which seems too difficult; return to it after all other questions have been answered
      4. Apportion your time properly; do not spend too much time on any single question or group of questions

5. Note and underline key words – *all, most, fewest, least, best, worst, same, opposite,* etc.
6. Pay particular attention to negatives
7. Note unusual option, e.g., unduly long, short, complex, different or similar in content to the body of the question
8. Observe the use of "hedging" words – *probably, may, most likely,* etc.
9. Make sure that your answer is put next to the same number as the question
10. Do not second-guess unless you have good reason to believe the second answer is definitely more correct
11. Cross out original answer if you decide another answer is more accurate; do not erase until you are ready to hand your paper in
12. Answer all questions; guess unless instructed otherwise
13. Leave time for review

   b. Essay questions
1. Read each question carefully
2. Determine exactly what is wanted. Underline key words or phrases.
3. Decide on outline or paragraph answer
4. Include many different points and elements unless asked to develop any one or two points or elements
5. Show impartiality by giving pros and cons unless directed to select one side only
6. Make and write down any assumptions you find necessary to answer the questions
7. Watch your English, grammar, punctuation and choice of words
8. Time your answers; don't crowd material

8) Answering the essay question

Most essay questions can be answered by framing the specific response around several key words or ideas. Here are a few such key words or ideas:

M's: manpower, materials, methods, money, management
P's: purpose, program, policy, plan, procedure, practice, problems, pitfalls, personnel, public relations

   a. Six basic steps in handling problems:
1. Preliminary plan and background development
2. Collect information, data and facts
3. Analyze and interpret information, data and facts
4. Analyze and develop solutions as well as make recommendations
5. Prepare report and sell recommendations
6. Install recommendations and follow up effectiveness

   b. Pitfalls to avoid
1. *Taking things for granted* – A statement of the situation does not necessarily imply that each of the elements is necessarily true; for example, a complaint may be invalid and biased so that all that can be taken for granted is that a complaint has been registered

2. *Considering only one side of a situation* – Wherever possible, indicate several alternatives and then point out the reasons you selected the best one
3. *Failing to indicate follow up* – Whenever your answer indicates action on your part, make certain that you will take proper follow-up action to see how successful your recommendations, procedures or actions turn out to be
4. *Taking too long in answering any single question* – Remember to time your answers properly

IX. AFTER THE TEST

Scoring procedures differ in detail among civil service jurisdictions although the general principles are the same. Whether the papers are hand-scored or graded by machine we have described, they are nearly always graded by number. That is, the person who marks the paper knows only the number – never the name – of the applicant. Not until all the papers have been graded will they be matched with names. If other tests, such as training and experience or oral interview ratings have been given, scores will be combined. Different parts of the examination usually have different weights. For example, the written test might count 60 percent of the final grade, and a rating of training and experience 40 percent. In many jurisdictions, veterans will have a certain number of points added to their grades.

After the final grade has been determined, the names are placed in grade order and an eligible list is established. There are various methods for resolving ties between those who get the same final grade – probably the most common is to place first the name of the person whose application was received first. Job offers are made from the eligible list in the order the names appear on it. You will be notified of your grade and your rank as soon as all these computations have been made. This will be done as rapidly as possible.

People who are found to meet the requirements in the announcement are called "eligibles." Their names are put on a list of eligible candidates. An eligible's chances of getting a job depend on how high he stands on this list and how fast agencies are filling jobs from the list.

When a job is to be filled from a list of eligibles, the agency asks for the names of people on the list of eligibles for that job. When the civil service commission receives this request, it sends to the agency the names of the three people highest on this list. Or, if the job to be filled has specialized requirements, the office sends the agency the names of the top three persons who meet these requirements from the general list.

The appointing officer makes a choice from among the three people whose names were sent to him. If the selected person accepts the appointment, the names of the others are put back on the list to be considered for future openings.

That is the rule in hiring from all kinds of eligible lists, whether they are for typist, carpenter, chemist, or something else. For every vacancy, the appointing officer has his choice of any one of the top three eligibles on the list. This explains why the person whose name is on top of the list sometimes does not get an appointment when some of the persons lower on the list do. If the appointing officer chooses the second or third eligible, the No. 1 eligible does not get a job at once, but stays on the list until he is appointed or the list is terminated.

X. HOW TO PASS THE INTERVIEW TEST

The examination for which you applied requires an oral interview test. You have already taken the written test and you are now being called for the interview test – the final part of the formal examination.

You may think that it is not possible to prepare for an interview test and that there are no procedures to follow during an interview. Our purpose is to point out some things you can do in advance that will help you and some good rules to follow and pitfalls to avoid while you are being interviewed.

What is an interview supposed to test?

The written examination is designed to test the technical knowledge and competence of the candidate; the oral is designed to evaluate intangible qualities, not readily measured otherwise, and to establish a list showing the relative fitness of each candidate – as measured against his competitors – for the position sought. Scoring is not on the basis of "right" and "wrong," but on a sliding scale of values ranging from "not passable" to "outstanding." As a matter of fact, it is possible to achieve a relatively low score without a single "incorrect" answer because of evident weakness in the qualities being measured.

Occasionally, an examination may consist entirely of an oral test – either an individual or a group oral. In such cases, information is sought concerning the technical knowledges and abilities of the candidate, since there has been no written examination for this purpose. More commonly, however, an oral test is used to supplement a written examination.

Who conducts interviews?

The composition of oral boards varies among different jurisdictions. In nearly all, a representative of the personnel department serves as chairman. One of the members of the board may be a representative of the department in which the candidate would work. In some cases, "outside experts" are used, and, frequently, a businessman or some other representative of the general public is asked to serve. Labor and management or other special groups may be represented. The aim is to secure the services of experts in the appropriate field.

However the board is composed, it is a good idea (and not at all improper or unethical) to ascertain in advance of the interview who the members are and what groups they represent. When you are introduced to them, you will have some idea of their backgrounds and interests, and at least you will not stutter and stammer over their names.

What should be done before the interview?

While knowledge about the board members is useful and takes some of the surprise element out of the interview, there is other preparation which is more substantive. It *is* possible to prepare for an oral interview – in several ways:

1) Keep a copy of your application and review it carefully before the interview

This may be the only document before the oral board, and the starting point of the interview. Know what education and experience you have listed there, and the sequence and dates of all of it. Sometimes the board will ask you to review the highlights of your experience for them; you should not have to hem and haw doing it.

2) Study the class specification and the examination announcement

Usually, the oral board has one or both of these to guide them. The qualities, characteristics or knowledges required by the position sought are stated in these documents. They offer valuable clues as to the nature of the oral interview. For example, if the job involves supervisory responsibilities, the announcement will usually indicate that knowledge of modern supervisory methods and the qualifications of the candidate as a supervisor will be tested. If so, you can expect such questions, frequently in the form of a hypothetical situation which you are expected to solve. NEVER go into an oral without knowledge of the duties and responsibilities of the job you seek.

3) Think through each qualification required

Try to visualize the kind of questions you would ask if you were a board member. How well could you answer them? Try especially to appraise your own knowledge and background in each area, *measured against the job sought*, and identify any areas in which you are weak. Be critical and realistic – do not flatter yourself.

4) Do some general reading in areas in which you feel you may be weak

For example, if the job involves supervision and your past experience has NOT, some general reading in supervisory methods and practices, particularly in the field of human relations, might be useful. Do NOT study agency procedures or detailed manuals. The oral board will be testing your understanding and capacity, not your memory.

5) Get a good night's sleep and watch your general health and mental attitude

You will want a clear head at the interview. Take care of a cold or any other minor ailment, and of course, no hangovers.

What should be done on the day of the interview?

Now comes the day of the interview itself. Give yourself plenty of time to get there. Plan to arrive somewhat ahead of the scheduled time, particularly if your appointment is in the fore part of the day. If a previous candidate fails to appear, the board might be ready for you a bit early. By early afternoon an oral board is almost invariably behind schedule if there are many candidates, and you may have to wait. Take along a book or magazine to read, or your application to review, but leave any extraneous material in the waiting room when you go in for your interview. In any event, relax and compose yourself.

The matter of dress is important. The board is forming impressions about you – from your experience, your manners, your attitude, and your appearance. Give your personal appearance careful attention. Dress your best, but not your flashiest. Choose conservative, appropriate clothing, and be sure it is immaculate. This is a business interview, and your appearance should indicate that you regard it as such. Besides, being well groomed and properly dressed will help boost your confidence.

Sooner or later, someone will call your name and escort you into the interview room. *This is it.* From here on you are on your own. It is too late for any more preparation. But remember, you asked for this opportunity to prove your fitness, and you are here because your request was granted.

What happens when you go in?

The usual sequence of events will be as follows: The clerk (who is often the board stenographer) will introduce you to the chairman of the oral board, who will introduce you to the other members of the board. Acknowledge the introductions before you sit down. Do not be surprised if you find a microphone facing you or a stenotypist sitting by. Oral interviews are usually recorded in the event of an appeal or other review.

Usually the chairman of the board will open the interview by reviewing the highlights of your education and work experience from your application – primarily for the benefit of the other members of the board, as well as to get the material into the record. Do not interrupt or comment unless there is an error or significant misinterpretation; if that is the case, do not hesitate. But do not quibble about insignificant matters. Also, he will usually ask you some question about your education, experience or your present job – partly to get you to start talking and to establish the interviewing "rapport." He may start the actual questioning, or turn it over to one of the other members. Frequently, each member undertakes the questioning on a particular area, one in which he is perhaps most competent, so you can expect each member to participate in the examination. Because time is limited, you may also expect some rather abrupt switches in the direction the questioning takes, so do not be upset by it. Normally, a board member will not pursue a single line of questioning unless he discovers a particular strength or weakness.

After each member has participated, the chairman will usually ask whether any member has any further questions, then will ask you if you have anything you wish to add. Unless you are expecting this question, it may floor you. Worse, it may start you off on an extended, extemporaneous speech. The board is not usually seeking more information. The question is principally to offer you a last opportunity to present further qualifications or to indicate that you have nothing to add. So, if you feel that a significant qualification or characteristic has been overlooked, it is proper to point it out in a sentence or so. Do not compliment the board on the thoroughness of their examination – they have been sketchy, and you know it. If you wish, merely say, "No thank you, I have nothing further to add." This is a point where you can "talk yourself out" of a good impression or fail to present an important bit of information. Remember, *you close the interview yourself.*

The chairman will then say, "That is all, Mr. _____, thank you." Do not be startled; the interview is over, and quicker than you think. Thank him, gather your belongings and take your leave. Save your sigh of relief for the other side of the door.

How to put your best foot forward

Throughout this entire process, you may feel that the board individually and collectively is trying to pierce your defenses, seek out your hidden weaknesses and embarrass and confuse you. Actually, this is not true. They are obliged to make an appraisal of your qualifications for the job you are seeking, and they want to see you in your best light. Remember, they must interview all candidates and a non-cooperative candidate may become a failure in spite of their best efforts to bring out his qualifications. Here are 15 suggestions that will help you:

1) Be natural – Keep your attitude confident, not cocky

If you are not confident that you can do the job, do not expect the board to be. Do not apologize for your weaknesses, try to bring out your strong points. The board is interested in a positive, not negative, presentation. Cockiness will antagonize any board member and make him wonder if you are covering up a weakness by a false show of strength.

2) Get comfortable, but don't lounge or sprawl

Sit erectly but not stiffly. A careless posture may lead the board to conclude that you are careless in other things, or at least that you are not impressed by the importance of the occasion. Either conclusion is natural, even if incorrect. Do not fuss with your clothing, a pencil or an ashtray. Your hands may occasionally be useful to emphasize a point; do not let them become a point of distraction.

3) Do not wisecrack or make small talk

This is a serious situation, and your attitude should show that you consider it as such. Further, the time of the board is limited – they do not want to waste it, and neither should you.

4) Do not exaggerate your experience or abilities

In the first place, from information in the application or other interviews and sources, the board may know more about you than you think. Secondly, you probably will not get away with it. An experienced board is rather adept at spotting such a situation, so do not take the chance.

5) If you know a board member, do not make a point of it, yet do not hide it

Certainly you are not fooling him, and probably not the other members of the board. Do not try to take advantage of your acquaintanceship – it will probably do you little good.

6) Do not dominate the interview

Let the board do that. They will give you the clues – do not assume that you have to do all the talking. Realize that the board has a number of questions to ask you, and do not try to take up all the interview time by showing off your extensive knowledge of the answer to the first one.

7) Be attentive

You only have 20 minutes or so, and you should keep your attention at its sharpest throughout. When a member is addressing a problem or question to you, give him your undivided attention. Address your reply principally to him, but do not exclude the other board members.

8) Do not interrupt

A board member may be stating a problem for you to analyze. He will ask you a question when the time comes. Let him state the problem, and wait for the question.

9) Make sure you understand the question

Do not try to answer until you are sure what the question is. If it is not clear, restate it in your own words or ask the board member to clarify it for you. However, do not haggle about minor elements.

10) Reply promptly but not hastily

A common entry on oral board rating sheets is "candidate responded readily," or "candidate hesitated in replies." Respond as promptly and quickly as you can, but do not jump to a hasty, ill-considered answer.

11) Do not be peremptory in your answers

A brief answer is proper – but do not fire your answer back. That is a losing game from your point of view. The board member can probably ask questions much faster than you can answer them.

12) Do not try to create the answer you think the board member wants

He is interested in what kind of mind you have and how it works – not in playing games. Furthermore, he can usually spot this practice and will actually grade you down on it.

13) Do not switch sides in your reply merely to agree with a board member

Frequently, a member will take a contrary position merely to draw you out and to see if you are willing and able to defend your point of view. Do not start a debate, yet do not surrender a good position. If a position is worth taking, it is worth defending.

14) Do not be afraid to admit an error in judgment if you are shown to be wrong

The board knows that you are forced to reply without any opportunity for careful consideration. Your answer may be demonstrably wrong. If so, admit it and get on with the interview.

15) Do not dwell at length on your present job

The opening question may relate to your present assignment. Answer the question but do not go into an extended discussion. You are being examined for a *new* job, not your present one. As a matter of fact, try to phrase ALL your answers in terms of the job for which you are being examined.

Basis of Rating

Probably you will forget most of these "do's" and "don'ts" when you walk into the oral interview room. Even remembering them all will not ensure you a passing grade. Perhaps you did not have the qualifications in the first place. But remembering them will help you to put your best foot forward, without treading on the toes of the board members.

Rumor and popular opinion to the contrary notwithstanding, an oral board wants you to make the best appearance possible. They know you are under pressure – but they also want to see how you respond to it as a guide to what your reaction would be under the pressures of the job you seek. They will be influenced by the degree of poise you display, the personal traits you show and the manner in which you respond.

ABOUT THIS BOOK

This book contains tests divided into Examination Sections. Go through each test, answering every question in the margin. We have also attached a sample answer sheet at the back of the book that can be removed and used. At the end of each test look at the answer key and check your answers. On the ones you got wrong, look at the right answer choice and learn. Do not fill in the answers first. Do not memorize the questions and answers, but understand the answer and principles involved. On your test, the questions will likely be different from the samples. Questions are changed and new ones added. If you understand these past questions you should have success with any changes that arise. Tests may consist of several types of questions. We have additional books on each subject should more study be advisable or necessary for you. Finally, the more you study, the better prepared you will be. This book is intended to be the last thing you study before you walk into the examination room. Prior study of relevant texts is also recommended. NLC publishes some of these in our Fundamental Series. Knowledge and good sense are important factors in passing your exam. Good luck also helps. So now study this Passbook, absorb the material contained within and take that knowledge into the examination. Then do your best to pass that exam.

EXAMINATION SECTION

EXAMINATION SECTION
TEST 1

DIRECTIONS: Each question or incomplete statement is followed by several suggested answers or completions. Select the one that BEST answers the question or completes the statement. *PRINT THE LETTER OF THE CORRECT ANSWER IN THE SPACE AT THE RIGHT.*

1. A type of depression or pit that may serve to drain, collect or store liquids is called a   1.____
   A. ditch   B. gutter   C. sump   D. trench

2. The general name applied to the material that is spread on the ground around plants to   2.____
   prevent evaporation of water from the soil or the freezing of the roots is
   A. mulch   B. mullock   C. fertilizer   D. mullion

3. The wire, rope, chain or rod that is attached to a tree, and which is used to steady the   3.____
   tree, is called a
   A. guy   B. davit   C. hoist   D. bitt

4. A chemical used to kill weeds is called a   4.____
   A. pesticide   B. herbicide   C. fungicide   D. arborcide

5. A mixture of cement or lime with sand and water which is used between bricks or stones   5.____
   in buildings is called
   A. epoxy   B. putty   C. concrete   D. mortar

6. Coarse aggregate is the same as   6.____
   A. pumice   B. cement
   C. crushed stone   D. sand

7. The process of keeping the surface of concrete as wet as possible after the concrete is   7.____
   placed and hardened in order to prevent loss of water through evaporation is called
   A. floating   B. damping   C. curing   D. checking

8. Plants that live for more than two years are called   8.____
   A. annuals   B. perennials   C. biennials   D. semi-annuals

9. Which piece of equipment is run by compressed air?   9.____
   A. Drill press   B. Impact wrench
   C. Soldering gun   D. Jack hammer

QUESTIONS 10-13.

Answer questions 10-13 SOLELY on the basis of the information given in the paragraphs below.

NITROGEN AND PLANT GROWTH

Nitrogen is an essential element for plant growth. Its most important function is to stimulate vegatative development and it is, therefore, particularly necessary in the production of leaves and stems. If an excess of nitrogen is applied to the soil, it will result in an excessive growth of foliage at the expense of flowers and fruit. The cell walls of the stems will also become weakened and the plant's resistance to disease will be lowered.

Nitrogen is seldom found in the soil in a free state but is usually in combination with other elements. Soils are usually lowest in available nitrogen during the early spring months. It is at this season that quickly available nitrogenous fertilizers are of particular value.

10. According to the paragraph, an excess of nitrogen in plants is *likely to* produce

    A. strong healthy stems
    B. stronger resistance to disease
    C. too many leaves and stems
    D. too many flowers and fruit.

11. Weakened cell walls and decreased resistance to disease in plants are *likely to* occur because

    A. there is too much foliage on the plant
    B. there is not enough nitrogen in the soil
    C. there is too much nitrogen in the soil
    D. there are too many flowers or too much fruit on the plant

12. According to the above passage, one of the properties of nitrogen is that it

    A. seldom combines with other elements in the soil
    B. increase the production of flowers
    C. increases the growth of roots
    D. increases vegetative growth in a plant

13. In which months would soil *most likely* be LOWEST in nitrogen? Late

    A. March and early April
    B. June and early July
    C. September and early October
    D. December and early January

14. A person may appear to be accident-prone for a number of reasons. Which of the following would NOT usually be particularly associated with frequent accidents?

    A. Slow work habits
    B. Improper training
    C. Lack of physical coordination
    D. Working in cramped quarters

15. When removing a large branch from a tree, a pruner usually includes an undercut on the branch.
    The SPECIFIC purpose of the undercut is to

    A. stimulate the flow of sap to the area where the branch is taken off in order to stimulate growth of new branches
    B. prevent the branch that is being taken off from tearing off a strip of bark down the tree
    C. aid the wound from the cut off branch to heal quickly without decay or infection
    D. prevent an excessive growth of new branches from where the branch had been

    15.____

16. A foreman sees one of his men start to cut a hedge so that it will be narrower at the bottom than at the top. The foreman stops the man and tells him to cut hedges in general so that they are narrower at the top than at the bottom. "Why?" asks the man.
    The foreman gave him the *generally accepted* reason, which is that

    A. rainfall will be able to run down the sides, and moisture will reach other parts of the hedge more quickly
    B. the broad base of the hedge will keep the hedge from being top-heavy and prevent it from toppling over during heavy winds
    C. sunlight will be able to reach all parts of the hedge, thereby helping to keep the growth of the entire hedge dense
    D. the hedge will be uniform from top to bottom since the top grows out much faster than the bottom

    16.____

17. Concrete sidewalks are usually laid with a divider space every four or six feet rather than as one long ribbon.
    The reason for allowing the space is that in the summer the concrete in the sidewalk is *most likely* to

    A. contract   B. expand   C. sweat   D. soften

    17.____

18. Some degree of shock accompanies all injuries. Symptoms of shock include all of the following EXCEPT

    A. a warm dry skin   B. a rapid, weak pulse
    C. enlarged pupils   D. irregular breathing

    18.____

19. You are going to plant ivy in the circular flower bed pictured in Figure I. You have decided to plant them on the border of each of circles A, B, and C. The distance around each of the circles is as follows:
    A = 32 feet
    B = 20 feet
    C = 6 feet
    If you can plant 3 plants per foot, how many plants will you need?

    A. 100   B. 135   C. 156   D. 174

    19.____

20. Nine out of ten people have never used a fire extinguisher. A trained person used a fire extinguisher 2 1/2 times more effectively than the average person does.
    These facts should motivate a foreman of a new crew exposed to possible fire hazards to

    20.____

A. have a substitute for fire extinguishers on the job
B. rely only on experienced firemen for extinguishing fires
C. try to get men into his crew who are experienced in the use of fire extinguighers
D. give training to his men on the use of fire extinguishers

21. The crowbar, pick and shovel are three hand tools that can all be used *effectively* and *safely* in the process of

   A. splitting logs
   B. prying heavy objects
   C. making holes in stone
   D. digging up earth

21.____

22. Those tools which require the user to twist or turn one end in one direction while the other end is held fast in order to apply a force on an object are classified as torsion tools. Of the following, the one which would NOT be classified as a torsion tool is

   A. pliers   B. wrench   C. pinchbar   D. screw driver

22.____

23. A portable heater used widely in severe weather to protect masonry, concrete and plaster from freezing and to provide warmth for workmen is the

   A. blowtorch
   B. salamander
   C. plumbers' furnace
   D. metal forge

23.____

24. In loading and unloading materials a variety of equipment is used.
Of the following, the one which is generally NOT an accessory in moving materials onto and off trucks is a

   A. power shovel
   B. clam shell
   C. grease rack
   D. lift truck

24.____

25. Which one of the following pictures shows the top of a Phillips-type screw?

25.____

26. Which one of the following is called a box-end wrench?

26.____

27. A chisel is a hammer-struck tool. Some workmen grip the chisel with the fist to steady it and minimize the chances of glancing blows. The turn "glancing" refers here to the

    A. hammer striking the chisel off angle, thereby hitting the hand holding the chisel
    B. chisel bending or warping under the pressure of hammer blows
    C. hammer hitting with uneven force each time it contacts the chisel
    D. chisel striking the material to be cut straight on, instead of at an angle

28. Which one of the following BEST describes a *counters ink*? A

    A. tool designed to balance weight
    B. hammer used to shape sheet metal
    C. tool that enlarges the top part of a hole
    D. tool used to dig holes rapidly

29. Of the following, the MAIN reason that some electrical tools require the use of a 3-pronged plug is to

    A. prolong the life of the fuse
    B. avoid wasting electricity
    C. prolong the life of the cord
    D. properly ground them

30. Which of the following statements applies BEST to the care and use of a shovel?

    A. A shovel should not be waxed or greased immediately before using it.
    B. Dipping a shovel into a pail of water occasionally, while digging, makes the shovel easier to use.
    C. The leg muscles should not be permitted to take most of the load when shovelling.
    D. A shovel should lie flat on the ground when it is not being used.

31. Which is the SAFEST distance between the base of a 24-foot fully extended ladder and the base of the building against which it is placed?

    A. 3 feet   B. 6 feet   C. 9 feet   D. 12 feet

32. When instructing a man on how to lift a heavy object, you should advise him to

    A. stand as far from the load as possible
    B. keep the back as straight as possible
    C. lift by straightening his legs first and then his back
    D. lift from a full crouch

33. Suppose that, of 14 men assigned to a shop, 3 are absent. The percentage of men absent is, *most nearly,*

    A. 19%   B. 20%   C. 21%   D. 22%

34. The sum of 5 1/6 + 7 1/3 + 4 1/2 + 3 1/8 is

    A. 19 7/8   B. 20 1/2   C. 20 3/4   D. 20 7/8

35. A foreman must order enough sod to cover a dirt area 36 feet wide by 28 feet long. Each piece of sod is 3 feet long by 12 inches wide.
How many pieces of sod should be ordered to cover that area?

   A. 192   B. 236   C. 304   D. 336

36. If each man works at the same speed and 6 men take 2 1/2 hours to do a particular job, how many men will it take to do the *same* job in 1 hour?

   A. 13   B. 15   C. 26   D. 30

37. An agency bought 115 hammers from Company A for $253.00. It later bought 80 hammers from Company B for $140.00 If the agency had bought all of its hammers from Company B, the TOTAL AMOUNT of money that would have been *saved* would have been

   A. $25.25   B. $45.00   C. $51.75   D. $63.25

38. In order to make up a particular mixture of concrete, a foreman mixes 2 parts of cement to 3 parts of sand and 4 parts of gravel.
If he wants to make up 405 lbs. of concrete, he would need

   A. 45 lbs. of cement, 170 lbs. of sand, and 190 lbs. of gravel
   B. 45 lbs, of cement, 160 lbs. of sand, and 200 lbs. of gravel
   C. 90 lbs. of cement, 140 lbs. of sand, and 175 lbs. of gravel
   D. 90 lbs. of cement, 135 lbs. of sand, and 180 lbs. of gravel

39. A tank that is 5/8 full is holding 200 gallons of gasoline. The amount of gasoline this tank can hold *when filled* to capacity is

   A. 270 gals.   B. 320 gals.   C. 360 gals.   D. 410 gals.

40.

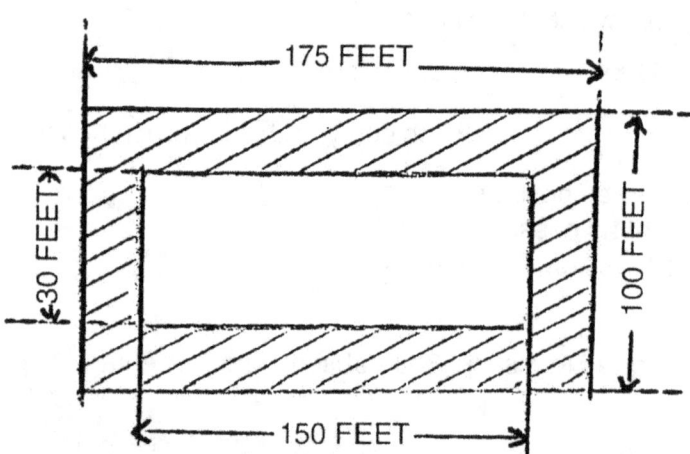

The shaded portion of the above drawing represents an icy walk surrounding a building. If it takes 1 lb. of rock salt to clear ice from every 100 square feet of walk, how many pounds of rock salt would be needed to clear the *entire* walk?

   A. 55   B. 60   C. 120   D. 175

KEY (CORRECT ANSWERS)

1.	C	11.	C	21.	D	31.	B
2.	A	12.	D	22.	C	32.	B
3.	A	13.	A	23.	B	33.	C
4.	B	14.	A	24.	C	34.	A
5.	D	15.	B	25.	B	35.	D
6.	C	16.	C	26.	C	36.	B
7.	C	17.	B	27.	A	37.	C
8.	B	18.	A	28.	C	38.	D
9.	D	19.	D	29.	D	39.	B
10.	C	20.	D	30.	B	40.	A

EXAMINATION SECTION
TEST 1

DIRECTIONS: Each question or incomplete statement is followed by several suggested answers or completions. Select the one that BEST answers the question or completes the statement. *PRINT THE LETTER OF THE CORRECT ANSWER IN THE SPACE AT THE RIGHT.*

1. What is a mulch?
   A
   A. fertilizer which is high in nitrogen
   B. material spread upon the surface of the soil to conserve moisture and inhibit weed growth
   C. chemical compound which is sprayed on the foliage of plants to prevent wilting
   D. mixture of coarse gravel, stones, and broken rock used for drainage in the bottom of flower pots and planting tubs

   1.____

2. A GOOD permanent grass seed mixture for a dry, shady lawn area is

   A. 2 parts Merion Blue grass, 1 part Kentucky Blue grass
   B. 1 part Merion Blue grass, 2 parts Rhode Island or Colonial Bent grass
   C. 1 part chewing fescue, 1 part Illahee fescue, 1 part Pennlawn fescue
   D. 2 part Perennial Rye grass, 1 part Italian Rye grass

   2.____

3. Which of the following is the BEST cutting height for the average lawn in the city area in hot weather?

   A. 1/4"   B. 1/2"   C. 1"   D. 2"

   3.____

4. Earthworms are MOST likely to

   A. make good soil from poor soil
   B. make good soil into even better soil
   C. ruin good soil
   D. indicate a lack of organic matter in the soil

   4.____

5. Before turning over a power rotary lawnmower to clean the underside and cutting blade, you SHOULD

   A. adjust the carburetor idle setting to low speed
   B. allow the engine to cool for at least 10 minutes
   C. remove the high-tension wire from the spark plug
   D. adjust the carburetor setting to full choke

   5.____

6. A 10-6-4 fertilizer contains

   A. 4% nitrogen   B. 10% potassium
   C. 6% potassium   D. 6% phosphorus

   6.____

7. Which of the following is *generally* the BEST pH range for a lawn soil?
   pH
   A. 2-3.5   B. 3-4.5   C. 6-6.5   D. 8-10.5

   7.____

9

8. Peat moss is BEST used as a(n)

   A. mulch
   B. organic soil amendment
   C. fertilizer
   D. substitute for lime

9. What does pH indicate?
   The _____ the soil.

   A. amount of nitrogen in
   B. amount of moisture in
   C. acidity or alkalinity of
   D. amount of organic matter in

10. In order to promote dense growth on all parts of a hedge, it is BEST to prune it so that the

    A. top is wider than the bottom
    B. bottom is wider than the top
    C. top and bottom are of equal width
    D. top and bottom are narrower than the middle

11. When should shrubs that bloom in the spring, such as Weigela and Lilac *generally* be pruned?

    A. As soon as they are finished blooming
    B. Just before they bloom
    C. While they are blooming
    D. When they are still dormant

12. Assume that you wish to cut a large limb off a tree trunk. In order to do this without damage to the tree, the MINIMUM number of separate saw cuts which should *usually* be made is

    A. 1   B. 2   C. 3   D. 4

13. The BEST method of controlling infestations of scale insects on young trees is by

    A. dusting the trees with a good fungicide
    B. removing and burning affected limbs and branches
    C. digging up and destroying the trees
    D. spraying the trees with dormant oil

14. In a slat house for shading plants, the direction in which the roof slats should run is a(n) _____ direction.

    A. east-west
    B. north-south
    C. northeast by southwest
    D. northwest by southeast

15. Which one of the following plants is a monocotyledon?

    A. Begonia   B. Geranium   C. Phlox   D. Iris

16. You are in charge of a small lawn area of 1850 sq.ft. You are asked to apply lime on this lawn at the rate of 40 pounds per 1000 sq.ft.
    The number of pounds of lime you will need to cover the entire area of the lawn is MOST NEARLY _____ lbs. 16._____

    A. 85   B. 86   C. 87   D. 89

17. A Kentucky Blue grass lawn requires 3 lbs. of actual nitrogen per 1000 square feet. How many pounds of 10-6-4 fertilizer will be needed to fertilize a 5000 square foot lawn of Kentucky Blue grass? _____ lbs. 17._____

    A. 15.5   B. 150   C. 555   D. 50

18. You need to fill a 32-oz. bottle with a solution contain-10% malathion, but all you have is a gallon of 50% malathion solution.
    How many ounces of the 50% malathion solution and how many ounces of water should you put in the bottle? _____ oz. of 50% malathion solution and _____ oz. of water. 18._____

    A. 3.2; 28.8   B. 6.4; 25.6
    C. 9.6; 22.4   D. 12.8; 19.2

19. The term *hardiness* is MOST often used to refer to the 19._____

    A. tensile strength of the plant's stem and branches
    B. ability of plants to endure low temperatures
    C. amount of wind force the plant can withstand
    D. length of time that plant can survive without water

20. Which one of the following is NOT a method of plant propagation? 20._____

    A. Layering   B. Budding   C. Chlorosis   D. Division

KEY (CORRECT ANSWERS)

1.	B	11.	A
2.	C	12.	C
3.	D	13.	D
4.	B	14.	B
5.	C	15.	D
6.	D	16.	A
7.	C	17.	B
8.	B	18.	B
9.	C	19.	B
10.	B	20.	C

TEST 2

DIRECTIONS: Each question or incomplete statement is followed by several suggested answers or completions. Select the one that BEST answers the question or completes the statement. *PRINT THE LETTER OF THE CORRECT ANSWER IN THE SPACE AT THE RIGHT.*

1. Clematis, wisteria, and ampelopsis are ALL

    A. indoor foliage plants
    B. outdoor annuals
    C. grown from bulbs planted each fall
    D. ornamental climbing plants

    1._____

2. In attaching a scion to a stock, you should use which one of the following methods?

    A. Whip or tongue
    B. Tack weld
    C. Pintle and gudgeon
    D. Clinch or rivet and burr

    2._____

3. *Pinching*, as performed by a gardener, is a method of

    A. grafting
    B. pruning
    C. propagation
    D. pollination

    3._____

4. In a project involving the laying of sod, the soil was properly cultivated, fertilized, and the turf laid and rolled in the approved fashion. Water was periodically applied in ample quantity. After a few days, the grass began to die around the edges of each rectangular piece of sod.
   The BEST method of avoiding such a problem is *probably* to

    A. add more fertilizer to the soil before the turf is laid
    B. apply lime before and after the sod has been laid
    C. brush a dressing of sandy loam into the joints between the sods
    D. water the sod only in bright sunlight

    4._____

5. A label on a plant was marked as follows: Abie nobilis glauca, Pinaceae.
   The name of this plant reveals that the

    A. species is Abies, the genus is nobilis, the family is glauca, and the variety is Pinaceae
    B. family is Abies, the variety is nobilis, the genus is glauca, and the species is Pinaceae
    C. genus is Abies, the family is nobilis, the species is glauca, and the variety is Pinaceae
    D. genus is Abies, the species is Nobilis, the variety is glauca, and the family is Pinaceae

    5._____

6. A small deciduous tree in leaf has just been dug from the ground and transplanted into a tub and then watered until the soil is saturated. It quickly shows symptoms of severe wilting.
   In trying to save this tree, which of the following would be the LEAST acceptable remedy?

    6._____

A. Remove some of the foliage, either by removing some of the leaves or some of the smaller branches with their foliage
B. Wet the plant's foliage and then place a plastic bag over the entire tree and place it either in a shady place or a darkened room
C. Remove the tree from the tub and remove all of the soil from the roots and then place the plant in a pail of water so the roots are completely submerged
D. Place the tree under the constant mist of a fine water spray

7. A certain broad-leaf evergreen tree had many flowers in the spring but it bore no fruit in the fall. The next spring a close examination of the flowers revealed only stamens and no pistils.
The *probable* reason for the failure of the tree to fruit is that the

   A. flowers were deformed
   B. tree was a male
   C. tree was a female and there was no male in the vicinity
   D. tree was planted too far north and the cold weather prevented it from fruiting

7.____

8. Which one of the following trees would be LEAST desirable for planting in a shady area?

   A. Dogwood   B. Pine   C. Hemlock   D. Holly

8.____

9. Brown patches are noticed in a sunny lawn area in the summer. A close examination reveals numerous brown insects around the grass roots in the patches about 1/6" long with white markings on their backs.
These insects MOST likely are

   A. aphids
   B. scale insects
   C. chinch bugs
   D. leaf hoppers

9.____

10. Many diseases of lawn grasses can be treated effectively with

    A. Benomyl (Benlate)
    B. 2,4-D
    C. DDT
    D. Rotenone

10.____

11. Of the following, the BEST way to reduce the acidity of soil is to apply

    A. limestone
    B. flowers of sulfur
    C. aluminum sulfate
    D. water

11.____

12. The MOST effective of the following actions to take to stop erosion of soil on steep embankments is to

    A. break the flow of water on the embankment
    B. dig several water channels from the top of the embankment to the bottom
    C. rototill the embankment
    D. spray the embankment with 2,4-D

12.____

13. A *complete* fertilizer contains

    A. nitrogen, phosphorus, and iron
    B. calcium, potassium, and sulfur
    C. nitrogen, phosphorus, and potassium
    D. calcium, carbon, and nitrogen

13.____

14. Plants produce seeds by means of

    A. pollination and fertilization
    B. cultivation and grafting
    C. hybridization and air-layering
    D. rooting and hydrogenation

15. If a tree is to be replanted in a heavy clay-loam soil with questionable drainage, it would be BEST to plant the tree

    A. three inches deeper than it was planted before
    B. six inches deeper than it was planted before
    C. at the same level as before and backfill with sand
    D. slightly higher in the soil than it was planted before

16. Suckers are MOST likely to develop from

    A. buds
    B. roots
    C. shoots
    D. leaf cuttings

17. All of the following are piercing-sucking insects EXCEPT the

    A. white fly
    B. leaf hopper
    C. lace bug
    D. black vine weevil

18. Knowing and using good horticultural books for reference is important in gardening work. Which of the following is a GOOD horticultural book?

    A. HORTUS SECOND, by Liberty Hyde Bailey
    B. PLANT LOCATION IN THEORY AND IN PRACTICE, by Melvin Greenhut
    C. HOW GREEN WAS MY VALLEY, by Richard Llewellyn
    D. THE GREENING OF AMERICA, by Charles Reich

19. The pine bark aphid is a pest of pines such as the Eastern White Pine (Pinus strobus). A superior-type emulsifiable oil spray can be applied during the early spring when the tree is still dormant.
    Which of the following conditions are BEST for applying the spray?

    A. There is no wind, the day temperature is 50° F or higher, the night temperature is above the mid 30's, no rain is predicted
    B. A slight wind is predicted, the day temperature does not exceed 48° F, the night temperature is predicted to fall below freezing
    C. A slight wind is predicted, the day temperature and the night temperature are both above 85° F, and the day is misty
    D. The aphids start to move

20. An excellent fungicide which not only has historical significance but is still highly recommended for control of certain fungus diseases contains copper sulfate, hydrated lime, and water.
    This fungicide is called

    A. Ferbam
    B. Bordeaux mixture
    C. Solution C.S.H.L.
    D. Captan

KEY (CORRECT ANSWERS)

1. D
2. A
3. B
4. C
5. D

6. C
7. B
8. B
9. C
10. A

11. A
12. A
13. C
14. A
15. D

16. A
17. D
18. A
19. A
20. B

TEST 3

DIRECTIONS: Each question or incomplete statement is followed by several suggested answers or completions. Select the one that BEST answers the question or completes the statement. *PRINT THE LETTER OF THE CORRECT ANSWER IN THE SPACE AT THE RIGHT.*

1. A heavy mulch is LEAST desirable for

    A. iris
    B. rhododendrons
    C. azaleas
    D. newly planted trees

2. You have noticed that a number of older leaves fall each year from a pine tree. This phenomenon is *probably* due to

    A. root rot
    B. insufficient fertilizer
    C. natural aging of the needles
    D. insufficient water

3. The BEST time to sow grass seed in the city is

    A. mid-August to mid-September
    B. mid-March to mid-April
    C. late April to mid-May
    D. late May to early June

4. In order to maintain natural growth, the BEST of the following methods of pruning forsythia is to remove

    A. half of the top growth
    B. only the apical buds
    C. up to one-third of the older stems
    D. all growth over two feet

5. Which one of the following trees can be *safely* pruned in spring when sap is flowing?

    A. Acer saccharium - Sugar Maple
    B. Ulmus species - Elms
    C. Cladrastis lutea - Yellow-wood
    D. Pinus thumbergii - Japanese Black Pine

6. Of the following, the BEST way to treat trees or shrubs with dead and diseased branches is to

    A. leave them alone
    B. prune to remove 1/3 of older wood
    C. prune back to healthy wood
    D. spray with 2,4-D

7. Anthracnose disease of Plantanus species (Plane trees) is more prevalent in wet spring weather.
   This disease is caused by a

    A. beetle   B. fungus   C. mildew   D. gas leak

8. Peat moss is frequently used in gardening to change soil conditions. Which of the following is the BEST definition of peat moss?

   A. A short, slow-growing plant
   B. Completely decomposed animal life
   C. Partially decomposed plant life
   D. A type of wood

9. A sprayer which has been used to spray insecticides and will be used for this purpose in the future should NEVER be used to apply

   A. fungicides
   B. miticides
   C. malathion
   D. herbicides

10. It is especially important that an excess of fertilizer not be applied to the soil because of the possibility of root damage.
    This is due to the fact that fertilizer is a(n)

    A. acid   B. base   C. salt   D. alkali

11. Of the following, the BEST time to apply fertilizer to lawn grasses is *usually* when the

    A. soil is *moist* and the grass is *wet*
    B. grass is *dry* and the soil is *moist*
    C. soil and the grass are *dry*
    D. soil is *dry* and the grass is *wet*

12. Assume that a child's rope swing has been attached to a tree by tying the rope securely around the lowest limb. Of the following, it is MOST important that

    A. girdling of the limb at the point of attachment of the rope does not eventually occur
    B. only a natural fiber rope is used
    C. the rope be lengthened as the tree grows in height
    D. as the limb grows in length, the swing be moved back toward the trunk to adjust for linear growth

13. An established lawn which requires watering during dry periods should be watered

    A. *lightly* twice a day in the morning and again at dusk
    B. *lightly* once a day in the morning unless the humidity is above 90%
    C. *thoroughly* to a depth of at least 4 inches early in the day
    D. *thoroughly* to a depth of 4 inches in the morning and again at dusk

14. A Rhododendron shows severe yellowing of leaves. The problem is due to an iron deficiency.
    To correct this deficiency, it is MOST effective to apply iron

    A. carbide   B. pyrites   C. chelate   D. oxide

15. The color of the flower of some species of plants is distinctly affected by soil alkalinity or acidity as well as the amount of aluminum or iron in the soil. When the soil is neutral or alkaline, the flower color is pinker, whereas under acid soil conditions the flower color is bluer.
    Which one of the following plants is BEST known to exhibit this response?

- A. Rose species - Roses
- B. Hydrangea macrophylla (hortensis) - House Hydrangea
- C. Chrysanthemum morifolium - Florist and Garden Chrysanthemums
- D. Begonia semperflorens - wax or fibrous-rooted begonias

16. Which one of the following terms refers to a method in which trees or shrubs can be trained into a special shape or form?

    - A. Abscission
    - B. Layering
    - C. Pricking-out
    - D. Espalier

17. Which one of the following is NOT a shrub?

    - A. Pieris japonica
    - B. Abelia grandiflora
    - C. Acer platanoides
    - D. Viburnum japonicum

18. You have just been told by your supervisor that your crew members must use a new method for accounting for the time spent on specific jobs. Some members of your crew complain to you that the previous method was better.
    Of the following, the BEST action to take FIRST is to

    - A. find out specifically to what your crew objects
    - B. suggest to your crew members that they are correct and that management does not really understand the effect of the change
    - C. tell your crew to try the new method and that if they still feel that way in a few weeks they can go back to the old method
    - D. take a vote among your crew to determine which method to use

19. Complaining to your crew about working conditions is

    - A. *advisable* ; it makes you
    - B. *advisable;* it allows you to get your feelings out in the open
    - C. *inadvisable,* it permits the crew to depend more on the attitudes and approval of their supervisor
    - D. *inadvisable,* it brings attention to problems but does not resolve them

20. Asking your crew for their suggestions on better gardening methods is

    - A. *inadvisable;* they may feel that you lack self-confidence
    - B. *inadvisable;* it is poor practice to become too friendly with those you supervise
    - C. *advisable;* it makes the men feel they have a hand in decision making
    - D. *advisable;* those who make the suggestions can be held responsible for results

KEY (CORRECT ANSWERS)

1.	A	11.	B
2.	C	12.	A
3.	A	13.	C
4.	C	14.	C
5.	D	15.	B
6.	C	16.	D
7.	B	17.	C
8.	C	18.	A
9.	D	19.	D
10.	C	20.	C

TEST 4

DIRECTIONS: Each question or incomplete statement is followed by several suggested answers or completions. Select the one that BEST answers the question or completes the statement. *PRINT THE LETTER OF THE CORRECT ANSWER IN THE SPACE AT THE RIGHT.*

1. For you, as a supervisor, to explain department objectives for the year ahead to a new employee is

   A. *inadvisable;* the new employee may leave before the year is up
   B. *inadvisable;* the new employee has nothing to do with the goals of the department
   C. *advisable;* it may enable the new employee to do the job with less training
   D. *advisable;* it may give the new employee a sense of personal involvement and motivation

   1.____

2. When a new laborer reports for duty for the first time, which of the following should be discussed with him FIRST?

   A. Departmental rules and regulations that relate to his employment
   B. The priorities that he should assign to his work
   C. The latest techniques of getting the technical work done
   D. The recognition of what constitutes an error in his work and its consequences

   2.____

3. While you are trimming some shrubs in the park, a woman comes up to you and tells you that her civic club is running a benefit for the handicapped and that it would be wonderful if the department would donate some flowers to this worthy cause. You do not know how this type of situation has been handled in the past.
Of the following, the BEST action for you to take is to tell the woman that you

   A. are sure the department will be happy to donate flowers, and take her name and address
   B. have nothing to do with department policy and cannot make that decision
   C. are not sure what the department policy is but you think she is wasting her time trying to get flowers from the department
   D. are not sure what department policy is but that you will tell her how to get more information

   3.____

4. One of your crew members has made an error in the care of bulbs, resulting in the loss of many expensive bulbs.
Of the following, the BEST way to handle this situation *initially* is to

   A. write a memo on the care of bulbs and post it where your crew can refer to it
   B. call your crew together and discuss the proper care of bulbs
   C. speak privately to the crew member who made the error and discuss his error and proper care of bulbs with him
   D. tell the crew member who made the error you will not report him at present, but if this type of error occurs again you will recommend his dismissal

   4.____

5. It has been brought to your attention that several expensive tools are missing from the tool cabinet. Since this had never before been a problem, the cabinet was always left unlocked.
Of the following, the BEST way to handle this situation is to

   5.____

A. lock the cabinet, and give keys to all your crew members, making them all responsible for the tools
B. lock the cabinet, and make one of your crew members responsible for the key to the cabinet and the tools inside
C. announce to your crew members that if a tool is missing they will all have to be charged an appropriate amount towards the purchase of a new tool
D. assign each crew member a particular tool and have him use this device exclusively

6. Of the following, the BEST reason for the practice of requiring your crew members to sign in and out for lunch is that

   A. the crew members are more productive when they are more strictly controlled
   B. it enables the supervisor to regulate the time and working hours of the crew members more directly
   C. it will prevent crew members from leaving the work area during their lunch period
   D. the supervisor will find out the preferred lunch period for each individual crew member

7. While pruning some shrubs, a crew member under your supervision trips over what he thinks was a loose cobblestone. After checking to make sure he has suffered no injury, of the following, the MOST advisable action for you to take NEXT is to

   A. tell him to be more careful in the future
   B. determine what actually caused the accident
   C. post safety rules where they can be seen by all crew members
   D. assign him to a different type of work at another location

8. One of the crew members under your supervision tells you that the lawnmower he has been using has just broken down. Of the following, the BEST reason for you to try operating the mower yourself is to

   A. test the worker's knowledge with his performance on the job
   B. keep the machines in need of repair in service as long as possible
   C. show that supervisors can do the work of the crew members
   D. determine whether a minor adjustment will bring the machine to operating condition

9. You have just explained to your most competent crew member a complicated root-pruning procedure that you wish him to follow. He tells you that he is a little uncertain about it and is not sure he can handle it.
Of the following, the BEST action for you to take is to

   A. show him how much confidence you have in him by leaving him alone to do the job
   B. have another crew member work with him to make sure that the job is done correctly
   C. stay with him while he does the job to assure yourself that he knows how to do it correctly
   D. drop the assignment until such time as he indicates that he is ready for it

10. While you are replanting some flowers, a man comes up to you and starts berating you for the condition of the park.
Of the following, the BEST way to handle this situation is to

A. suggest that he write to the department about his complaint
B. ask the man to leave and call for a police officer if he does not
C. explain to the man that those who use the park are primarily responsible for its condition
D. tell him that his opinions about the conditions of the park are wrong

11. Gardeners should be courteous to the public PRIMARILY because

    A. someone might report them if they are not
    B. this might earn them a merit increase
    C. a good relationship between the department and the public is important
    D. this makes for better morale among their crew members

12. Assume that you have been asked to evaluate the performance of one of your crew members.
    The one of the following which should be given the LEAST consideration when making this evaluation is the employee's attitude towards

    A. his co-workers   B. the organization
    C. his friends   D. you

Questions 13-15.

DIRECTIONS: Questions 13 through 15 are to be answered on the basis of the following report.

To: John Greene   Date: May 5
      General Park Foreman

From: Earl Jones   Subject:
      Gardener

    On May 3rd, as I was finishing a job six feet from the boathouse, I observed that the hole which had been filled in last week was now not level with the ground around it. This seems to be a hazardous condition because it might cause pedestrians to fall into it. I, therefore, suggest that this job be redone as soon as possible.

13. This report should be considered *poorly* written MAINLY because

    A. it does not give enough information to take appropriate action
    B. too many different tenses are used
    C. it describes no actual personal injury to anyone
    D. there is no recommendation in the report to remedy the situation

14. It is noted that the subject of the report has been left out.
    Which of the following statements would be BEST as the subject of this report?

    A. Observation made by Earl Jones, Gardener
    B. Deteriorating condition of park grounds
    C. Report of dangerous condition near boathouse
    D. A dangerous walk through the park

15. In order for John Greene to take *appropriate action*, ADDITIONAL information should be added to the report giving the

    A. exact date the repair was made
    B. exact location of the hole
    C. exact time the observation was made
    D. names of the crew who previously filled in the hole

15.____

Questions 16-20.

DIRECTIONS: Questions 16 through 20 are based on the Fact Situation and the Repair Request Report form below. Read the Fact Situation carefully and examine the blank report form. Questions 16 through 20 ask how the report form should be filled in based on the information given in the Fact Situation.

FACT SITUATION

John Smith is a gardener, permanently assigned to the greenhouse in Queens. On Tuesday morning, he arrives at the greenhouse at 8 A.M. and sees that seven panes of glass in the west wing of the greenhouse have been broken. Since several large rooks are found on the greenhouse floor, it appears that the panes of the windows have been broken by vandals. It is necessary to repair the windows immediately due to the cold weather. In order to arrange for the repair, John Smith must complete the following "Repair Request Report."

```
                    REPAIR REQUEST REPORT

  1.  Date of Request _____   2.  Time _____

  3.  Location of Needed Repair _____

  4.  Type of Repair Requested _____

  5.  Reason for Request _____
      _____

  6.  Signed _____   7.  Title _____

  8.  Additional Comments _____
      _____
```

16. Which of the following should be entered in Blank 4?

    A. Rock removal
    B. Broken glass
    C. Window pane replacement
    D. Heater installation

16.____

17. Based on the information given in the Pact Situation, it is *impossible* to fill in which one of the following blanks?
Blank _____.

    A. 1   B. 3   C. 5   D. 7

17.____

18. Which of the following would it be MOST appropriate to include in Blank 8? 18.____
    A. John Smith was on time for work on January 10, 1997.
    B. It seems that the windows were broken by vandals.
    C. The weather forecast for the next few days is unknown.
    D. Identity of vandals is unknown.

19. Of the following, the BEST way for John Smith to show his supervisor that the Repair Request Report was properly filled out is to 19.____

    A. personally deliver the report to the repair crew
    B. have two signatures instead of one required in Blank 6
    C. show his supervisor a duplicate copy of the report
    D. in Blank 8 include the dimensions of the panes of glass needed

20. It is necessary to emphasize the need to have the repair made quickly. The PROPER blank on the form to show the urgency of this request is Blank 20.____

    A. 2   B. 3   C. 7   D. '8

KEY (CORRECT ANSWERS)

1.	D	11.	C
2.	A	12.	C
3.	D	13.	A
4.	C	14.	C
5.	B	15.	B
6.	B	16.	C
7.	B	17.	A
8.	D	18.	B
9.	C	19.	C
10.	A	20.	D

EXAMINATION SECTION
TEST 1

DIRECTIONS: Each question consists of a statement. You are to indicate whether the statement is TRUE (T) or FALSE (F). *PRINT THE LETTER OF THE CORRECT ANSWER IN THE SPACE AT THE RIGHT.*

1. Weeds are USUALLY undesirable in a lawn because they take away plant food from the good grasses. 1.____

2. When flowering shrubs are planted, they should be crowded very close together so that weeds will not have room to grow. 2.____

3. It is USUALLY good practice to spade the soil when it is wet because it is easier to work it when it is in that condition. 3.____

4. The size of a hole in which a piece of nursery stock is to be planted should be determined by the time available to dig the hole rather than by the size of the plant and its roots. 4.____

5. Lawn clippings that are NOT too heavy may be left on a lawn after the lawn is mowed. 5.____

6. Chemical fertilizers in powdered form should be applied to a lawn on a windy day so that the wind will blow them into the ground. 6.____

7. To prevent rust, it is USUALLY good practice to put a coat of oil on garden tools when they are stored away for the winter. 7.____

8. When he transplants a plant from one place in the garden to another, the assistant gardener should be careful to avoid injury to the roots. 8.____

9. Freshly planted nursery stock is often pruned by cutting off part of the branches. The MAIN purpose of this pruning is usually to keep the plant from growing further. 9.____

10. Chemical sprays are often used to kill insect enemies of plants. 10.____

11. The purpose of adding chemical fertilizers to the soil is USUALLY to provide additional plant food. 11.____

12. An assistant gardener who does not know all the latest developments in gardening will NOT be able to do his work properly. 12.____

13. It is GOOD practice to keep the cutting edge of a garden tool slightly dull in order to prevent injury to the user of the tool. 13.____

14. An assistant gardener who is given a job he does NOT know how to do should ask for further instructions. 14.____

15. A shrub planted by an assistant gardener fails to grow. This proves that the shrub was NOT planted correctly. 15.____

16. Some garden insects are beneficial to plant life and should NOT be killed. 16.____

17. Plants MUST have light in order to grow properly. 17.____

18. If an assistant gardener accidentally sticks the point of a sharp tool into the bark of a tree, the tree will die within a few years.

18.____

19. During a long dry spell, it is advisable to water carefully recently planted nursery stock.

19.____

20. An IMPORTANT reason why an assistant gardener should know the proper use of each garden tool is that if he uses a tool improperly, he may spoil it.

20.____

21. An assistant gardener should carry out his superior's orders only if he knows that the orders are correct according to the best gardening practice.

21.____

22. An assistant gardener, whenever he suffers a slight cut or scratch while at work, should immediately go to the NEAREST doctor to be treated.

22.____

23. An assistant gardener who always finds a lot of rubbish in the park area to which he is assigned should issue a warning to every person who uses the area.

23.____

24. If a passerby asks an assistant gardener who is at work in a park for directions on how to get to another part of the park, the assistant gardener should refer him to the nearest policeman so that his work will not be interrupted.

24.____

25. An assistant gardener should never help a fellow employee with his work unless he has received permission in writing from the supervisor.

25.____

26. An assistant gardener is assigned a job by his supervisor and told that it must be finished by a certain time. If, after working on the job for a while, the assistant gardener is sure that he will NOT be able to finish on time, he should immediately let his supervisor know.

26.____

27. You have an unwrapped shrub with bare roots which you are all ready to plant when you receive a call to go to another part of the park. Before you leave, it would be advisable for you to temporarily cover the roots of the plant with soil so as to prevent them from drying out.

27.____

28. After plants are established and growing, they require no further attention.

28.____

Questions 29-33.

DIRECTIONS: Your answers to Questions 29 to 33 must be based only on the information given in the following paragraph and NOT upon any other information you may have.

To insure thick growth from the ground up, hedges should be out back to a few inches from the ground when planted. The properly shaped hedge is narrower at the top than at the bottom, and the top should be rounded rather than flat. The sloping sides admit much light to the lower branches. A somewhat narrow and rounded top also sheds snow instead of accumulating a heavy load and sometimes bending or breaking under it.

29. Hedges should be cut down to a few inches from the ground after they have grown dense at the bottom.

29.____

30. Trimming of hedges should be done in such a way as to give them a rounded top.

30.____

31. A hedge shaped wider at the top than at the bottom will admit much light to the bottom branches. 31.____

32. Snow will tend to accumulate and stay on a hedge with a wide, flat top. 32.____

33. A hedge can sometimes be broken by the weight of the snow accumulated on top of it. 33.____

Questions 34-43.

DIRECTIONS: Your answers to Questions 34 to 43 must be based only on the information given in the following paragraph and NOT upon any other information you may have.

Arsenate of lead, the best known and most widely used stomach poison, comes in two forms, basic and acid. The basic form is less likely to burn tender growth but stays in suspension poorly and kills insects more slowly. Most commercial preparations are the acid form usually sold as a powder, sometimes as a paste. For general spraying, use the powder at the rate of 3 lbs. to 100 gallons of water; or in small quantities, use one heaping tablespoon to one gallon of water. If the paste form is available, use twice the amount recommended.

34. There is an acid form of arsenate of lead and a basic form of arsenate of lead. 34.____

35. No stomach poison is better known than arsenate of lead. 35.____

36. No other stomach poison is used as much as arsenate of lead. 36.____

37. The basic form of arsenate of lead kills insects more quickly than the acid form. 37.____

38. There are many forms of arsenate of lead. 38.____

39. The basic form of arsenate of lead is MORE likely to burn plants than the acid form. 39.____

40. The acid form of arsenate of lead is USUALLY sold as a paste. 40.____

41. Commercially prepared arsenate of lead is USUALLY of the acid form. 41.____

42. The paste of the acid form of arsenate of lead, when used for general spraying, should be mixed at the rate of 3 lbs. to 100 gallons of water. 42.____

43. The powder of the acid form of arsenate of lead, when used for general spraying, should be used at the rate of one heaping teaspoon to a gallon of water. 43.____

44. *The instructions received were contradictory.*
    In this sentence, the word *contradictory* means NEARLY the same as *alike*. 44.____

45. *His application for the job was rejected.*
    In this sentence, the word *rejected* means NEARLY the same as *accepted*. 45.____

46. *This plant reaches maturity quickly.*
    In this sentence, the word *maturity* means NEARLY the same as *full development*. 46.____

47. *The garden was provided with a system of underground irrigation.*
    In this sentence, the word *irrigation* means NEARLY the same as *watering*. 47.____

48. *In some plants, the flowers often appear before the foliage.* 48.___
In this sentence, the word *foliage* refers to the leaves of the plant.

49. *The new horticultural society was organized through the merger of two previous groups.* 49.___
In this sentence, the word *merger* means NEARLY the same as *breakup*.

50. *The stem of the plant measured three inches in diameter.* 50.___
In this sentence, the word *diameter* means NEARLY the same as *height*.

KEY (CORRECT ANSWERS)

1. T	11. T	21. F	31. F	41. T
2. F	12. F	22. F	32. T	42. F
3. F	13. F	23. F	33. T	43. F
4. F	14. T	24. F	34. T	44. F
5. T	15. F	25. F	35. T	45. F
6. F	16. T	26. T	36. T	46. T
7. T	17. T	27. T	37. F	47. T
8. T	18. F	28. F	38. F	48. T
9. F	19. T	29. F	39. F	49. F
10. T	20. T	30. T	40. F	50. F

TEST 2

DIRECTIONS: Each question consists of a statement. You are to indicate whether the statement is TRUE (T) or FALSE (F). *PRINT THE LETTER OF THE CORRECT ANSWER IN THE SPACE AT THE RIGHT.*

Questions 1-10.

DIRECTIONS: Your answers to Questions 1 to 10 must be based only on the information given in the following paragraph and NOT upon any other information you may have.

A commercial fertilizer may be a single substance such as nitrate of soda, or it may be a combination of such materials which contains a definite ratio of the three main plant-food elements, nitrogen, phosphorus, and potassium. Such a mixture is said to be complete. And if the proportions of the three elements are such as to meet the full needs of a certain plant, the fertilizer is said to be balanced as well as complete. As the plant food compounds in commercial fertilizers are in highly soluble form, they should not be applied too heavily nor allowed to come in contact with plant parts. Small frequent applications are safest and least wasteful as they give less chance for the soluble salts to be dissolved and leached out of the soil before the plant roots can get them. It is usually advisable to water the soil after adding commercial fertilizer, both to put the fertilizer in solution so that the plants can take it up and to prevent the fertilizer from absorbing the moisture in the soil.

1. All commercial fertilizers consist of a combination of the three main plant food elements.   1.____
2. Nitrate of soda is available as a commercial fertilizer.   2.____
3. The three main plant food elements are nitrate of soda, nitrogen, and phosphorus.   3.____
4. A complete fertilizer contains nitrogen, potassium, and phosphorus.   4.____
5. Any fertilizer which contains nitrogen, potassium, and phosphorus is said to be balanced.   5.____
6. The plant food elements in commercial fertilizers are very soluble.   6.____
7. A commercial fertilizer should be mixed right in among the roots of a plant so that it becomes available quickly.   7.____
8. Commercial fertilizers should be applied to the soil in large amounts.   8.____
9. Commercial fertilizer must be in solution before it can be taken up by plants.   9.____
10. If the soil is not watered when commercial fertilizer is applied, the fertilizer may absorb the moisture that is already in the soil.   10.____

Questions 11-25.

DIRECTIONS: Your answers to Questions 11 to 25 must be based only on the information given in the following paragraph and NOT upon any other information you may have.

2 (#2)

Bent grass is the common name for Agrostis, a large class of mostly low-growing and spreading grasses, including some valuable, high-class lawn grasses as well as the important pasture grass, Redtop. Bent grasses are annual or perennial, have somewhat rough, flat, or slightly rolled leaves and bear loose panicles of small reddish flowers. While some of the forms are grown from seed, those used for fine lawns and golf courses are of the creeping type and are increasingly being grown from stolons, which are simply the chopped-up stems. Bent grasses will do well in sun or partial shade, but are not in any sense a shady-spot variety. The soil should be well supplied with thoroughly rotted manure and receive a good application of a balanced complete fertilizer before planting time. In sowing, use about one pound of seed to 250 square feet; if stolons are used, broadcast them at the rate of 25 square feet of stolons to 200 square feet of area. They must then be covered lightly with soil, rotted and watered.

11. Agrostis is the common name for Bent grass.

12. Redtop is a pasture grass.

13. Agrostis is a variety of Redtop.

14. Most Bent grasses are low growing.

15. Not all Bent grasses are perennial.

16. All Bent grasses are annual.

17. Bent grasses bear flowers.

18. Creeping Bent grasses are used from seed.

19. All Bent grass lawns are grown from seed.

20. A stolon is a chopped-up Bent grass seed.

21. Bent grasses are good for planting in heavily shaded areas.

22. Before Bent grass is planted, rotted manure and a balanced complete fertilizer should be added to the soil.

23. Bent grass may be sown at the rate of $\frac{1}{2}$ pound of seed to 125 square feet.

24. When Bent grass is planted by means of stolons, 25 pounds of stolons should be broadcast to 200 square feet of area.

25. After being broadcast, stolons should be covered with at least three inches of soil.

26. *For proper growth, the plant needs plenty of water, supplemented with liquid manure.* In this sentence, the word *supplemented* means NEARLY the same as *replaced*.

27. *One reason why aphids are undesirable is that they transmit plant diseases.* In this sentence, the word *transmit* means NEARLY the same as *pass on*.

28. *When the trees are young, the spaces between them may be utilized for other plantings.* In this sentence, the word *utilized* means NEARLY the same as *used*.

29. *The cuttings will take root readily.*
    In this sentence, the word *readily* means NEARLY the same as *quickly*.

30. *The seedlings should be transplanted at least once to stimulate growth.*
    In this sentence, the word *stimulate* means NEARLY the same as *encouraged*.

31. *The water evaporates through cracks in the soil.*
    In this sentence, the word *evaporates* means NEARLY the same as *flows in*.

32. *Hardy native vines were planted.*
    In this sentence, the word *hardy* means NEARLY the same as *few*.

33. *The insects were present in moderate numbers.*
    In this sentence, the word *moderate* means NEARLY the same as *large*.

34. *The beetle is injurious to garden crops.*
    In this sentence, the word *injurious* means NEARLY the same as *harmful*.

35. *With proper care, the plants will survive the winter.*
    In this sentence, the word *survive* means NEARLY the same as *live through*.

36. *An arbor should be inconspicuous.*
    In this sentence, the word *inconspicuous* means NEARLY the same as *made of wood*.

37. *The plants are indifferent as to soil.*
    In this sentence, the word *indifferent* means NEARLY the same as *not particular*.

38. *The plant produces fragrant flowers.*
    In this sentence, the word *fragrant* means NEARLY the same as *sweet smelling*.

39. An assistant gardener assigned to do a job did $\frac{1}{4}$ of it on Tuesday, $\frac{1}{2}$ of it on Wednesday, and the remainder on Thursday.
    The part of the job done by the assistant gardener on Thursday was $\frac{1}{4}$ of the whole job.

40. In a park department, 55 plants were planted each day for a period of 12 days.
    The total number of plants planted by this park department in these 12 days was between 600 and 700.

41. Suppose that 524 plants were planted in a city. Of these plants, 302 were planted in Zone A. The rest were planted in Zone B.
    The number of plants planted in Zone B was between 200 and 250.

42. Suppose that 25% of 400 employees were on vacation in July.
    The number of employees who were on vacation in July was 200.

43. A park department planted 3760 plants in 1999, 1876 plants in 1998, 922 plants in 1997, 4001 plants in 1996, and 3301 plants in 1995.
    The total number of plants planted by this park department in these five years was more than 15,000.

44. In one division of the park department of a large city, there are the following employees: Assistant Gardeners - 1,739, Gardeners - 687, Laborers - 1,452, Climbers and Pruners - 796, Foremen - 69, Auto Enginemen - 38, and Attendants - 543.
The total number of these employees is between 5,315 and 5,320.

45. Suppose that in Park A, there are 8,796 trees. In Park B, there are 13,435 trees. Therefore, in Park B there are 4,459 more trees than in Park A.

46. Suppose that a total of 595,563 street trees was planted on 2,354 city streets. If the same number of trees was planted on each street, the number of trees planted on each street was between 250 and 255.

47. Suppose the Park Department bought 35,796 plants at a cost of $2.49 for each plant. The total cost of all of these plants was less than $85,000.

48. The Park Department receives 120 rose bushes for planting. You are assigned to plant 20% of these bushes.
Therefore, you must plant 24 of these bushes.

49. In order to completely fence in a playground which is 100 feet long and 100 feet wide, 200 feet of fence would be needed.

50. If a gardener divided 56 pounds of seed equally among 8 assistant gardeners, each assistant gardener would get seven pounds of seed.

KEY (CORRECT ANSWERS)

1. F	11. F	21. F	31. F	41. T
2. T	12. T	22. T	32. F	42. F
3. F	13. F	23. T	33. F	43. F
4. T	14. T	24. F	34. T	44. F
5. F	15. T	25. F	35. T	45. T
6. T	16. F	26. F	36. F	46. T
7. F	17. T	27. T	37. T	47. F
8. F	18. T	28. T	38. T	48. T
9. T	19. F	29. T	39. T	49. F
10. T	20. F	30. T	40. T	50. T

TEST 3

DIRECTIONS: Each question consists of a statement. You are to indicate whether the statement is TRUE (T) or FALSE (F). *PRINT THE LETTER OF THE CORRECT ANSWER IN THE SPACE AT THE RIGHT.*

1. If you see a new employee doing a job the wrong way, you should show this employee the right way to do this job. 1.____

2. If your supervisor gives you an assignment which you do not like, you should ask him to assign another employee to do this work. 2.____

3. If your supervisor gives you instructions for a job which you do not understand, you should do the job the BEST you can and not take up his time by asking him to explain the instructions. 3.____

4. A new employee can sometimes learn how to do a job just by watching an experienced employee actually do the job. 4.____

5. If you cannot get along with a fellow employee, the PROPER thing for you to do is to ask your supervisor to transfer this employee to another assignment. 5.____

6. Even though an assistant gardener has had gardening experience before coming to the Park Department, a short period of training in Park Department methods and procedures would PROBABLY be helpful to him. 6.____

7. If you know in advance that you will not be able to come to work on a certain day, you should telephone your supervisor at about 11 o'clock on the morning of that day. 7.____

8. At the end of the working day, only those tools that are not going to be used the next day should be put back in their regular storage place. 8.____

9. If some work that you did is criticized by your supervisor because of mistakes that you made, you should try to avoid these mistakes the next time you do such work. 9.____

10. Your supervisor instructs you to do a job in a certain way but you believe that there is a better way to do this job. You should disregard the supervisor's instructions and do the job in your own way. 10.____

Questions 11-19.

DIRECTIONS: Your answers to Questions 11 to 19 must be based only on the information contained in the following quotation and NOT upon any other information you may have.

Before laying sod, prepare the soil as in making a lawn, rake it smooth and leave it, when loose and uncompacted, just about as high as the desired finished level. Lay the sods carefully, first along the margin of the area, then side by side toward the center. Fit the edges close together, adding or removing a little soil beneath as may be necessary to produce a level surface. When an area a few sods wide is laid, pound it down hard, using a heavy flat wooden block on a handle or the back of a spade. A plank should be laid to walk on while doing this so as to avoid making footprints in the new turf. Do not attempt to roll the sod but pound it well, especially where the edges join. Then soak it thoroughly.

11. After a piece of sod has been laid, it should be stamped down with the feet or with a heavy flat wooden block on a handle. 11.___

12. To allow for expansion as a result of pounding, a very small space should be left between individual pieces of sod when they are laid. 12.___

13. An area on which sod is to be laid should be prepared in the same way as an area which is to be seeded for a lawn. 13.___

14. Rolling the sod after laying, especially where the edges join, is desirable. 14.___

15. The level of an area which has been prepared for the laying of sod should be about the same as the final level that is desired after the sod has been laid. 15.___

16. A spade is sometimes used in one of the operations connected with the laying of sod. 16.___

17. If, when a piece of sod is laid down, it is lower than the piece next to it, some additional soil should be put under it to bring it to the necessary level. 17.___

18. After the sod has been laid and pounded down, it is desirable to give it a good watering. 18.___

19. In laying sod over a prepared area, the BEST procedure to follow is to start in the center of the area and work outwards, laying the sods side by side. 19.___

Questions 20-27.

DIRECTIONS: Your answers to Questions 20 to 27 must be based only on the information contained in the following quotation and NOT upon any other information you may have.

Unpack and prune trees delivered from a nursery as soon as they arrive. Before planting them, shorten slightly every root of the thickness of a lead pencil and cut injured roots back to sound wood. Make the cuts on a slant and with the surface of the wound facing down. After planting, reduce the tops of all except one year trees at least 50 percent, and preferably 75 percent, to balance the reduction of the feeding root area. Let the main branches start a foot or more apart on the trunk and point in different directions. Three or four are enough to start with. Shorten these limbs from 33 to 50 percent and cut off all the others. It is not desirable to cut the leader or main stem because branches will tend to develop in a bunch just below the cut.

20. After a tree delivered from a nursery is planted, its MAIN branches should be cut back from 1/3 to 1/2. 20.___

21. The tops of one year trees should be cut back 75% after planting. 21.___

22. Branches will develop in a bunch below the cut if the leader of a tree is cut after planting. 22.___

23. Before planting trees received from the nursery, slightly shorten every root. 23.___

24. The top of a transplanted tree is reduced in order to offset the reduction of the feeding root area. 24._____

25. When roots are cut, the surface of the cut should face down. 25._____

26. Not more than four main branches should be left on the trunk as a start. 26._____

27. When nursery stock is transplanted, injured roots should be cut off at the base of the trunk. 27._____

Questions 28-33.

DIRECTIONS: Your answers to Questions 28 to 33 must be based only on the information contained in the following quotation and NOT upon any other information you may have.

The best way to apply nitrate of soda and other readily soluble fertilizers is to divide the total quantity recommended for the given area into several equal parts; to scatter one part broadcast after the ground is plowed or dug and rake or harrow it into the surface just before planting; to apply a second part two or three weeks later and others at similar intervals.

28. The second application of the fertilizer should be made just before planting. 28._____

29. When a readily soluble fertilizer is applied to a given area, the total quantity of fertilizer should be divided into two equal parts. 29._____

30. The first application of the fertilizer should be raked into the ground. 30._____

31. Nitrate of soda is a fertilizer that is readily soluble. 31._____

32. The fertilizer should be applied with a spreader in order to get a uniform rate of application. 32._____

33. The first application of the fertilizer should be made after the ground is plowed. 33._____

Questions 34-37.

DIRECTIONS: Your answers to Questions 34 to 37 must be based only on the information contained in the following quotation and NOT upon any other information you may have.

Avoid light surface sprinkling of outdoor plants and lawns. Such applications of water are worse than giving none at all because the moistened layer of soil is very shallow. The plants are thereby encouraged to develop roots near the surface, and the result is disaster when sprinkling is discontinued for a few days or when a dry hot spell occurs to dry the roots.

34. Light sprinkling of outdoor plants causes them to develop roots near the surface. 34._____

35. Light watering of lawns is desirable during dry hot spells. 35._____

36. It is sometimes better to give plants no water at all than to give them very little water. 36._____

37. Shallow rooting systems are severely injured during hot spells.   37.____

Questions 38-46.

DIRECTIONS: Your answers to Questions 38 to 46 must be based only on the information contained in the following quotation and NOT upon any other information you may have.

Fall bulbs are dormant and should be planted during the summer and fall. Spring bulbs are dormant over the winter and must be planted in the early spring. Fall bulbs include Tulip and Narcissus. Spring bulbs include Gladiolus and Dahlia. September and October are the best months for planting fall bulbs. April and May are the best months for planting spring bulbs. A good plan to follow is to allow twice the diameter of a bulb between every two bulbs and to plant the bulb three inches deep if it is a large bulb or corm such as Gladiolus, and one and a half to two inches deep if it is a small bulb or corm such as Crocus.

38. Dahlias should be planted in September or October.   38.____
39. Bulbs may be planted in the fall if they are dormant in the fall.   39.____
40. When bulbs are planted, they should be spaced six inches apart.   40.____
41. Crocus should be planted two and one half inches deep.   41.____
42. Bulbs should be planted in the spring if they are dormant in the winter.   42.____
43. The bigger the bulb, the deeper it should be planted.   43.____
44. Tulips should be planted in the spring.   44.____
45. It is desirable to plant Narcissus in October.   45.____
46. Gladiolus and Crocus are also known as corms.   46.____

Questions 47-50.

DIRECTIONS: Your answers to Questions 47 to 50 must be based only on the information contained in the following quotation and NOT upon any other information you may have.

A hotbed is a bottomless box with a transparent, removable top used to grow plants out of local season. It is different from a cold-frame mainly in that it is artificially heated so that it can be used earlier and operated during more severe weather. When the source of artificial heat of a hotbed is removed, a hotbed becomes the same as a coldframe.

47. The MAIN difference between a hotbed and a coldframe is the source of heat.   47.____
48. It is possible to see through the top of a hotbed.   48.____
49. The MAIN purpose of a hotbed is to grow plants during the summer season.   49.____
50. A hotbed is heated by artificial means.   50.____

KEY (CORRECT ANSWERS)

1. T	11. F	21. F	31. T	41. F
2. F	12. F	22. T	32. F	42. T
3. F	13. T	23. F	33. T	43. T
4. T	14. F	24. T	34. T	44. F
5. F	15. T	25. T	35. F	45. T
6. T	16. T	26. T	36. T	46. T
7. F	17. T	27. F	37. T	47. T
8. F	18. T	28. F	38. F	48. T
9. T	19. F	29. F	39. T	49. F
10. F	20. T	30. T	40. F	50. T

TEST 4

DIRECTIONS: Each question consists of a statement. You are to indicate whether the statement is TRUE (T) or FALSE (F). *PRINT THE LETTER OF THE CORRECT ANSWER IN THE SPACE AT THE RIGHT.*

Questions 1-9.

DIRECTIONS: Your answers to Questions 1 to 9 must be based only on the information contained in the following quotation and NOT upon any other information you may have.

Insecticides kill insects by poisoning, suffocation, or paralysis. They are grouped into three classes: stomach poisons, contact poisons, and fumigants. Fumigants are the most effective type to use when the insects are in a greenhouse or other enclosure. Occasionally, they are used in the open under tents placed over the plant. Commonly used fumigants are nicotine and carbon bisulphide. Stomach poisons are used against insects with biting and chewing mouth parts, such as beetles and caterpillars. There are two types of stomach poisons, poison baits and protectants. The most widely used stomach poisons are composed of some form of arsenic.

1. Nicotine is used as a stomach poison. 1.____
2. Fumigants are best to use on plants growing outdoors. 2.____
3. An insecticide kills insects in one of three ways. 3.____
4. When fumigants are used outdoors, the plant is covered with a tent. 4.____
5. A protectant is another name for a fumigant. 5.____
6. Beetles have the same kind of mouth parts as caterpillars. 6.____
7. Most contact poisons contain arsenic. 7.____
8. Carbon disulphide is used against beetles and caterpillars. 8.____
9. A protectant is a type of stomach poison. 9.____

Questions 10-19.

DIRECTIONS: Your answers to Questions 10 to 19 must be based only on the information contained in the following quotation and NOT upon any other information you may have.

The Japanese beetle is nearly a half inch long, is bright shining green with bronze or reddish wing covers. There are five white spots made of tufts of white hairs along the sides of the abdomen and two distinct white spots at the tip of the abdomen below the tips of the wing covers. The larva is a white grub resembling that of the common May beetle or June bug, but only about half as big. The beetles begin to emerge from the soil the latter part of June and may be present until the first of October, but the period of greatest density lasts only from the middle of July to early August. The eggs, laid in the soil chiefly during July and August, hatch in 12 days, and the grubs soon begin to feed on grass roots near the surface. Toward the winter, they move downward about a foot to hibernate.

10. The larva of the June bug is half as large as the larva of the Japanese beetle.   10.____

11. The Japanese beetle has seven white spots on its abdomen.   11.____

12. The grubs of the Japanese beetle come up to the surface right after they hatch in order   12.____
    to feed on the grass.

13. The Japanese beetle is reddish bronze in color.   13.____

14. The Japanese beetles begin to come out of the soil after June.   14.____

15. The larva of the May beetle resembles the larva of the Japanese beetle.   15.____

16. The Japanese beetle ranges in size from 1/4 to 3/4 of an inch.   16.____

17. During the winter, Japanese beetle grubs live about a foot underground.   17.____

18. Japanese beetles are most plentiful from about July 15 to about August 10th.   18.____

19. The Japanese beetle lays its eggs in the ground.   19.____

Questions 20-25.

DIRECTIONS: Your answers to Questions 20 to 25 must be based only on the information contained in the following quotation and NOT upon any other information you may have.

Soils may be either acid, neutral, or alkaline. The degree of acidity or alkalinity of the soil has an important influence on the health of many plants. Acids and alkalis are opposites, and if mixed together, tend to neutralize each other so that a combination may be neither acid nor alkaline, but neutral. Acetic acid, which gives sourness to vinegar, is a well-known acid. Lime is a familiar, mild alkali. Caustic soda is a more powerful alkali. Compounds containing both lime and acetic acid occur in soils, but acid soils contain more of carbonic, tannic, and other acids.

20. All soils are either neutral, acid, or alkaline.   20.____

21. Alkalis and acids mixed together neutralize each other.   21.____

22. Tannic acid gives vinegar its sour taste.   22.____

23. If a plant is not growing well, this may be due to the acidity of the soil.   23.____

24. Caustic soda is a mild alkali.   24.____

25. Acid soils contain mainly acetic acid.   25.____

26. A metal bow rake is generally the BEST tool to use for raking light litter from the lawn.   26.____

27. A dibble is a tool generally used to make holes in soft ground for planting bulbs or setting   27.____
    small plants.

28. The average lawn mower can be adjusted to vary the height above the ground at which it will cut the grass. 28.____
29. The common garden spade USUALLY has a flat metal blade. 29.____
30. A spading fork USUALLY has a single, broad, curved metal blade. 30.____
31. A *oomplete fertilizer* is one which contains phosphorus, potassium, and iron. 31.____
32. A 10-6-4 fertilizer is suitable for feeding lawns. 32.____
33. When lime is added to the soil, it will make the soil more acid. 33.____
34. An organic fertilizer is one which is produced by animals or derived from plants. 34.____
35. The sub-soil is GENERALLY richer in plant nutrients than the top-soil. 35.____
36. Humus is an important ingredient of any good, fertile soil that is in good condition. 36.____
37. Acid soils MUST be made alkaline before they will support any plant life. 37.____
38. Shrubs that bloom during early spring should be pruned within a week or two after the flowers have fallen. 38.____
39. Plants which live more than two years are known as perennials. 39.____
40. A deciduous tree sheds its leaves in winter. 40.____
41. Forsythia is a shrub that flowers early in the spring. 41.____
42. Daffodils should be planted in the fall. 42.____
43. MOST lilacs flower in September. 43.____
44. Nicotine is COMMONLY used as a contact insecticide against sucking insects. 44.____
45. Sulphur is COMMONLY used as a fungicide. 45.____
46. The BEST time to sow lawn grass seed is in the spring. 46.____
47. California privet is COMMONLY used for hedge material. 47.____
48. Broad-leaved weeds in a lawn may be effectively destroyed by the application of 2,4-D. 48.____
49. Crab grass is a desirable lawn grass. 49.____
50. The Norway Maple is a tree COMMONLY used for street plantings in this area. 50.____

KEY (CORRECT ANSWERS)

1. F	11. T	21. T	31. F	41. T
2. F	12. F	22. F	32. T	42. T
3. T	13. F	23. T	33. F	43. F
4. T	14. F	24. F	34. T	44. T
5. F	15. T	25. F	35. F	45. T
6. T	16. F	26. F	36. T	46. T
7. F	17. T	27. T	37. F	47. T
8. F	18. T	28. T	38. T	48. T
9. T	19. T	29. T	39. T	49. F
10. F	20. T	30. F	40. T	50. T

EXAMINATION SECTION
TEST 1

DIRECTIONS: Each question consists of a statement. You are to indicate whether the statement is TRUE (T) or FALSE (F). *PRINT THE LETTER OF THE CORRECT ANSWER IN THE SPACE AT THE RIGHT.*

1. Fence posts sunk into the soil need no wood preservative below the soil line because the earth itself is a natural preservative. 1.____

2. An assistant gardener who sees a man drop papers on a lawn should say nothing and pick the papers up himself in order to keep the goodwill of the public. 2.____

3. One reason for wrapping newly planted trees with burlap cloth when they are over 2 inches in diameter is to cut down on loss of water through the bark of the tree. 3.____

4. When a large branch is cut from a tree-like shrub, the cut should USUALLY be left open to the healing powers of the air. 4.____

5. If you find that a lawn area your foreman has sent you to mow has just been mowed by another assistant gardener, you should say nothing about this and mow the lawn anyway. 5.____

6. A sandy soil USUALLY holds water longer than a clay soil. 6.____

7. Pole pruners are used MAINLY for sawing down posts. 7.____

8. A fan-shaped bamboo rake is a good rake for gathering leaves on a lawn. 8.____

9. If your foreman asks you to help a gang of Park Department laborers who are digging a trench, you should refuse to do so because digging is NOT one of the duties of an assistant gardener. 9.____

10. Before using a chisel which has *mushroomed* from constant use, an assistant gardener should lay the chisel on a hard piece of steel and hammer the *mushroomed* edges until they disappear. 10.____

11. If you wish to dig up a plant from one place in order to plant it in another place, you should do this on a sunny day so that the roots receive some of the sunlight they seldom get. 11.____

12. Lime is USUALLY added to the soil to make the soil more acid. 12.____

13. The leaf is USUALLY the part of the plant that makes food for the plant. 13.____

14. Gasoline is one of the SAFEST cleaning liquids to use for greasy, dirty, metal equipment. 14.____

15. An assistant gardener should work steadily but slowly so that there will be enough work to go around. 15.____

16. When a dump truck brings brush to a spot to be burned, the truck should USUALLY dump the brush at a place some distance from the fire rather than right on the fire. 16.____

17. If the sod you are cutting to plant in another place seems to be infected with fungus, you should report this to your foreman as soon as possible. 17.____

18. The BEST trees for planting on streets are those with roots that can get into sewers for water.   18.____

19. To let the sunlight get to the lower branches, a hedge should USUALLY be trimmed so that it is wider at the top than at the bottom.   19.____

20. To help grass on a lawn become deep rooted, it is better to soak the lawn with water when the lawn needs it than to water it lightly every day.   20.____

21. If you should overhear several teenagers plotting a gang fight in the park to which you are assigned, you should notify your foreman so that he can take action.   21.____

22. MOST northern grasses should usually be cut much shorter than usual in a summer drought because shorter grass leaves require less water.   22.____

23. You notice that a mechanic working in the park is doing his work in a way you consider inefficient. You, as the assistant gardener, should report this mechanic for inefficiency.   23.____

24. A newly planted bed of lawn seed should be watered with a fine spray rather than a heavy spray to keep from washing the seed away.   24.____

25. A scythe is MAINLY used to trim hedges.   25.____

26. If you see a child annoying squirrels in the park in which you work, you should call a policeman to arrest the child.   26.____

27. A sickle is MAINLY used to cut tall grass and weeds.   27.____

Questions 28-36.

DIRECTIONS: Your answers to Questions 28 through 36 must be based only on the information given in the following paragraph and NOT on any other information you may have.

Plant reproduction is called propagation. Methods of propagation can be divided into two classes, those methods which depend on seed and those depending on the use of buds. Buds are the small swellings on plant stems from which shoots, clusters of leaves, or flowers develop. Propagation by seed is called sexual, while propagation by buds is called asexual. Asexual propagation depends primarily upon the activity of the cambium. This is a layer of very thin tissue consisting entirely of young, easily broken cells filled with protoplasm, the basic stuff found in all living things. This cambium layer forms new plant tissues under the proper circumstances. It plays an important part in growth, in healing, and in asexual reproduction. When a bud is cut from a parent plant and inserted into water, sand, or other material suitable for starting growth, the cambium promotes root formation on the bud. When a branch is cut from one tree and grafted onto another of the same kind, the cambium from the branch unites with that of the tree and develops an additional protective covering. Propagation by asexual rather than sexual means is used because it is the most certain means of producing an offspring closely resembling the parent.

28. One example of propagation by sexual means is the growing of a plant from a bud.   28.____

29. Several forms of growth can develop from buds which are on a plant stem.   29.____

30. The cambium layer is made up of tough cells which help protect the tree.   30.____

31. A special quality of the cambium layer is that it will form new plant tissues under any circumstances.   31.____

32. Cambium activity is important in asexual reproduction.   32.____

33. All living animals have protoplasm in them.   33.____

34. Roots may start to grow from a bud cut from a parent plant only when the bud is placed in sand.   34.____

35. When a branch from one tree is grafted onto another tree of the same kind, the cambium of the first tree joins with that of the second tree.   35.____

36. The surest way of obtaining plants which look very much like the parent plant is to grow such plants from the seeds of the parent.   36.____

Questions 37-41.

DIRECTIONS: Your answers to Questions 37 through 41 must be based only on the information given in the following paragraph and NOT on any other information you may have.

The soil around young trees and shrubs is often cultivated the first two or three years in order to insure a good start. Cultivation helps to control and eliminate weeds but has no other value in stimulating plant growth. Deep cultivation is done in the spring. As the growing season progresses, cultivation should be gradually shallower. This method may result in the destruction of feeding roots formed the previous year in the same cultivated areas, but it does not disturb the carrier roots from which the feeding roots came. If the tree or shrub is not cultivated for a few years, however, these feeding roots grow into carrier roots with feeding roots growing mainly from their ends. When cultivation is resumed after such an interval, extra precaution must be taken not to prune the carrier roots too severely. Injurious results of severe root pruning may be partially offset by a correspondingly severe pruning of the top at the time of root pruning.

37. Cultivating the earth around young trees for the first two or three years helps plant growth by letting air get to the roots.   37.____

38. Even though the method of cultivating a young tree may be the right one, some feeding roots of the tree may be destroyed.   38.____

39. Cultivation of young trees at the beginning of the growing season should be more shallow than cultivation late in the growing season.   39.____

40. If several seasons of growth of a tree have gone by without cultivation, some feeding roots grow into carrier roots.   40.____

41. Cutting a lot from the top of a tree makes up partly for the bad effects of cutting a lot from the roots.   41.____

Questions 42-46.

DIRECTIONS: Your answers to Questions 42 through 46 must be based only on the information given in the following paragraph and NOT upon any other information you may have.

Low shrubs need no guys to maintain their position. But newly planted trees and tree-like shrubs, unless they are staked or guyed at once, may be pushed out of alignment by the wind or other forces. When pulled by a wire back to a vertical position, such trees continue to exert a force against the pull. In such cases, not only will all the strain usually be put on one stake or guy wire but, most important, air pockets may form around the roots. To best maintain the stability of the tree, the tension on all stakes and guy wires should be approximately equal at the time of planting. Although the tension on individual wires will then vary with the conditions met later, the position of the tree is not likely to be affected.

42. To keep the wind from bending low shrubs, they should be staked or guyed right after planting. 42.____

43. If a tree pushed out of line is then pulled straight by one wire, the chances are that the tree will snap back out of line if the wire is cut. 43.____

44. The most important result of guying straight a tree which has been knocked out of line is that most of the strain is usually put on one guy wire. 44.____

45. Straightening out a tree after it has been pushed from its vertical position helps to remove air pockets around the roots. 45.____

46. If three guy wires are used to support a small tree after planting, the tension on one guy wire should be approximately one-third of the total tension on all three guy wires. 46.____

Questions 47-50.

DIRECTIONS: Your answers to Questions 47 through 50 MUST be based only on the information given in the following paragraph and NOT on any other information you may have.

Sun often injures trees by burning their trunks and main branches. Especially susceptible to such injury are those trees growing in well-cultivated orchards. In the Northern Hemisphere, such injury usually occurs on the south side, although it often also occurs on the east side, less often on the west, and never on the north side. The damage is sometimes confined to these exposed bark areas, but such limitation to exposed bark areas only is seldom found. When the tissues in the inner bark are destroyed, the downward flow of plant food is impeded, and the roots to which these tissues lead are deprived of nourishment.

47. One method of protecting trees from sun injury is to cultivate well the orchard in which they grow. 47.____

48. In the United States, one side of the tree on which sun injury usually occurs is the north side. 48.____

49. Sun damage to trees is sometimes restricted to the outer bark of the tree. 49.____

50. Root nourishment depends on the downward flow of plant food in the inner bark. 50.____

KEY (CORRECT ANSWERS)

1. F	11. F	21. T	31. F	41. T
2. F	12. F	22. F	32. T	42. F
3. T	13. T	23. F	33. T	43. T
4. F	14. F	24. T	34. F	44. F
5. F	15. F	25. F	35. T	45. F
6. F	16. T	26. F	36. F	46. T
7. F	17. T	27. T	37. F	47. F
8. T	18. F	28. F	38. T	48. F
9. F	19. F	29. T	39. F	49. T
10. F	20. T	30. F	40. T	50. T

TEST 2

DIRECTIONS: Each question consists of a statement. You are to indicate whether the statement is TRUE (T) or FALSE (F). *PRINT THE LETTER OF THE CORRECT ANSWER IN THE SPACE AT THE RIGHT.*

Questions 1-3.

DIRECTIONS: Your answers to Questions 1 through 3 must be based only on the information given in the following paragraph and NOT on any other information you may have.

The belt should always be taut when clutch is fully engaged and at no other time. To check the belt for proper tension, first start the engine, and then bear down lightly on the handle of the mower in order to raise the mower wheels off the ground. While in this position, engage the clutch; then stop the engine by shorting the sparkplug with the stop switch, leaving the clutch engaged. If the belt is not taut, loosen the nut which holds the countershaft pedestal in order to make the countershaft pedestal movable. Then slide the countershaft pedestal to the back to tighten the belt. Sliding the countershaft pedestal forward loosens the belt.

1. The only time the belt should be tight is when the clutch is engaged completely.   1.____

2. In testing the belt for correct tension, the clutch should be engaged after the mower wheels are raised off the ground.   2.____

3. To make the belt looser, tighten the nut holding the countershaft pedestal.   3.____

Questions 4-10.

DIRECTIONS: Your answers to Questions 4 through 10 must be based only on the information given in the following paragraph and NOT on any other information you may have.

The soil around actively growing delphiniums should receive a thorough soaking at least once a week. Delphiniums can be transplanted either in the autumn or in the spring. The fine and fibrous root system of these plants facilitates their removal. Since delphiniums are among the first herbaceous plants to start growth in the spring, autumn transplanting is generally recommended because the plants then undoubtedly suffer less shock. If the work is done with extreme care, it is possible to move quite large plants when they are just coming into bloom. Large plants must be lifted with a generous quantity of earth in order that the root system remain intact. The use of a plastic spray will prevent wilting if applied before the plants are moved.

4. Delphiniums must be watered more than once a week.   4.____

5. Delphiniums are difficult to remove because of their thick, tough roots.   5.____

6. Delphiniums start growth earlier in the spring than many other herbaceous plants.   6.____

7. Delphiniums experience more shock from transplanting in the spring than in the fall.   7.____

8. To keep the root system together when large delphiniums are moved, a large amount of earth should be taken up with the roots.   8.____

9. One way of preventing a delphinium from wilting when moved is to apply a plastic spray to the plant beforehand.   9.____

10. Large delphinium plants are MOST easily moved at the time they are beginning to bloom.   10.____

11. *Formal shearing destroys the plant's individuality.* In this sentence, the word *formal* means NEARLY the same as *irregular*.   11.____

12. *The entire tree is covered with a film which is flexible, colorless, and lasting.* In this sentence, the word *flexible* means NEARLY the same as *tough*.   12.____

13. *All of the equipment is mobile.* In this sentence, the word *mobile* means NEARLY the same as the word *movable*.   13.____

14. *Just enough asphalt adheres to make a mat.* In this sentence, the word *adheres* means NEARLY the same as the word *sticks*.   14.____

15. *Efforts at proper maintenance were nullified by this act.* In this sentence, the word *nullified* means NEARLY the same as *brought to nothing*.   15.____

16. Saying that a hose is *perforated* is another way of saying that a hose is *bent*.   16.____

17. *Do not injure the foliage of a plant* means NEARLY the same as *do not injure the plant's roots*.   17.____

18. *Pulverizing* soil is breaking it down into very small bits.   18.____

19. Humus is the part of the soil which is very often called clay in gardening practice.   19.____

20. *Aerating* a turf area is NEARLY the same as *sodding* the area.   20.____

21. *To mechanically agitate* means NEARLY the same as *to seed by mechanical power*.   21.____

22. *To eliminate hand pumping* means NEARLY the same as *to do away with hand pumping*.   22.____

23. *Discarding a ladder with a cracked rung* means NEARLY the same as *repairing a ladder with a cracked rung*.   23.____

24. A *projecting* stub is USUALLY a stub which sticks out.   24.____

25. A *nitrogen deficiency* in the soil is an oversupply of nitrogen in the soil.   25.____

26. Saying that a soil has a heavy *texture* is NEARLY the same as saying that the soil has a deep color.   26.____

27. A *neutral* soil is one in which no useful plants will grow.   27.____

28. A plant which is *dormant* is USUALLY in an inactive period of growth.   28.____

29. Saying that sun is *detrimental* to ferns is NEARLY the same as saying that sun is harmful to ferns.   29.____

30. *Vendors are permitted only in certain park areas.* In this sentence, the word *vendors* means NEARLY the same as *sellers*.   30.____

31. *The assistant gardener was confident that he would be able to learn the new work quickly.* In this sentence, the word *confident* means NEARLY the same as *sure*.   31.____

32. *The employee's behavior on the job was improper.* In this sentence, the word *improper* means NEARLY the same as *good*.   32.____

33. *The foreman's oral instructions were always clear and to the point.* In this sentence, the word *oral* means NEARLY the same as *spoken*.   33.____

34. *A covering with paper will prevent excessive loss of moisture from the surface soil.* In this sentence, the word *excessive* means NEARLY the same as *unnecessary*.   34.____

35. *In making a permanent hotbed, the ground should be excavated to a depth of fifteen inches.* In this sentence, the word *excavated* means NEARLY the same as *dug out*.   35.____

36. *After the seed has been sown, an application of water will help it to germinate.* In this sentence, the word *germinate* means NEARLY the same as *start growing*.   36.____

37. *A sandy soil may be greatly improved through the incorporation of organic materials.* In this sentence, the word *incorporation* means NEARLY the same as *removal*.   37.____

38. *Manures are considered a concentrated form of fertilizer.* In this sentence, the word *concentrated* means NEARLY the same as *natural*.   38.____

39. *Ventilation of some kind must be given the plants.* In this sentence, the word *ventilation* means NEARLY the same as *heat*.   39.____

40. *When rain water enters soil, it penetrates air spaces.* In this sentence, the word *penetrates* means NEARLY the same as *fills*.   40.____

41. If 100 pounds of a certain artificial fertilizer does a job equal to that done by 1 ton of a certain kind of manure, then 125 pounds of this fertilizer should do the same job as $1\frac{1}{2}$ tons of the manure.   41.____

42. If an assistant gardener digs up an average of 73 square yards of lawn area per hour, then the total area dug in eight hours by this assistant gardener should be 574 square yards.   42.____

43. From a total of 245 shrubs in a nursery, 56 shrubs are taken away the first day and 62 shrubs are brought into the nursery on the second day. The number of shrubs in the nursery at the beginning of the third day should be 251.   43.____

44. An assistant gardener finished 1/3 of a job on the first day, 1/2 of the job on the second day, and the balance on the third day. The part of the job done by the assistant gardener on the third day was equal to the part done on the first day.   44.____

45. If there are 231 cubic inches in a gallon, then in 1/3 of a gallon there are 77 cubic inches.   45.____

46. If $12\frac{1}{2}$% of a total force of 8,080 employees are laborers, then there are 1,010 laborers in this force. 46.____

47. If a bill for gardening materials lists $15.40 for rose bushes, $78.45 for lawn seed, $24.15 for fertilizer, and $27.10 for bulbs and corms, then the total cost of these items is $145.10. 47.____

48. An assistant gardener must distribute a certain number of plants equally among a certain number of parks. To find the number of plants to give to each park, he should divide the number of parks by the number of plants. 48.____

49. A lawn 47 feet wide and 93 feet long has an area of 4,471 square feet. 49.____

50. If 14 out of a total of 114 shrubs are evergreens, then 14% of the total are evergreens. 50.____

KEY (CORRECT ANSWERS)

1. T	11. F	21. F	31. T	41. F
2. T	12. F	22. T	32. F	42. F
3. F	13. T	23. F	33. T	43. T
4. F	14. T	24. T	34. F	44. F
5. F	15. T	25. F	35. T	45. T
6. T	16. F	26. F	36. T	46. T
7. T	17. F	27. F	37. F	47. T
8. T	18. T	28. T	38. F	48. T
9. T	19. F	29. T	39. F	49. F
10. F	20. F	30. T	40. F	50. F

TEST 3

DIRECTIONS: Each question consists of a statement. You are to indicate whether the statement is TRUE (T) or FALSE (F). *PRINT THE LETTER OF THE CORRECT ANSWER IN THE SPACE AT THE RIGHT.*

1. A bed of leaves or straw on the surface of the ground around plants helps to keep down loss of moisture from the soil. 1.____

2. An evergreen tree is one which does NOT shed its leaves each year. 2.____

3. All insects are harmful to plant life. 3.____

4. Hedges should NEVER be used as a border around walks and other landscaped areas. 4.____

5. When hedges are pruned, it is considered good practice to cut them wider at the top than at the bottom in order to allow light to reach the bottom branches. 5.____

6. Leaves mixed with the soil will in time rot and add plant food to the soil. 6.____

7. The usual reason why a tree guard is placed around a young tree is to protect the tree from possible injury. 7.____

8. During periods of hot weather, it is desirable to give lawns a light watering. 8.____

9. The fall is USUALLY the BEST time to sow lawn grass seed. 9.____

10. If a plant loses its leaves in the fall of every year, it shows that the plant has not been planted properly. 10.____

11. Sandy soils drain quickly and dry rapidly. 11.____

12. Animal manures added to the soil improve the condition of the soil. 12.____

13. It is often hard to grow grass under a tree because the roots of the tree take away most of the water and plant food from the grass. 13.____

14. Any rust found on garden tools during the summer should be removed the following spring. 14.____

15. An assistant gardener should know the tool BEST suited for each type of work so that the work involved will be made easier. 15.____

16. After use in gardening, tools should be stored in a cellar or basement because the dampness there is good for the metal parts. 16.____

17. As a help in keeping a good edge on tools, earth and grass clippings should be removed from the tools immediately after they are used. 17.____

18. A four-pronged spading fork is a good tool for digging up a garden area. 18.____

19. Chemicals used to kill plant insects USUALLY can be applied only in a dissolved liquid form. 19.____

20. If a growing plant is to be moved from one spot to another, it is good practice to first dig the new hole before digging up the plant that is to be moved in order to lessen the drying out of the roots.

    20._____

21. Rapidly running water from an unattended hose can cause soil to wash off sloping planted areas.

    21._____

22. An assistant gardener who comes late to work often should expect his superiors to pay no attention to this lateness if his work is excellent.

    22._____

23. It is all right for an assistant gardener to give members of the public parts of plants growing in city parks provided he cuts off the parts very carefully.

    23._____

24. An assistant gardener at work who sees a person throwing rubbish on the ground in a park should pay no attention as this is a matter for the Sanitation Department.

    24._____

25. If your superior gives you an assignment which you do not like, you should try to do a good job anyway.

    25._____

26. If you know in advance that you will not be able to report for work next Thursday, you should tell your superior immediately rather than wait to telephone him on the day of your absence.

    26._____

Questions 27-29.

DIRECTIONS: Your answers to Questions 27 through 29 must be based only on the information given in the following paragraph and NOT on any other information you may have.

It has long been customary to wrap damp sphagnum moss, peat moss, or wood shavings around the roots and crowns of plants to prevent loss of moisture from living tissues during storage or in transit. The use of these materials have two major disadvantages. They make heavy, bulky packages which adds to the cost in mail-order shipping. And, in the case of dormant stock, if the moisture content of the packing is too high, the plants may prematurely start into new growth.

27. It has been customary to wrap sphagnum moss around the roots and crowns of plants to prevent loss of moisture during storage or in transit.

    27._____

28. A cost factor in mail-order shipping is the bulkiness of the package.

    28._____

29. Plants cannot start into new growth if the moisture content of the packing is too high.

    29._____

Questions 30-35.

DIRECTIONS: Your answers to Questions 30 through 35 must be based only on the information given in the following paragraph and NOT on any other information you may have.

Lawnmowers, as well as lawns, suffer when the grass is cut too short. There is much more dust and dirt on the base of the blades of grass, near the soil, than there is higher up. This grit wears away the blades and the strike bar and quickly dulls them. Other bad practices are leaving the mower out overnight and failing to wipe the cutting edges dry after each mowing. A couple of dewy nights, a session with wet grass, and the sharp edge has rusted. The simple measure of wiping an oily rag across the edges of the blades and the cutting bar will prevent rusting of these important surfaces.

30. When the grass is cut too short, the lawnmower suffers.   30._____
31. There is more dirt on the base of a blade of grass than there is higher up.   31._____
32. The blades and the strike bar of a lawnmower are sharpened by the grit of the soil.   32._____
33. It is bad practice to leave the mower out overnight.   33._____
34. After each mowing, the cutting edges of a mower should be wiped dry.   34._____
35. Wiping the edges of the blades and the cutting bar with an oily rag will NOT prevent rusting.   35._____

Questions 36-42.

DIRECTIONS: Your answers to Questions 36 through 42 must be based only on the information given in the following paragraph and NOT on any other information you may have.

There are many organic fertilizers that can be used not only to add nutrients to the soil, but also to help build up humus content and thus increase its water-holding capacity. The organic fertilizers are those derived entirely from animal or vegetable sources, while inorganic kinds are chemical. The most readily available, complete organic fertilizers are the manures and these alone do not contain enough nutrients to satisfy a garden for a whole season. Application of one or more kinds of manure to the soil is excellent in the spring and again in the fall.

36. Organic fertilizers can be used to help build up the humus content of the soil.   36._____
37. Nutrients cannot be added to the soil through the use of organic fertilizers.   37._____
38. Inorganic fertilizers are chemical ones.   38._____
39. The organic fertilizers are derived from vegetable or animal sources.   39._____
40. The manures are the MOST readily available, complete organic fertilizer.   40._____
41. The manures contain enough nutrients to satisfy a garden for a whole season.   41._____
42. Application of manure to the soil is excellent in the spring and in the fall.   42._____

Questions 43-55.

DIRECTIONS: Your answers to Questions 43 through 55 must be based only on the information given in the following paragraph and NOT on any other information you may have.

If the roses are to bloom well, they should not be neglected. Of the several measures to be taken, watering is one of the most important. A weekly soil soaking is recommended. Moisture should go down to the roots of the plants, where it is vitally needed, to a depth of about six inches. Taking the nozzle off the hose and letting water trickle into the soil is one way to do this.

A four-inch layer of mulch on the surface of the soil will protect the roots of the rose plants against heat, cold, and draught. Suitable mulches for roses include partly rotted stable manure, peat moss, compost, and even grass clippings. Peat moss is best worked lightly into the surface of the soil; otherwise, it is apt to form a crust.

Rose plants are susceptible to black spot, mildew, and the ravages of insects. It is advisable, therefore, to dust or spray rose plants at least once a week. Regular applications are necessary, covering both upper and under sides of the foliage. A well-nourished rose plant is more likely to resist disease than a weakened one. Any of the well-balanced commercially prepared rose foods will stimulate growth and bloom. It should be applied around the base of the plants at intervals of about three weeks and watered in well. It is not advisable to fertilize rose plants after September first.

43. Watering of roses is the LEAST important of the measures to be taken to insure good rose bloom. 43._____

44. Moisture should go down around the rose plant to a depth of about three inches. 44._____

45. Removing the nozzle from the hose and letting the water trickle into the soil is a method of getting water to the roots of the plants. 45._____

46. The roots of rose plants will be protected against heat, cold, and drought by a four-inch layer of mulch on the surface of the soil. 46._____

47. Grass clippings are NOT suitable as a mulch for roses. 47._____

48. Peat moss which is NOT worked into the surface of the soil is apt to form a crust. 48._____

49. Rose plants are susceptible to black spot and mildew. 49._____

50. Rose plants should NOT be dusted or sprayed more than once a month. 50._____

51. It is necessary to apply a spray or dust on the under side of the foliage only. 51._____

52. A rose plant is MORE likely to resist disease if it is well-nourished. 52._____

53. A well-balanced commercially prepared rose food will stimulate growth and bloom of the rose plant. 53._____

54. The rose food should be applied to the plant once during the growing season. 54._____

55. Rose plants should be fertilized up to November 1st. 55._____

KEY (CORRECT ANSWERS)

1. T	11. T	21. T	31. T	41. F
2. T	12. T	22. F	32. F	42. T
3. F	13. T	23. F	33. T	43. F
4. F	14. F	24. F	34. T	44. F
5. F	15. T	25. T	35. F	45. T
6. T	16. F	26. T	36. T	46. T
7. T	17. T	27. T	37. F	47. F
8. F	18. T	28. T	38. T	48. T
9. T	19. F	29. F	39. T	49. T
10. F	20. T	30. T	40. T	50. F

51. F
52. T
53. T
54. F
55. F

TEST 4

DIRECTIONS: Each question consists of a statement. You are to indicate whether the statement is TRUE (T) or FALSE (F). *PRINT THE LETTER OF THE CORRECT ANSWER IN THE SPACE AT THE RIGHT.*

Questions 1-7.

DIRECTIONS: Your answers to Questions 1 through 7 must be based only on the information given in the following paragraph and NOT on any other information you may have.

    In dry weather, after a few minutes of light sprinkling, the surface soil may become muddy and the inexperienced gardener is fooled into believing that enough water has been applied. Actually, the water may not even reach the roots. The roots may be in an almost powdery dry earth below a thin layer of mud from which the water quickly evaporates. Deep roots thus get no benefit while shallow roots are attracted to the upper surface of the soil and are worse off than if no sprinkling had been done. Sprinkling should always be continued on any one spot until the soil has become drenched. The best time of the day to sprinkle is toward or during the evening because usually the air is cooler and evaporation losses will be reduced to a minimum.

1. A few minutes of light sprinkling in dry weather may make the surface of the soil become muddy. 1.____

2. After a few minutes of light sprinkling in dry weather, the water may not even reach the roots. 2.____

3. Deep roots get no benefit from a light sprinkling. 3.____

4. Shallow roots are better off with a light sprinkling than with no sprinkling. 4.____

5. Sprinkling should not be continued on any one spot for so long that the soil becomes drenched. 5.____

6. The BEST time of day to sprinkle is toward or during evening. 6.____

7. The LEAST amount of evaporation loss occurs during the evening because the air is usually cooler then. 7.____

8. *Some plants are grown for the decorative value of their leaves.* In this sentence, the word *decorative* means NEARLY the same as *ornamental*. 8.____

9. *They made a circular flower garden.* In this sentence, the word *circular* means NEARLY the same as *square*. 9.____

10. *The gardener was a conscientious worker.* In this sentence, the word *conscientious* means NEARLY the same as *lazy*. 10.____

11. *A decaying branch is dangerous to the life of a tree.* In this sentence, the word *decaying* means NEARLY the same as *rotting*. 11.____

12. *Shearing helps keep the plants in the shape required.* In this sentence, the word *shearing* means NEARLY the same as *watering*. 12._____

13. *Some shrubs have vigorous growth and early flowering.* In this sentence, the word *vigorous* means NEARLY the same as *weak*. 13._____

14. *The lawn retained its healthy green color.* In this sentence, the word *retained* means NEARLY the same as *kept*. 14._____

15. *The soil is combined with an acid plant food.* In this sentence, the word *combined* means NEARLY the same as *mixed* 15._____

16. *Gardening can be tiring without the right tools.* In this sentence, the word *tiring* means NEARLY the same as *amusing* 16._____

17. *With the ground saturated, the roots may die.* In this sentence, the word *saturated* means NEARLY the same as *soaked*. 17._____

18. *Air can penetrate freely if holes are made in the soil.* In this sentence, the word *penetrate* means NEARLY the same as *follows*. 18._____

19. *With some plants, flowers precede the growth of leaves.* In this sentence, the word *precede* means NEARLY the same as *follow*. 19._____

20. *The gardener anticipated frost.* In this sentence, the word *anticipated* means NEARLY the same as *expected*. 20._____

21. *Tools are assembled when the job is finished.* In this sentence, the word *assembled* means NEARLY the same as *cleaned*. 21._____

22. *Part of the area was set aside for a miniature rock garden.* In this sentence, the word *miniature* means NEARLY the same as *beautiful*. 22._____

23. *Cheap tools are seldom durable.* In this sentence, the word *durable* means NEARLY the same as *long-lasting*. 23._____

24. *Concrete walks are maintained clean easily.* In this sentence, the word *maintained* means NEARLY the same as *kept*. 24._____

25. *Each morning the assistant gardener was punctual in reporting to work.* In this sentence, the word *punctual* means NEARLY the same as *prompt*. 25._____

26. *The landscaping work was a prolonged task.* In this sentence, the word *prolonged* means NEARLY the same as *difficult*. 26._____

27. *A transparent removable cover was placed over the flower bed.* In this sentence, the word *transparent* means NEARLY the same as *wooden*. 27._____

28. If a group of assistant gardeners planted 1,278 plants in Zone A, 1,262 plants in Zone B, 1,020 plants in Zone C, and 793 plants in Zone D, then the total number of plants planted by this group in these four zones was between 4,450 to 4,500. 28._____

29. If an assistant gardener assigned to a job does 1/3 of the work on Monday, 1/3 of the work on Wednesday, and the remainder on Friday, then the part of the work done by him on Friday is 1/3 of the whole job. 29._____

30. If an assistant gardener can dig up 150 square yards of lawn area every 3 hours, then in 5 hours he can dig up 350 square yards of lawn area. 30._____

31. If a gardener rejects 12 spades out of a total shipment of 48, then the number of spades that he rejected is 25 percent of the total. 31._____

32. If 4 assistant gardeners planted a total of 60 shrubs a day for a period of 22 days, then the total number of shrubs planted by these 4 in these 22 days was between 1,300 and 1,400. 32._____

33. If a park department spent $14.50 for rose bushes, $76.15 for lawn seed, $20.00 for lime, and $36.80 for tulip bulbs, then the total amount of money spent by the department for these items was $137.45. 33._____

34. If 165 plants are distributed equally among 15 parks, then each park will get 11 plants. 34._____

35. The decimal .125 expressed as a fraction is 1/4. 35._____

36. The quantity 25% expressed as a decimal is .40. 36._____

37. An employee who sweeps a path 12 feet wide and 50 feet long sweeps a total area of 600 square feet. 37._____

38. If a man who can walk at the rate of a mile in 20 minutes has a letter to deliver $3\frac{1}{2}$ miles away, it will take an hour and a half to deliver his letter. 38._____

39. If a square room is 900 square feet in area, then each side is 30 feet long. 39._____

40. If it is necessary to use a gallon of water in watering 50 square feet of garden, then 80 gallons are needed to water the balance of the area 20 feet wide and 200 feet long. 40._____

41. If a room holding twelve chairs is two-thirds full, there are nine persons present. 41._____

42. First aid is the immediate and temporary care given a victim of an accident or sudden illness until the services of a physician can be obtained. 42._____

43. A first action to take when taking care of an injured person is to sit him up so that you can talk to him directly. 43._____

44. If the injured person is unconscious, try to bring him around by offering a liquid stimulant at once. 44._____

45. When there is severe injury to any part of the body from any cause, the injured person will probably develop shock. 45._____

46. A sterile dressing is one that is free from germs. 46._____

47. Absorbent cotton may be applied directly over wounds to help control bleeding. 47._____

48. A compound fracture indicates that more than one bone is broken. 48.____

49. A first aider's duties are to relieve pain, prevent infection, and treat shock. 49.____

50. The best first aid treatment for a hernia is to lay the patient on his back. 50.____

KEY (CORRECT ANSWERS)

1. T	11. T	21. F	31. T	41. F
2. T	12. F	22. F	32. T	42. T
3. T	13. F	23. T	33. F	43. F
4. F	14. T	24. T	34. T	44. F
5. F	15. T	25. T	35. F	45. T
6. T	16. F	26. F	36. F	46. T
7. T	17. T	27. F	37. T	47. F
8. T	18. F	28. F	38. F	48. F
9. F	19. F	29. T	39. T	49. T
10. F	20. T	30. F	40. T	50. T

EXAMINATION SECTION
TEST 1

DIRECTIONS: Each question or incomplete statement is followed by several suggested answers or completions. Select the one that BEST answers the question or completes the statement. *PRINT THE LETTER OF THE CORRECT ANSWER IN THE SPACE AT THE RIGHT.*

1. Assume that the ticket agent at the bathhouse cannot dispense tickets from his machine because of a mechanical failure.
 You should authorize the ticket agent to

 A. sell tickets by hand from the bundle only
 B. stop selling tickets and await the installation of a stand-by machine
 C. collect cash from the patrons and have them escorted through the bathhouse entrance gate
 D. let the patrons deposit admission fees in a box at the bathhouse entrance gate

1.____

2. If an operator of a four-wheel drive beach buggy leaves the sand portion of a beach and neglects to disengage his forward gears when he starts to drive over area streets to the dump or drop area, he will

 A. cause his transmission to lose linkage
 B. excessively wear his emergency brake
 C. jam up his front differential
 D. seriously damage the springs of the vehicle

2.____

3. Inventories and replacement of material, supplies, and equipment required for pre-season preparation of beaches is normally scheduled to begin immediately after

 A. April 1st B. Memorial Day
 C. Labor Day D. New Year's Day

3.____

4. On an Emerson Resuscitator, the cylinder is considered full when the cylinder volume indicator shows AT LEAST _____ lbs. pressure per square inch or more.

 A. 900 B. 1300 C. 1800 D. 2800

4.____

5. The term *deadman,* when used in training courses for lifeguards assigned to oceanfront beaches, refers to

 A. a rope splicing tool
 B. beach cradles
 C. upland anchorage
 D. a fixed warning sign on a stone jetty

5.____

6. The appropriate arm signal for a lifeguard to give from a standing position on his tower to call for delivery of a resuscitator is:

 A. Pump one arm up and down from an overhead position
 B. Rotary motion in front of chest
 C. Arms extended up -- straight overhead
 D. Arms clasped overhead

6.____

7. The standard technique for executing the back pressure - arm lift method of artificial respiration requires the operator to adhere to a cycle consisting of a prescribed series of motions.
   This cycle should be repeated about _____ times per minute.

   A. two   B. four   C. six   D. twelve

8. Assume that an elderly swimmer has collapsed while swimming. His friend, who is with him, states that the victim has a long history of heart failure. The victim is brought to the first aid station showing signs of shock and labored breathing.
   You should take which one of the following actions?

   A. Apply an oxygen mask tightly to the victim's face
   B. Using the resuscitator, turn on the inhalator valve and apply the face mask
   C. Get him dressed and send him to a hospital with his friend
   D. Wrap him in blankets to keep warm and give him a hot beverage

9. The symptoms of heat prostration MOST usually are:

   A. Face pale, pulse weak; perspiration profuse on forehead, face, and hands; faintness and nausea
   B. Face red, hot, and dry; pulse strong and fast, high fever; perhaps nausea
   C. Face purplish; pulse erratic; feet and hands cold
   D. Face pale; respiration rate down to six; patient violent

10. Of the following, the BEST method for controlling algae growth in outdoor swimming pools is to

    A. treat with heavy dosages of chlorine
    B. raise the pH with additional amounts of calcium carbonate
    C. apply standard rates of copper sulphate
    D. lower the pool level and add fresh water from the main

11. To improve the capabilities of swimming pool filters, a jelly-like substance called a *flock* must be deposited on the surface of the filter bed.
    The flock is formed by adding which of the following two chemicals to the water in the treatment tank?

    A. Anhydrous ammonia and sodium dichromate
    B. Aluminum sulphate and sodium carbonate
    C. Orthotolidine and copper sulphate
    D. Iodides and calcium chloride

12. Pool water returning from the center drain of an outdoor swimming pool is called the

    A. confluent   B. effluent   C. influent   D. affluent

13. Backwashing in a conventional water treatment plant is USUALLY performed by the plant operator when the loss of head reaches _____ pounds per square inch.

    A. 3 1/2-4   B. 5 1/2-7   C. 8-10   D. 11-12

14. Most outdoor swimming pool operations have large heating boilers. These boilers have water columns with look-through water gauges, showing the water level in the boiler. The manual on maintenance and operation of heating plants and auxiliary equipment specifies that, while the boiler is in operation, the water column and gauge glass should be blown down   14._____

   A. daily   B. weekly   C. bi-weekly   D. monthly

15. Conventional gun-type oil burners used at park facilities are required to utilize as fuel   15._____

   A. #2 oil
   B. #4 oil
   C. #6 oil
   D. a kerosene mixture

16. Chlorine residual in municipally operated pools as required by the department of health shall be kept at NOT LESS THAN _____ ppm.   16._____

   A. 0.01   B. 0.25   C. 0.45   D. 1.0

17. Which of the following should be used to test the pH range (alkaline range) of swimming pool water?   17._____

   A. Ultraviolet light
   B. Iodides
   C. Orthotolodine
   D. Bromthymol blue

18. The filtration rate per square foot for a conventional filter is _____ gallons per square foot.   18._____

   A. 8   B. 6   C. 5   D. 3

19. Chlorine gas in steel cylinders is used as a sterilant in most outdoor swimming pools. If chlorine gas leaks occur from faulty connections, valve packings, etc., the STANDARD procedure for locating the leaks promptly is to use   19._____

   A. a lighted sulphur taper
   B. a soapy mixture
   C. acetone, applied with a camel hair brush
   D. concentrated ammonia

20. The MOST desirable time to apply lime to fairways on a golf course that is high in the acid range is   20._____

   A. during the rainy season
   B. after a long, dry spell
   C. in the fall or spring
   D. in late January

21. A bag of commercial fertilizer with a 10-6-4 classification on the printed face of the bag contains which of the following combination of chemicals by weight?   21._____

   A. 10% phosphoric acid, 6% nitrogen, and 4% potash
   B. 10% potash, 6% phosphoric acid, and 4% nitrogen
   C. 10% nitrogen, 6% phosphoric acid, and 4% potash
   D. 10% potash, 6% nitrogen, and 4% phosphoric acid

22. The turf on a tee with 15,000 square feet is badly worn because of traffic density and must be completely rehabilitated. You have completed the step requiring the application of a soil sterilant, and you are ready to apply nitrogen to the soil at a rate of two pounds of available nitrogen per thousand square feet.
    How many 100 pound bags of 10-6-4 fertilizer must be applied to adequately supply the nitrogen requirements?

    A. 10　　　　B. 8　　　　C. 5　　　　D. 3

23. According to regulations relating to lawn-making, which of the following pH ratings of fertilizer is desirable?

    A. 4.5 to 5.0　　　　B. 5.5 to 6.0
    C. 6.5 to 7.0　　　　D. 7.5 to 8.0

24. To facilitate photosynthesis for normal growth, grass should be mowed often enough so that clippings are

    A. equal to mowing height
    B. shorter than mowing height
    C. longer than mowing height
    D. two inches long

25. Of the following, the MOST suitable grass seed mixture for a play field is one containing Kentucky bluegrass and

    A. colonial bent　　　　B. Bermuda grass
    C. zoysia　　　　D. creeping red fescue

26. Red fescue is USUALLY added to a seed mixture because of its

    A. drought resistance　　　　B. fast germination
    C. slow germination　　　　D. coarse texture

27. The four basic procedures generally considered as constituting the minimum maintenance for turf are: (1) selection of adapted grasses; (2) fertilization; (3) watering; and (4)

    A. aerification　　　　B. mowing
    C. plugging　　　　D. rolling

28. The BEST method for improving the soil structure of a heavily compacted playfield is to apply organic top-dressing first and then proceed with

    A. pesticide application　　　　B. mowing and watering
    C. fertilization　　　　D. aerification

29. A fairway should be maintained so that its width averages _____ to _____ feet.

    A. 60; 110　　　　B. 120; 210　　　　C. 220; 260　　　　D. 270; 310

30. A good supplemental program to aid the grass that is already growing and to establish new grass in the thin, worn-out areas of an athletic field is

    A. overseeding　　　　B. rolling
    C. plugging　　　　D. watering

KEY (CORRECT ANSWERS)

1. A	11. B	21. C
2. C	12. B	22. D
3. C	13. B	23. C
4. C	14. A	24. B
5. C	15. A	25. D
6. C	16. D	26. A
7. D	17. D	27. B
8. B	18. D	28. D
9. A	19. D	29. B
10. C	20. C	30. A

TEST 2

DIRECTIONS: Each question or incomplete statement is followed by several suggested answers or completions. Select the one that BEST answers the question or completes the statement. *PRINT THE LETTER OF THE CORRECT ANSWER IN THE SPACE AT THE RIGHT.*

1. Traps are customarily surfaced with a layer of sand about _____ inches deep. 1.____
   A. 6 B. 12 C. 18 D. 24

2. A GOOD medium sandy loam for a putting green should contain _____ organic content. 2.____
   A. 5-10% B. 10-15% C. 20-30% D. 30-50%

3. In the maintenance of a putting green, the LEAST necessary piece of equipment is 3.____
   A. putting green mower
   B. power sprayer
   C. aerator
   D. fertilizer spreader

4. The BEST way to maintain a green so that it holds a pitched ball is by 4.____
   A. overwatering
   B. good soil structure
   C. underwatering
   D. high mowing

5. The surface soil on a green should be a medium sandy loam placed _____ to _____ inches deep. 5.____
   A. 2; 4 B. 4; 6 C. 8; 10 D. 12; 18

6. The BEST turf fertilizers today contain about 6.____
   A. 85% slow-release phosphorus
   B. 16% fast-release nitrogen
   C. 50% slow-release nitrogen
   D. 20% phosphorus

7. Since golf course grasses are heavy users of phosphorus, potassium, magnesium, and calcium, the BEST pH range for turf, where maximum quantities of these chemicals are available, is 7.____
   A. 4.2 to 4.8
   B. 5.0 to 5.8
   C. 6.0 to 7.0
   D. 7.2 to 8.2

8. Damage on golf greens and other turf areas caused by the *Fusarium nivale* fungus (snow mold) can BEST be prevented or adequately checked by treatment with 8.____
   A. ammonium methyl arsenates
   B. aluminum sulphate
   C. hydrated lime
   D. cadminates

9. To prevent snow mold, treatment should GENERALLY start 9.____
   A. in early spring
   B. after a heavy rain
   C. in late winter
   D. after a heavy snow

10. Chlordane is used in turf management to

    A. eradicate goose grass
    B. control brown patch
    C. grub-proof soil
    D. stimulate root growth

11. Artificial rinks have refrigerants to cool the brine which is constantly circulated through the wrought-iron pipes imbedded in the floor of the rink.
    The brine can be chilled to below zero degrees Fahrenheit because it contains a chemical salt known as

    A. sodium chloride
    B. calcium chloride
    C. calcium carbonate
    D. ammonium chloride

12. The MINIMUM ice thickness generally considered safe for ice skating on a lake or pond whose depth does not exceed 3 feet is _____ inches.

    A. 2   B. 3   C. 5   D. 6

13. In the operation of an ice skating rink, prior to starting the process of ice building, the slab surface should be painted with _____ paint.

    A. white water
    B. white epoxy
    C. blue water
    D. blue epoxy

14. Crowd control in an ice skating rink includes all phases of the patrons' activities from admissions line-up to the time the patrons leave the rink.
    According to regulations, during special sessions, guards should

    A. skate in a clockwise direction
    B. skate in a counterclockwise direction
    C. be positioned on the ice near the entrances
    D. be positioned off the ice near the entrances

15. When a rink slab has been chilled below freezing temperature, ice can be built to the desired thickness by spraying a fine layer of water onto the slab with a

    A. Toro sprayer
    B. Skinner sprinkler
    C. Rainboni
    D. Zamboni

16. The following is a description of the cooling system of a skating rink: The refrigerant (ammonia or freon) absorbs the heat from the circulating brine which, in turn, lowers the temperature of the skating slab; when the brine is returned to the chiller after leaving the rink floor with absorbed heat, the compressor pumps the refrigerant gases to the condenser.
    The condenser does which of the following?
    It

    A. cools the refrigerant gas to a liquid and returns it to the chiller
    B. heats up the refrigerant gas
    C. transforms the gas into ice crystals
    D. cools the circulating water within the condenser

17. At indoor rinks where atmospheric temperatures remain stable and are not affected by outdoor weather conditions, brine should be circulated at a temperature of APPROXIMATELY _____ degrees Fahrenheit.

    A. 7   B. 10   C. 15   D. 25

18. Conditioning ice surfaces on outdoor rinks in early fall or late spring is BEST accomplished

    A. after each session
    B. after the sun sets
    C. at 8 A.M.
    D. at 12 noon

19. The standard of thickness for safe skating on lakes and ponds with water depths over three feet is _____ inches.

    A. two
    B. three
    C. five
    D. seven

20. Assume that a heavy snowstorm has reached the area at the start of the evening session of outdoor rink operations. The one of the following actions that should be taken is to

    A. send all the skaters home, telling them the rink is closed
    B. let them skate until the snow is too deep to move
    C. cone off one-half of the rink at a time for snow removal operations
    D. give snow shovels to as many skaters as possible and put them to work clearing the rink

21. Of the following trees, the one which is NOT recommended for street tree planting is

    A. London plane
    B. Gingko
    C. Yellow Pine
    D. Pin Oak

22. Before useful measures can be applied to control a tree disease epidemic in a park, it is FIRST necessary to

    A. obtain an appropriation for spraying
    B. have a correct diagnosis made of the disease
    C. make an inventory of the diseased trees
    D. wait until winter when the trees are dormant

23. Of the following trees, the one which is generally MOST often recommended for sandy soils is

    A. American elm
    B. Japanese maple
    C. Chinese poplar
    D. Japanese black pine

24. About 75 percent of all tree diseases, including all mildews, rusts, anthracnoses, and sooty molds, are caused by

    A. fungi
    B. viruses
    C. nematodes
    D. bacteria

25. Tree crews should be instructed to ALWAYS

    A. trim the leader of a tree to improve its vitality
    B. prune trees by removing at least 50% of the crowns
    C. remove all injured and diseased wood
    D. fertilize a tree before pruning it

26. Three techniques that you can use to evaluate maintenance activities and determine whether they can be done better are work simplification, work measurement, and

    A. establishment of work performance standards
    B. use of labor saving devices
    C. increased supervision
    D. computerization

27. Staffing is BEST indicated by which of the following activities?

    A. Selection and training of personnel and maintaining favorable conditions of work
    B. Structuring an organization for unity of command, span of control, and lines of authority
    C. Writing task lists for the different titles working at a facility
    D. Working out in broad outline the things that need to be done and the methods for doing them to accomplish the mission of the agency

28. Generally, the MOST practical way to ascertain most readily the number of man-hours it takes to do a job is by

    A. referring to a management analysis handbook
    B. making a detailed analysis of the job
    C. asking the operator performing the job
    D. reviewing job specifications

29. Any violation of the rules or regulations for the government and protection of public parks and property shall be punishable by NOT MORE THAN _____ imprisonment or by a fine of not more than _____ dollars, or by both.

    A. thirty days'; fifty
    B. sixty days'; one hundred
    C. ninety days'; two hundred fifty
    D. one year's; five hundred

30. One workman can hand-rake leaves at the rate of approximately 1,000 square feet in 20 minutes.
    How many men would you assign to a crew to hand rake a grove of trees covering 40,000 square feet in order to accomplish the job within three hours?

    A. 3   B. 30   C. 50   D. 5

KEY (CORRECT ANSWERS)

1.	A	11.	B	21.	C
2.	C	12.	B	22.	B
3.	B	13.	A	23.	D
4.	B	14.	D	24.	A
5.	C	15.	D	25.	C
6.	C	16.	A	26.	A
7.	C	17.	C	27.	A
8.	D	18.	A	28.	C
9.	A	19.	C	29.	A
10.	C	20.	C	30.	D

TOOLS

EXAMINATION SECTION
TEST 1

DIRECTIONS: Each question or incomplete statement is followed by several suggested answers or completions. Select the one that BEST answers the question or completes the statement. *PRINT THE LETTER OF THE CORRECT ANSWER IN THE SPACE AT THE RIGHT.*

1. It is NOT good practice to cut thin-walled copper tubing with an ordinary three-wheel pipe cutter because

    A. the cutters will be dulled
    B. too much time is required
    C. the tubing end must be reamed after cutting
    D. the tubing is likely to collapse

2. Wedges are used under vertical shoring timbers to

    A. utilize scrap wood
    B. permit the use of very short timbers
    C. obtain rigid shoring
    D. absorb construction noise

3. The LONGEST nail of the following is a _____-penny nail.

    A. 12   B. 10   C. 6   D. 4

4. A commonly used priming coat for structural steel is

    A. enamel   B. varnish   C. red lead   D. lacquer

5. A nail set is a tool used for

    A. straightening bent nails
    B. cutting nails to specified size
    C. sinking a nail head in wood
    D. measuring nail size

6. The sketch at the right shows a gauge used to
    A. measure the depth of a hole
    B. determine if a board has been smoothly planed
    C. check the width of a brick
    D. scribe a line on a board parallel to its edge

7. The gauge box shown at the right is used for measuring the dry volume of a concrete mix. If the gauge box is to have a volume of 1 cubic yard, dimension H must be APPROXIMATELY _____ feet.
   A. 2.39
   B. 1.69
   C. 1.45
   D. .63

Questions 8-27.

DIRECTIONS: Questions 8 through 27 refer to the use of tools shown below. Refer to these tools when answering these questions.

3 (#1)

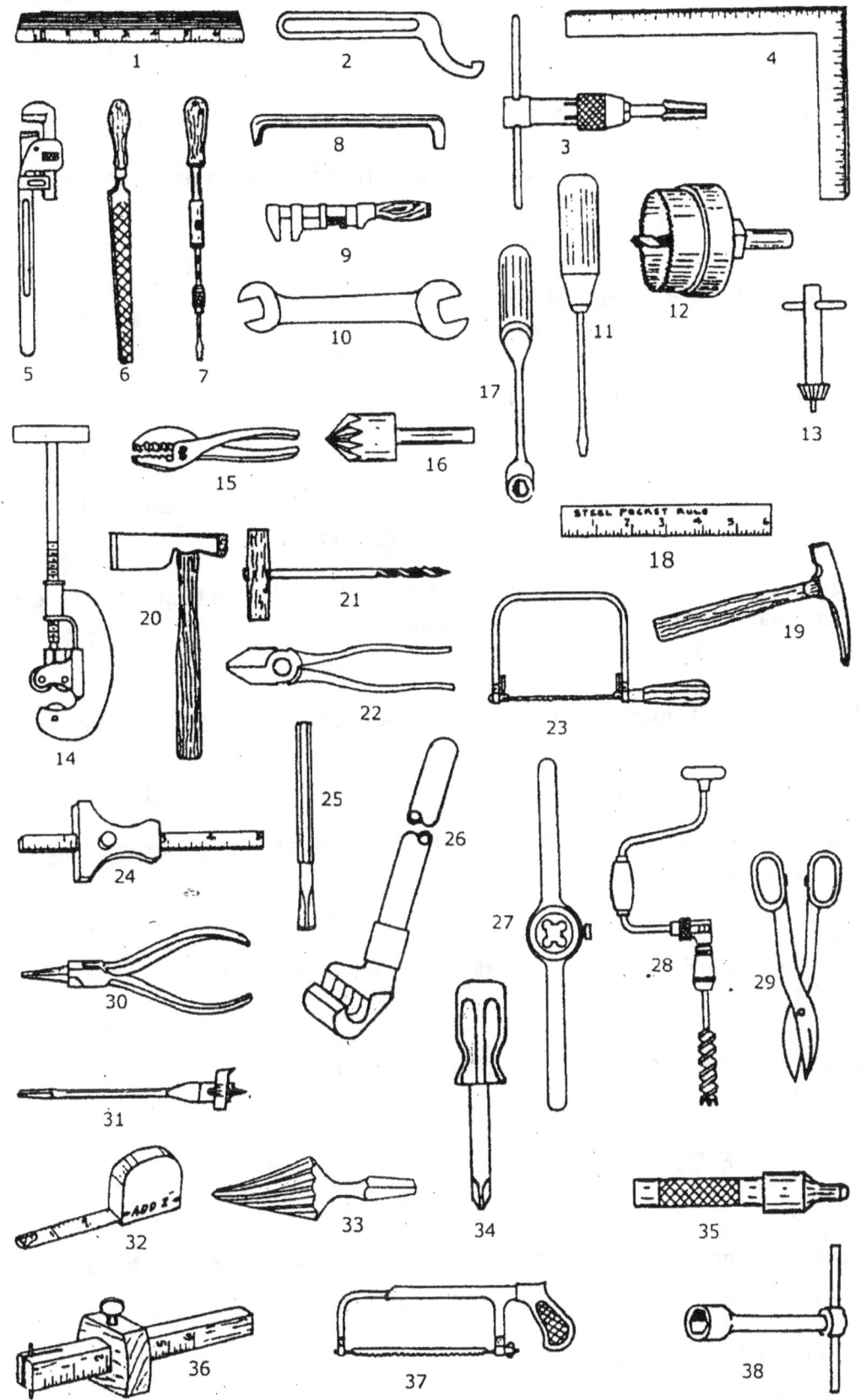

4 (#1)

8. Tool number 38 is properly called a(n) _____ wrench.
   A. box   B. open-end   C. socket   D. tool

9. Two tools which are used for cutting large circular holes in thin sheets are numbers _____ and _____.
   A. 12; 31   B. 28; 33   C. 12; 28   D. 31; 33

10. If there is a possible danger of electric shock when you are taking measurements, it would be BEST to use number
    A. 1   B. 4   C. 18   D. 32

11. A 1/2-inch steel pipe is preferably cut with number
    A. 14   B. 23   C. 27   D. 29

12. A nut for a #8 machine screw should be tightened using number
    A. 9   B. 15   C. 17   D. 38

13. The hexagon nut for a 1/2-inch diameter machine bolt should be tightened using number
    A. 5   B. 10   C. 22   D. 26

14. If a small piece must be chipped off a brick in order to clear an obstruction when a brick wall is being built, the MOST suitable tool to use is number
    A. 16   B. 19   C. 20   D. 33

15. A large number of wood screws can be screwed into a board MOST quickly by using number
    A. 7   B. 8   C. 11   D. 17

16. A number of different diameter holes can be MOST easily bored through a heavy wood plank by using number
    A. 3   B. 13   C. 21   D. 31

17. The tool to use in order to form threads in a hole in a steel block is number
    A. 2   B. 3   C. 27   D. 31

18. Curved designs in thin wood are preferably cut with number
    A. 12   B. 23   C. 29   D. 37

19. The driving of Phillips-head screws requires the use of number
    A. 7   B. 8   C. 11   D. 34

20. In order to properly flare one end of a piece of copper tubing, the tool to use is number
    A. 13   B. 25   C. 33   D. 35

21. Tool number 16 is used for
    A. counterboring   B. cutting concrete
    C. countersinking   D. reaming

22. A tool that can be used to drill a hole in a concrete wall to install a lead anchor is number   22.____
    A. 3   B. 16   C. 21   D. 25

23. After cutting a piece of steel pipe, the burrs are BEST removed from the inside edge with number   23.____
    A. 6   B. 13   C. 16   D. 33

24. The MOST convenient tool for measuring the depth of a 1/2-inch diameter hole is number   24.____
    A. 24   B. 31   C. 32   D. 36

25. A 1" x 1" x 1/8" angle iron would usually be cut using number   25.____
    A. 12   B. 26   C. 29   D. 37

26. Wood screws located in positions NOT accessible to an ordinary screwdriver would be removed using number   26.____
    A. 2   B. 8   C. 13   D. 30

27. A small hole can be quickly bored through an 1/8-inch thick plywood board with number   27.____
    A. 3   B. 7   C. 21   D. 31

28. The hammer shown to the right would be used by a   28.____
    A. carpenter
    B. bricklayer
    C. tinsmith
    D. plumber

29. Which of the following pairs of tools would be used to tighten a nut on a screw?   29.____
    A. Two open-end wrenches
    B. One open-end wrench and one adjustable wrench
    C. A screwdriver and a wrench
    D. A vise wrench and an adjustable screwdriver

30. In order to determine if a surface is truly horizontal, it should be checked with a   30.____
    A. carpenter's square   B. plumb bob
    C. steel rule   D. spirit level

KEY (CORRECT ANSWERS)

1.	D	16.	D
2.	C	17.	B
3.	A	18.	B
4.	C	19.	D
5.	C	20.	D
6.	D	21.	C
7.	B	22.	D
8.	C	23.	D
9.	A	24.	A
10.	A	25.	D
11.	A	26.	B
12.	C	27.	C
13.	B	28.	B
14.	B	29.	C
15.	A	30.	D

TEST 2

DIRECTIONS: Each question or incomplete statement is followed by several suggested answers or completions. Select the one that BEST answers the question or completes the statement. *PRINT THE LETTER OF THE CORRECT ANSWER IN THE SPACE AT THE RIGHT.*

1. After a wedge-shaped hole has been cut into the large stone, the three-legged lifting device is inserted to lift the stone. The CORRECT order for inserting the three legs is
    A. 1, 2, 3
    B. 3, 2, 1
    C. 2, 3, 1
    D. 1, 3, 2

1.____

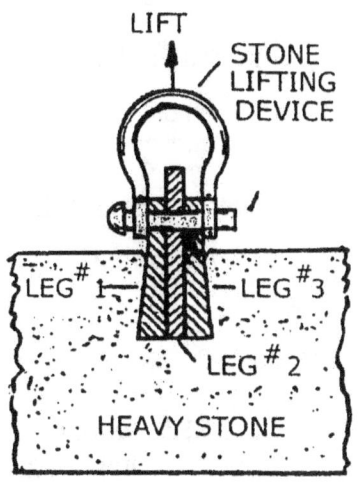

2. Brushes which have been used to apply shellac are BEST cleaned with

    A. alcohol
    B. water
    C. carbon tetrachloride
    D. acetic acid

2.____

3. When timbers are bolted together, a flat washer is GENERALLY used under the head of the bolt to

    A. prevent the bolt from turning
    B. increase the strength of the bolt
    C. reduce crushing of the wood when the bolt is tightened
    D. make it easier to turn the bolt

3.____

4. A claw hammer is PROPERLY used for

    A. driving a cold chisel
    B. driving brads
    C. setting rivets
    D. flattening a 1/4" metal bar

4.____

5. Open-end wrenches are made with the sides of the jaws at about a 15° angle to the line of the handle. This angle

    A. is useful when working the wrench in close quarters
    B. increases the strength of the jaws
    C. prevents extending the handle with a piece of pipe
    D. serves only to improve the appearance of the wrench

5.____

77

6. It is BEST to cut a piece of sheet metal with a pair of snips by starting each cut with the metal sheet

    A. out near the points of the snips
    B. as far back in the jaws as possible
    C. midway between the snip points and the pivot
    D. one-quarter the way between the snip points and the pivot

6.___

7. Cement-lined drain pipe should be cut with a

    A. chisel   B. file
    C. star drill   D. hacksaw

7.___

8. A riser is GENERALLY a pipe run which is

    A. horizontal   B. curved
    C. vertical   D. at a 45 angle

8.___

Questions 9-18.

DIRECTIONS: Questions 9 through 18 refer to the use of the tools shown below. Read the item, and for the operation given, select the PROPER tool to be used from those shown.

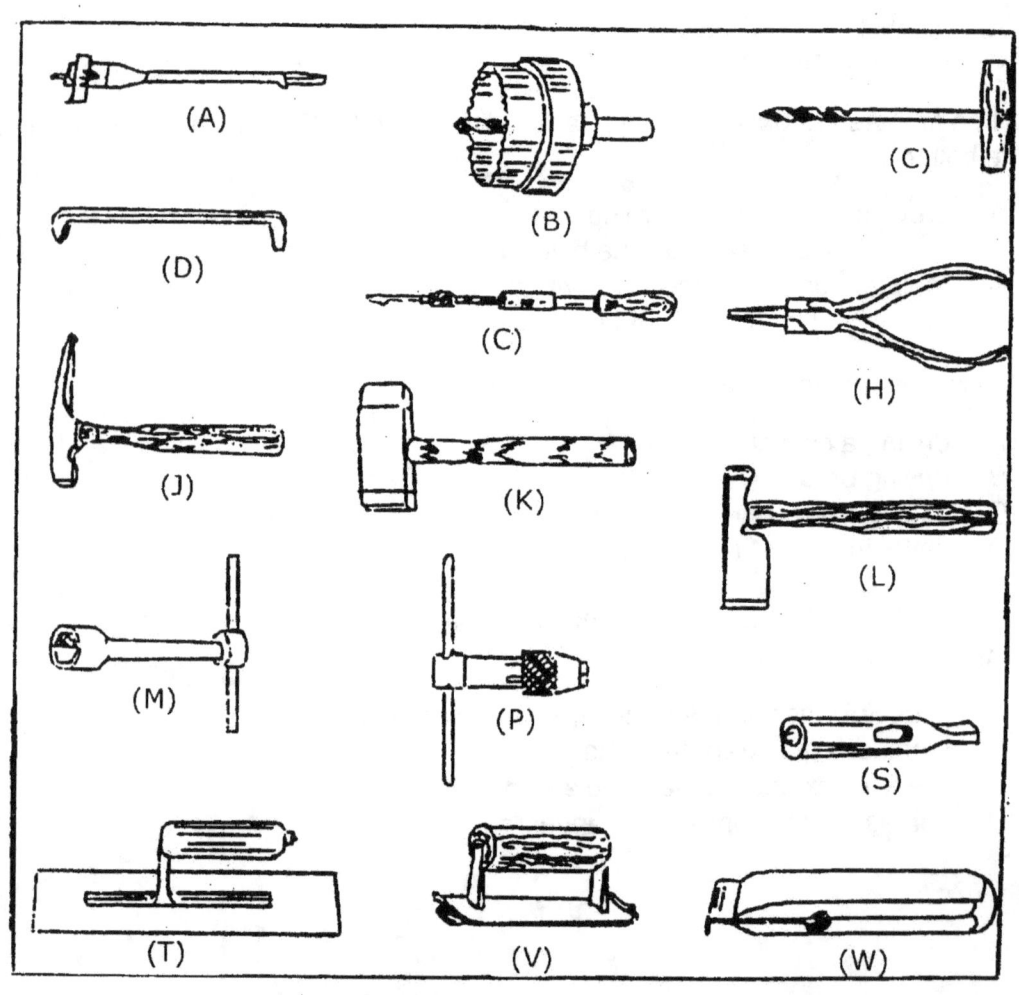

9. Turning a screw tap when threading a hole in a steel block. 9.____

10. Boring a number of different diameter holes through a heavy wood plank. 10.____

11. Quickly screwing a number of wood screws into a board. 11.____

12. Setting a groove in a cement floor before hardening of the cement. 12.____

13. Plastering a wall. 13.____

14. Chipping a small piece out of a brick to clear a projecting steel rod when building a brick wall. 14.____

15. Tightening a large nut. 15.____

16. Quickly boring a small hole through a 1/8" board. 16.____

17. Unfastening wood screws located in a position inaccessible to an ordinary screwdriver. 17.____

18. Making a 1 1/2" hole in a steel plate. 18.____

19. A pneumatic bucker is used in 19.____

    A. riveting   B. brazing
    C. soldering   D. reinforcing concrete

20. To make certain two points separated by a vertical distance of 8 feet are in perfect vertical alignment, it would be BEST to use a 20.____

    A. surface gage   B. height gage
    C. protractor   D. plumb bob

21. When repair work is being done on the elevated structure, canvas spreads are suspended under the working area MAINLY to 21.____

    A. reduce noise   B. discourage crowds
    C. protect the structure   D. protect pedestrians

22. When grinding a weld smooth, it is MOST important to avoid. 22.____

    A. overheating the surrounding metal
    B. grinding too much of the weld away
    C. grinding too slowly
    D. grinding after the weld has cooled off

23. A gouge is a tool used for 23.____

    A. planing wood smooth   B. grinding metal
    C. drilling steel   D. chiseling wood

24. The tool that should be used to cut a 1" x 4" plank down to a 3" width is a 24.____

    A. hacksaw   B. crosscut saw
    C. rip saw   D. backsaw

25. Threads are cut on the ends of a length of steel pipe by the use of a

    A. brace and bit
    B. counterbore
    C. stock and die
    D. doweling jig

26. A bit brace can be locked so that the bit will turn in only one direction by means of a

    A. feed screw
    B. rachet device
    C. universal chuck
    D. ball-bearing device

27. A reamer is used to

    A. enlarge drilled holes to an exact size
    B. punch holes to desired size
    C. line up adjacent holes
    D. lay out holes before drilling

28. The tool shown at the right is a
    A. countersink
    B. counterbore
    C. star drill
    D. burring reamer

29. The saw shown at the right would be used to cut
    A. curved designs in thin wood
    B. strap iron
    C. asphalt tiles to fit against walls
    D. soft lead pipe

30. The tool shown at the right is a
    A. float
    B. finishing trowel
    C. hawk
    D. roofing seamer

KEY (CORRECT ANSWERS)

1.	D	16.	C
2.	A	17.	D
3.	C	18.	B
4.	B	19.	B
5.	A	20.	D
6.	B	21.	C
7.	D	22.	B
8.	C	23.	D
9.	P	24.	C
10.	A	25.	C
11.	E	26.	B
12.	V	27.	A
13.	T	28.	D
14.	J	29.	A
15.	M	30.	A

TEST 3

DIRECTIONS: Each question or incomplete statement is followed by several suggested answers or completions. Select the one that BEST answers the question or completes the Statement. *PRINT THE LETTER OF THE CORRECT ANSWER IN THE SPACE AT THE RIGHT.*

Questions 1-8.

DIRECTIONS: Questions 1 through 8 are to be answered on the basis of the following items. The sizes of the items shown are NOT their actual sizes. Each item is identified by a number, For each question, select the answer which gives the identifying number of the item that BEST answers the question.

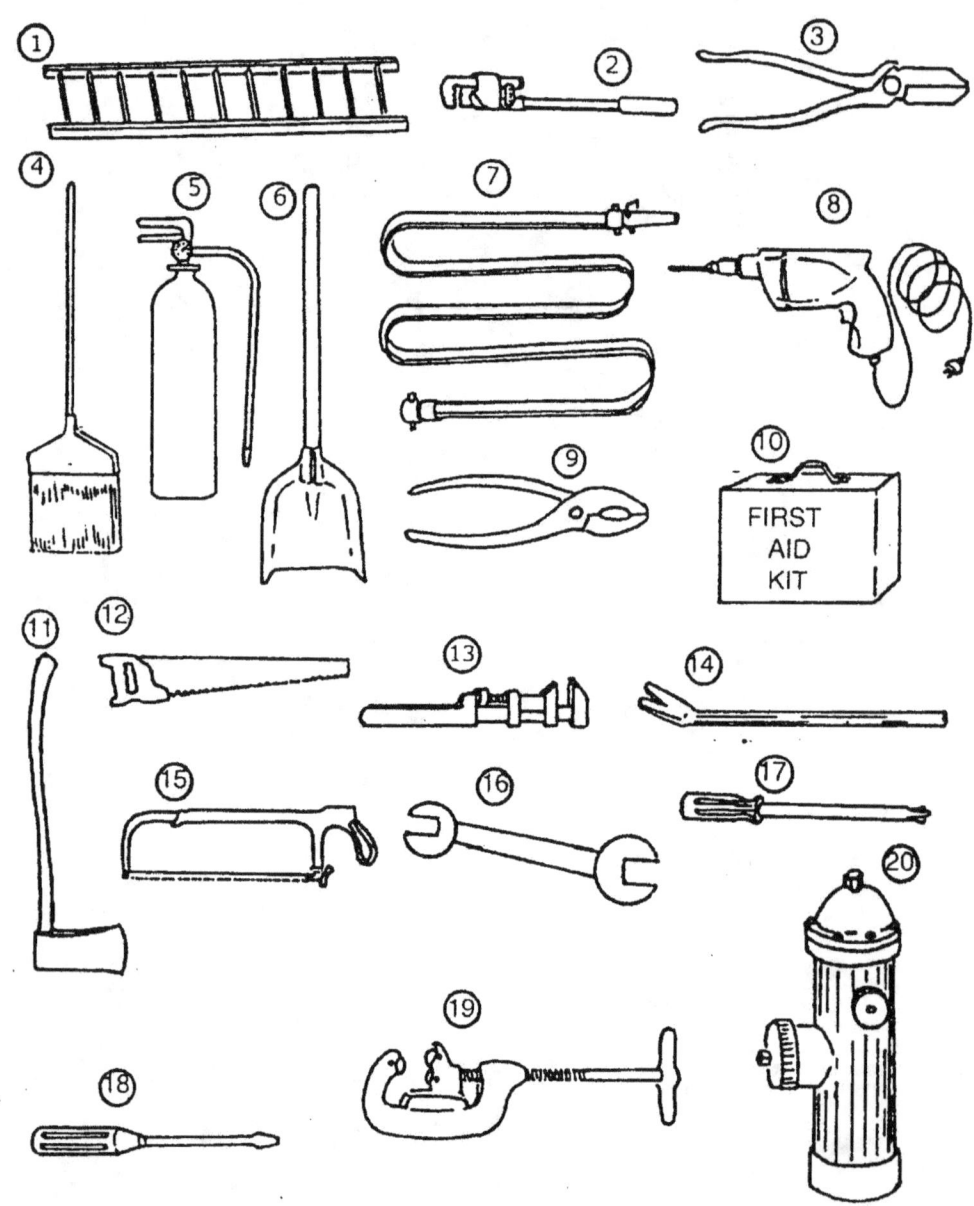

1. Which one of the following items should be connected to a hydrant and used to put out a fire?
   A. 5   B. 7   C. 8   D. 17

2. Which one of the following pairs of items should be used after a fire to clean a floor covered with small pieces of burned material?
   A. 1 and 14   B. 4 and 6   C. 10 and 12   D. 11 and 13

3. Which one of the following pairs of items should be used for cutting a branch from a tree?
   A. 2 and 3   B. 8 and 9   C. 11 and 12   D. 14 and 15

4. Which one of the following items should be used to rescue a victim from a second floor window?
   A. 1   B. 10   C. 15   D. 20

5. Which one of the following pairs of items should be used to tighten a nut on a screw?
   A. 2 and 3   B. 8 and 19   C. 9 and 14   D. 16 and 18

6. Which one of the following items should be used to repair a leaky faucet?
   A. 4   B. 5   C. 12   D. 13

7. Which one of the following items should be used as a source of water at a fire?
   A. 2   B. 6   C. 9   D. 20

8. Which item should be used for cutting metal?
   A. 6   B. 13   C. 15   D. 18

Questions 9-18.

DIRECTIONS: Questions 9 through 18, inclusive, in Column I are articles or terms used in structure maintenance and repair work, each of which is associated primarily (though not exclusively) with one of the trade specialties listed in Column II. For each article or term in Column I, select the trade specialty from Column II in which it is in greatest use. Indicate in the space at the right, the letter preceding your selected trade specialty.

COLUMN I
(Articles or Terms)

COLUMN II
(Trade Specialties)

9. Drift pin
10. Studding
11. Elbow
12. Header course
13. Dowel
14. Screeding
15. Cleanout
16. Air jam
17. Curing
18. Mortise and tenon

A. Carpentry
B. Masonry
C. Ironwork
D. Plumbing

19. Practically all valves used in plumbing work are made so that the handwheel is turned clockwise instead of counterclockwise to close the valve.
    The PROBABLE reason is that

    A. it is easier to remember since screws and nuts move inward when turned clockwise
    B. the handwheel is less likely to loosen
    C. greater force can be exerted
    D. most people are righthanded

20. Sharpening a hand saw consists of

    A. jointing, shaping, setting, and filing
    B. adzing, clinching, forging, and machining
    C. brazing, chiseling, grinding, and mitering
    D. bushing, dressing, lapping, and machining

21. A hacksaw blade having 32 teeth to the inch is the BEST blade to use when cutting

    A. cold rolled steel shafting
    B. wrought iron pipe
    C. stainless steel plate
    D. copper tubing

22. Good practice dictates that an adjustable open-end wrench should be used PRIMARILY when the

    A. nut to be turned is soft and must not be scored
    B. extra leverage is needed
    C. proper size of fixed wrench is not available
    D. location is cramped permitting only a small turning angle

23. When a hacksaw blade is designated as an 18-32, the numbers 18 and 32 refer to, respectively, the blade's

    A. stroke and thickness
    B. thickness and length
    C. length and teeth per inch
    D. teeth per inch and stroke

24. When a machine screw is designated as a 10-32, the numbers 10 and 32 refer to, respectively, the screw's

    A. length and head type
    B. threads per inch and length
    C. diameter and threads per inch
    D. head type and diameter

25. An offset screwdriver is MOST useful for turning a wood screw when

    A. a strong force needs to be applied
    B. the screw head is marred
    C. space is limited
    D. speed is desired

26. Of the following orders for tools or materials used in the building trades, the one which is INCOMPLETE is 26.____

   A. 1 paintbrush, flat, 2 in. wide
   B. 1 drill, twist, straight shank, high speed, 3/8 in.
   C. 1 snake, steel, 3/4 in. wide by 1/8 in. thick
   D. 1 keg of nails, 10 penny, common wire, galvanized

27. The tool that is GENERALLY used to slightly elongate a round hole in strap-iron is a 27.____

   A. rat-tail file   B. reamer
   C. drill   D. rasp

28. The BEST way to locate a point on the floor directly below a given point on the ceiling is by using a 28.____

   A. plumber's snake   B. plumb bob
   C. flashlight   D. chalk line

29. The wrench that would prove LEAST useful in uncoupling several pieces of pipe is a _____ wrench. 29.____

   A. socket   B. chain   C. strap   D. stillson

30. Of the following, the tool that is LEAST easily broken is a 30.____

   A. file   B. pry bar
   C. folding rule   D. hacksaw blade

KEY (CORRECT ANSWERS)

1.	B		16.	C
2.	B		17.	B
3.	C		18.	A
4.	A		19.	A
5.	D		20.	A
6.	D		21.	D
7.	D		22.	C
8.	C		23.	C
9.	C		24.	C
10.	A		25.	C
11.	B		26.	C
12.	D		27.	A
13.	A		28.	B
14.	B		29.	A
15.	D		30.	B

PREPARING WRITTEN MATERIALS
EXAMINATION SECTION
TEST 1

DIRECTIONS: Each question consists of a sentence which may be classified appropriately under one of the following four categories:
- A. Incorrect because of faulty grammar or sentence structure;
- B. Incorrect because of faulty punctuation;
- C. Incorrect because of faulty capitalization;
- D. Correct

Examine each sentence carefully. Then, in the space at the right, indicate the letter preceding the category which is the BEST of the four suggested above. Each incorrect sentence contains only one type of error. Consider a sentence correct if it contains no errors, although there may be other correct ways of expressing the same thought.

1. All the employees, in this office, are over twenty-one years old.   1.____

2. Neither the clerk nor the stenographer was able to explain what had happened.   2.____

3. Mr. Johnson did not know who he would assign to type the order.   3.____

4. Mr. Marshall called her to report for work on Saturday.   4.____

5. He might of arrived on time if the train has not been delayed.   5.____

6. Some employees on the other hand, are required to fill out these forms every month.   6.____

7. The supervisor issued special instructions to his subordinates to prevent their making errors.   7.____

8. Our supervisor Mr. Williams, expects to be promoted in about two weeks.   8.____

9. We were informed that prof. Morgan would attend the conference.   9.____

10. The clerks were assigned to the old building; the stenographers, to the new building.   10.____

11. The supervisor asked Mr. Smith and I to complete the work as quickly as possible.   11.____

12. He said, that before an employee can be permitted to leave, the report must be finished.   12.____

13. A calculator, in addition to the three computers, are needed in the new office. 13.____

14. Having made many errs in her work, the supervisor asked the typist to be more careful. 14.____

15. "If you are given an assignment," he said, "you should begin work on it as quickly as possible." 15.____

16. All the clerks, including those who have been appointed recently are required to work on the new assignment. 16.____

17. The office manager asked each employee to work one Saturday a month. 17.____

18. Neither Mr. Smith nor Mr. Jones was able to finish his assignment on time. 18.____

19. The task of filing these cards is to be divided equally between you and he. 19.____

20. He is an employee whom we consider to be efficient. 20.____

21. I believe that the new employees are not as punctual as us. 21.____

22. The employees, working in this office, are to be congratulated for their work. 22.____

23. The delay in preparing the report was caused, in his opinion, by the lack of proper supervision and coordination. 23.____

24. John Jones accidentally pushed the wrong button and then all the lights went out. 24.____

25. The investigator ought to of had the witness sign the statement. 25.____

KEY (CORRECT ANSWERS)

1. B
2. D
3. A
4. C
5. A

6. B
7. D
8. B
9. C
10. D

11. A
12. B
13. A
14. A
15. D

16. B
17. C
18. D
19. A
20. D

21. A
22. B
23. D
24. D
25. A

TEST 2

Questions 1-10.

DIRECTIONS: Each of the following sentences may be classified under one of the following four options:
  A. Faulty; contains an error in grammar only
  B. Faulty; contains an error in spelling only
  C. Faulty; contains an error in grammar and an error in spelling
  D. Correct; contains no error in grammar or in spelling

Examine each sentence carefully to determine under which of the above four options it is BEST classified. Then, in the space at the right, write the letter preceding the option which is the best of the four listed above.

1. A recognized principle of good management is that an assignment should be given to whomever is best qualified to carry it out. 1.____

2. He considered it a privilege to be allowed to review and summarize the technical reports issued annually by your agency. 2.____

3. Because the warehouse was in an inaccessible location, deliveries of electric fixtures from the warehouse were made only in large lots. 3.____

4. Having requisitioned the office supplies, Miss Brown returned to her desk and resumed the computation of petty cash disbursements. 4.____

5. One of the advantages of this chemical solution is that records treated with it are not inflamable. 5.____

6. The complaint of this employee, in addition to the complaints of the other employees, were submitted to the grievance committee. 6.____

7. A study of the duties and responsibilities of each of the various categories of employees was conducted by an unprejudiced classification analyst. 7.____

8. Ties of friendship with this subordinate compels him to withold the censure that the subordinate deserves. 8.____

9. Neither of the agencies are affected by the decision to institute a program for rehabilitating physically handi-caped men and women. 9.____

10. The chairman stated that the argument between you and he was creating an intolerable situation. 10.____

2 (#2)

Questions 11-25.

DIRECTIONS: Each of the following sentences may be classified under one of the following four options:
A. Correct
B. Sentence contains an error in spelling
C. Sentence contains an error in grammar
D. Sentence contains errors in both grammar and spelling.

11. He reported that he had had a really good time during his vacation although the farm was located in a very inaccessible portion of the country. 11.____

12. It looks to me like he has been fasinated by that beautiful painting. 12.____

13. We have permitted these kind of pencils to accumulate on our shelves, knowing we can sell them at a profit of five cents apiece any time we choose. 13.____

14. Believing that you will want an unexagerated estimate of the amount of business we can expect, I have made every effort to secure accurate figures. 14.____

15. Each and every man, woman and child in that untrammeled wilderness carry guns for protection against the wild animals. 15.____

16. Although this process is different than the one to which he is accustomed, a good chemist will have no trouble. 16.____

17. Insensible to the fuming and fretting going on about him, the engineer continued to drive the mammoth dynamo to its utmost capacity. 17.____

18. Everyone had studied his lesson carefully and was consequently well prepared when the instructor began to discuss the fourth dimention. 18.____

19. I learned Johnny six new arithmetic problems this afternoon. 19.____

20. Athletics is urged by our most prominent citizens as the pursuit which will enable the younger generation to achieve that ideal of education, a sound mind in a sound body. 20.____

21. He did not see whoever was at the door very clearly but thinks it was the city tax appraiser. 21.____

22. He could not scarsely believe that his theories had been substantiated in this convincing fashion. 22.____

23. Although you have displayed great ingenuity in carrying out your assignments, the choice for the position still lies among Brown and Smith. 23.____

24. If they had have pleaded at the time that Smith was an accessory to the crime, it would have lessened the punishment.   24._____

25. It has proven indispensible in his compilation of the facts in the matter.   25._____

KEY (CORRECT ANSWERS)

1.	A		11.	A
2.	D		12.	D
3.	B		13.	C
4.	D		14.	B
5.	B		15.	D
6.	A		16.	C
7.	D		17.	A
8.	C		18.	B
9.	C		19.	C
10.	A		20.	A

21.	B
22.	D
23.	C
24.	D
25.	B

TEST 3

Questions 1-5.

DIRECTIONS: Questions 1 through 5 consist of sentences which may or may not contain errors in grammar or spelling or both. Sentences which do not contain errors in grammar or spelling or both are to be considered correct, even though there may be other correct ways of expressing the same thought. Examine each sentence carefully. Then, in the space at the right, write the letter of the answer which is the BEST of those suggested below.
    A. If the sentence is correct
    B. If the sentence contains an error in spelling
    C. If the sentence contains an error in grammar
    D. If the sentence contains errors in both grammar and spelling.

1. Brown is doing fine although the work is irrevelant to his training. 1.____

2. The conference of sales managers voted to set its adjournment at one o'clock in order to give those present an opportunity to get rid of all merchandise. 2.____

3. He decided that in view of what had taken place at the hotel that he ought to stay and thank the benificent stranger who had rescued him from an embarassing situation. 3.____

4. Since you object to me criticizing your letter, I have no alternative but to consider you a mercenary scoundrel. 4.____

5. I rushed home ahead of schedule so that you will leave me go to the picnic with Mary. 5.____

Questions 6-15.

DIRECTIONS: Some of the following sentences contain an error in spelling, word usage, or sentence structure, or punctuation. Some sentences are correct as they stand although there may be other correct ways of expressing the same thought. All incorrect sentences contain only one error. Mark your answer to each question in the space at the right as follows:
    A. If the sentence has an error in spelling
    B. If the sentence has an error in punctuation or capitalization
    C. If the sentence has an error in word usage or sentence structure
    D. If the sentence is correct

6. Because the chairman failed to keep the participants from wandering off into irrelevant discussions, it was impossible to reach a consensus before the meeting was adjourned. 6.____

7. Certain employers have an unwritten rule that any applicant, who is over 55 years of age, is automatically excluded from consideration for any position whatsoever. 7.____

8. If the proposal to build schools in some new apartment buildings were to be accepted by the builders, one of the advantages that could be expected to result would be better communication between teachers and parents of schoolchildren. 8.____

9. In this instance, the manufacturer's violation of the law against deseptive packaging was discernible only to an experienced inspector. 9.____

10. The tenants' anger stemmed from the president's going to Washington to testify without consulting them first. 10.____

11. Did the president of this eminent banking company say; "We intend to hire and train a number of these disadvantaged youths?" 11.____

12. In addition, today's confidential secretary must be knowledgable in many different areas: for example, she must know modern techniques for making travel arrangements for the executive. 12.____

13. To avoid further disruption of work in the offices, the protesters were forbidden from entering the building unless they had special passes. 13.____

14. A valuable secondary result of our training conferences is the opportunities afforded for management to observe the reactions of the participants. 14.____

15. Of the two proposals submitted by the committee, the first one is the best. 15.____

Questions 16-25.

DIRECTIONS: Each of the following sentences may be classified MOST appropriately under one of the following three categories:
  A. Faulty because of incorrect grammar
  B. Faulty because of incorrect punctuation
  C. Correct

Examine each sentence. Then, print the capital letter preceding the BEST choice of the three suggested above. All incorrect sentences contain only one type of error. Consider a sentence correct if it contains none of the types of errors mentioned, even though there may be other ways of expressing the same thought.

16. He sent the notice to the clerk who you hired yesterday. 16.____

17. It must be admitted, however that you were not informed of this change. 17.____

18. Only the employees who have served in this grade for at least two years are eligible for promotion. 18.____

19. The work was divided equally between she and Mary. 19.____

20. He thought that you were not available at that time. 20.____
21. When the messenger returns; please give him this package. 21.____
22. The new secretary prepared, typed, addressed, and delivered, the notices. 22.____
23. Walking into the room, his desk can be seen at the rear. 23.____
24. Although John has worked here longer than she, he produces a smaller amount of work. 24.____
25. She said she could of typed this report yesterday. 25.____

KEY (CORRECT ANSWERS)

1.	D		11.	B
2.	A		12.	A
3.	D		13.	C
4.	C		14.	D
5.	C		15.	C
6.	A		16.	A
7.	B		17.	B
8.	D		18.	C
9.	A		19.	A
10.	D		20.	C

21. B
22. B
23. A
24. C
25. A

TEST 4

Questions 1-5.

DIRECTIONS: Each of the following sentences may be classified MOST appropriately under one of the following three categories:
    A. Faulty because of incorrect grammar
    B. Faulty because of incorrect punctuation
    C. Correct

Examine each sentence. Then, print the capital letter preceding the BEST choice of the three suggested above. All incorrect sentences contain only one type of error. Consider a sentence correct if it contains none of the types of errors mentioned, even though there may be other ways of expressing the same thought.

1. Neither one of these procedures are adequate for the efficient performance of this task.   1.____

2. The keyboard is the tool of the typist; the cash register, the tool of the cashier.   2.____

3. "The assignment must be completed as soon as possible" said the supervisor.   3.____

4. As you know, office handbooks are issued to all new employees.   4.____

5. Writing a speech is sometimes easier than to deliver it before an audience.   5.____

Questions 6-15.

DIRECTIONS: Each statement given in Questions 6 through 15 contains one of the faults of English usage listed below. For each, choose from the options listed the MAJOR fault contained.
    A. The statement is not a complete sentence.
    B. The statement contains a word or phrase that is redundant.
    C. The statement contains a long, less commonly used word when a shorter, more direct word would be acceptable.
    D. The statement contains a colloquial expression that normally is avoided in business writing.

6. The fact that this activity will afford an opportunity to meet your group.   6.____

7. Do you think that the two groups can join together for next month's meeting?   7.____

8. This is one of the most exciting new innovations to be introduced into our college.   8.____

9. We expect to consummate the agenda before the meeting ends tomorrow at noon.   9.____

10. While this seminar room is small in size, we think we can use it.   10.____

11. Do you think you can make a modification in the date of the Budget Committee meeting?   11.____

12. We are cognizant of the problem but we think we can ameliorate the situation.   12.____

13. Shall I call you around three on the day I arrive in the City?   13.____

14. Until such time that we know precisely that the students will be present.   14.____

15. The consensus of opinion of all the members present is reported in the minutes.   15.____

Questions 16-25.

DIRECTIONS: For each of Questions 16 through 25, select from the options given below the MOST applicable choice.
    A. The sentence is correct.
    B. The sentence contains a spelling error only.
    C. The sentence contains an English grammar error only.
    D. The sentence contains both a spelling error and an English grammar error.

16. Every person in the group is going to do his share.   16.____

17. The man who we selected is new to this University.   17.____

18. She is the older of the four secretaries on the two staffs that are to be combined.   18.____

19. The decision has to be made between him and I.   19.____

20. One of the volunteers are too young for his complicated task, don't you think?   20.____

21. I think your idea is splindid and it will improve this report considerably.   21.____

22. Do you think this is an exagerated account of the behavior you and me observed this morning?   22.____

23. Our supervisor has a clear idea of excelence.   23.____

24. How many occurences were verified by the observers?   24.____

25. We must complete the typing of the draft of the questionaire by noon tomorrow.

25.____

KEY (CORRECT ANSWERS)

1.	A		11.	C
2.	C		12.	C
3.	B		13.	D
4.	C		14.	A
5.	A		15.	B
6.	A		16.	A
7.	B		17.	C
8.	B		18.	C
9.	C		19.	C
10.	B		20.	D

21.	B
22.	D
23.	B
24.	B
25.	B

PREPARING WRITTEN MATERIAL

PARAGRAPH REARRANGEMENT
COMMENTARY

The sentences that follow are in scrambled order. You are to rearrange them in proper order and indicate the letter choice containing the correct answer at the space at the right.

Each group of sentences in this section is actually a paragraph presented in scrambled order. Each sentence in the group has a place in that paragraph; no sentence is to be left out. You are to read each group of sentences and decide upon the best order in which to put the sentences so as to form a well-organized paragraph.

The questions in this section measure the ability to solve a problem when all the facts relevant to its solution are not given.

More specifically, certain positions of responsibility and authority require the employee to discover connection between events sometimes, apparently, unrelated. In order to do this, the employee will find it necessary to correctly infer that unspecified events have probably occurred or are likely to occur. This ability becomes especially important when action must be taken on incomplete information.

Accordingly, these questions require competitors to choose among several suggested alternatives, each of which presents a different sequential arrangement of the events. Competitors must choose the MOST logical of the suggested sequences.

In order to do so, they may be required to draw on general knowledge to infer missing concepts or events that are essential to sequencing the given events. Competitors should be careful to infer only what is essential to the sequence. The plausibility of the wrong alternatives will always require the inclusion of unlikely events or of additional chains of events which are NOT essential to sequencing the given events.

It's very important to remember that you are looking for the best of the four possible choices, and that the best choice of all may not even be one of the answers you're given to choose from.

There is no one right way to solve these problems. Many people have found it helpful to first write out the order of the sentences, as they would have arranged them, on their scrap paper before looking at the possible answers. If their optimum answer is there, this can save them some time. If it isn't, this method can still give insight into solving the problem. Others find it most helpful to just go through each of the possible choices, contrasting each as they go along. You should use whatever method feels comfortable and works for you.

While most of these types of questions are not that difficult, we've added a higher percentage of the difficult type, just to give you more practice. Usually there are only one or two questions on this section that contain such subtle distinctions that you're unable to answer confidently. And you then may find yourself stuck deciding between two possible choices, neither of which you're sure about.

EXAMINATION SECTION
TEST 1

DIRECTIONS: Each question consists of several sentences which can be arranged in a logical sequence. For each question, select the choice which places the numbered sentences in the MOST logical sequence. *PRINT THE LETTER OF THE CORRECT ANSWER IN THE SPACE AT THE RIGHT.*

1.
   I. A body was found in the woods.
   II. A man proclaimed innocence.
   III. The owner of a gun was located.
   IV. A gun was traced.
   V. The owner of a gun was questioned.
   The CORRECT answer is:
   A. IV, III, V, II, I   B. II, I, IV, III, V   C. I, IV, III, V, II
   D. I, III, V, II, IV   E. I, II, IV, III, V

1.____

2.
   I. A man is in a hunting accident.
   II. A man fell down a flight of steps.
   III. A man lost his vision in one eye.
   IV. A man broke his leg.
   V. A man had to walk with a cane.
   The CORRECT answer is:
   A. II, IV, V, I, III   B. IV, V, I, III, II   C. III, I, IV, V, II
   D. I, III, V, II, IV   E. I, III, II, IV, V

2.____

3.
   I. A man is offered a new job.
   II. A woman is offered a new job.
   III. A man works as a waiter.
   IV. A woman works as a waitress.
   V. A woman gives notice.
   The CORRECT answer is:
   A. IV, II, V, III, I   B. IV, II, V, I, III   C. II, IV, V, III, I
   D. III, I, IV, II, V   E. IV, III, II, V, I

3.____

4.
   I. A train let the station late.
   II. A man was late for work.
   III. A man lost his job.
   IV. Many people complained because the train was late.
   V. There was a traffic jam.
   The CORRECT answer is:
   A. V, II, I, IV, III   B. V, I, IV, II, III   C. V, I, II, IV, III
   D. I, V, IV, II, III   E. II, I, IV, V, III

4.____

5. I. The burden of proof as to each issue is determined before trial and remains upon the same party throughout the trial.
    II. The jury is at liberty to believe one witness' testimony as against a number of contradictory witnesses.
    III. In a civil case, the party bearing the burden of proof is required to prove his contention by a fair preponderance of the evidence.
    IV. However, it must be noted that a fair preponderance of evidence does not necessarily mean a greater number of witnesses.
    V. The burden of proof is the burden which rests upon one of the parties to an action to persuade the trier of the facts, generally the jury, that a proposition he asserts is true.
    VI. If the evidence is equally balanced, or if it leaves the jury in such doubt as to be unable to decide the controversy either way, judgment must be given against the party upon whom the burden of proof rests.
    The CORRECT answer is:
    A. III, II, V, IV, I, VI   B. I, II, VI, V, III, IV   C. III, IV, V, I, II, VI
    D. V, I, III, VI, IV, II   E. I, V, III, VI, IV, II

5.____

6. I. If a parent is without assets and is unemployed, he cannot be convicted of the crime of non-support of a child.
    II. The term *sufficient ability* has been held to mean sufficient financial ability.
    III. It does not matter if his unemployment is by choice or unavoidable circumstances.
    IV. If he fails to take any steps at all, he may be liable to prosecution for endangering the welfare of a child.
    V. Under the penal law, a parent is responsible for the support of his minor child only if the parent is of *sufficient ability*.
    VI. An indigent parent may meet his obligation by borrowing money or by seeking aid under the provisions of the Social Welfare Law.
    The CORRECT answer is:
    A. VI, I, V, III, II, IV   B. I, III, V, II, IV, VI   C. V, II, I, III, VI, IV
    D. I, VI, IV, V, II, III   E. II, V, I, III, VI, IV

6.____

7. I. Consider, for example, the case of a rabble rouser who urges a group of twenty people to go out and break the windows of a nearby factory.
    II. Therefore, the law fills the indicated gap with the crime of *inciting to riot*.
    III. A person is considered guilty of inciting to riot when he urges ten or more persons to engage in tumultuous and violent conduct of a kind likely to create public alarm.
    IV. However, if he has not obtained the cooperation of at least four people, he cannot be charged with unlawful assembly.
    V. The charge of inciting to riot was added to the law to cover types of conduct which cannot be classified as either the crime of *riot* or the crime of *unlawful assembly*.
    VI. If he acquires the acquiescence of at least four of them, he is guilty of unlawful assembly even if the project does not materialize.
    The CORRECT answer is:
    A. III, V, I, VI, IV, II   B. V, I, IV, VI, II, III   C. III, IV, I, V, II, VI
    D. V, I, IV, VI, III, II   E. V, III, I, VI, IV, II

7.____

8.
  I. If, however, the rebuttal evidence presents an issue of credibility, it is for the jury to determine whether the presumption has, in fact, been destroyed.
  II. Once sufficient evidence to the contrary is introduced, the presumption disappears from the trial.
  III. The effect of a presumption is to place the burden upon the adversary to come forward with evidence to rebut the presumption.
  IV. When a presumption is overcome and ceases to exist in the case, the fact or facts which gave rise to the presumption still remain.
  V. Whether a presumption has been overcome is ordinarily a question for the court.
  VI. Such information may furnish a basis for a logical inference.
  The CORRECT answer is:
    A. IV, VI, II, V, I, III
    B. III, II, V, I, IV, VI
    C. V, III, VI, IV, II, I
    D. V, IV, I, II, VI, III
    E. II, III, V, I, IV, VI

9.
  I. An executive may answer a letter by writing his reply on the face of the letter itself instead of having a return letter typed.
  II. This procedure is efficient because it saves the executive's time, the typist's time, and saves office file space.
  III. Copying machines are used in small offices as well as large offices to save time and money in making brief replies to business letters.
  IV. A copy is made on a copying machine to go into the company files, while the original is mailed back to the sender.
  The CORRECT answer is:
    A. I, II, IV, III
    B. I, IV, II, III
    C. III, I, IV, II
    D. III, IV, II, I

10.
  I. Most organizations favor one of the types but always include the others to a lesser degree.
  II. However, we can detect a definite trend toward greater use of symbolic control.
  III. We suggest that our local police agencies are today primarily utilizing material control.
  IV. Control can be classified into three types: physical, material, and symbolic.
  The CORRECT answer is:
    A. IV, II, III, I
    B. II, I, IV, III
    C. III, IV, II, I
    D. IV, I, III, II

11.
  I. Project residents had first claim to this use, followed by surrounding neighborhood children.
  II. By contrast, recreation space within the project's interior was found to be used more often by both groups.
  III. Studies of the use of project grounds in many cities showed grounds left open for public use were neglected and unused, both by residents and by members of the surrounding community.
  IV. Project residents had clearly laid claim to the play spaces, setting up and enforcing unwritten rules for use.
  V. Each group, by experience, found their activities easily disrupted by other groups, and their claim to the use of space for recreation difficult to enforce.

The CORRECT answer is:
A. IV, V, I, II, III
B. V, II, IV, III, I
C. I, IV, III, II, V
D. III, V, II, IV, I

12. I. They do not consider the problems correctable within the existing subsidy formula and social policy of accepting all eligible applicants regardless of social behavior.
    II. A recent survey, however, indicated that tenants believe these problems correctable by local housing authorities and management within the existing financial formula.
    III. Many of the problems and complaints concerning public housing management and design have created resentment between the tenant and the landlord.
    IV. This same survey indicated that administrators and managers do not agree with the tenants.
    The CORRECT answer is:
    A. II, I, III, IV   B. I, III, IV, II   C. III, II, IV, I   D. IV, II, I, III

13. I. In single-family residences, there is usually enough distance between tenants to prevent occupants from annoying one another.
    II. For example, a certain small percentage of tenant families has one or more members addicted to alcohol.
    III. While managers believe in the right of individuals to live as they choose, the manager becomes concerned when the pattern of living jeopardizes others' rights.
    IV. Still others turn night into day, staging lusty entertainments which carry on into the hours when most tenants are trying to sleep.
    V. In apartment buildings, however, tenants live so closely together that any misbehavior can result in unpleasant living conditions.
    VI. Other families engage in violent argument.
    The CORRECT answer is:
    A. III, II, V, IV, VI, I
    B. I, V, II, VI, IV, III
    C. II, V, IV, I, III, VI
    D. IV, II, V, VI, III, I

14. I. Congress made the commitment explicit in the Housing Act of 194, establishing as a national goal the realization of a *decent home and suitable environment for every American family*.
    II. The result has been that the goal of decent home and suitable environment is still as far distant as ever for the disadvantaged urban family.
    III. In spite of this action by Congress, federal housing programs have continued to be fragmented and grossly underfunded.
    IV. The passage of the National Housing Act signaled a few federal commitment to provide housing for the nation's citizens.
    The CORRECT answer is:
    A. I, IV, III, II   B. IV, I, III, II   C. IV, I, II, III   D. II, IV, I, III

15. I. The greater expense does not necessarily involve *exploitation*, but it is often perceived as exploitative and unfair by those who are aware of the price differences involved, but unaware of operating costs.
II. Ghetto residents believe they are *exploited* by local merchants, and evidence substantiates some of these beliefs.
III. However, stores in low-income areas were more likely to be small independents, which could not achieve the economies available to supermarket chains and were, therefore, more likely to charge higher prices, and the customers were more likely to buy smaller-sized packages which are more expensive per unit of measure.
IV. A study conducted in one city showed that distinctly higher prices were charged for goods sold in ghetto stores in other areas.
The CORRECT answer is:
  A. IV, II, I, III   B. IV, I, III, II   C. II, IV, III, I   D. II, III, IV, I

15.____

KEY (CORRECT ANSWERS)

1.	C	6.	C	11.	D
2.	E	7.	A	12.	C
3.	B	8.	B	13.	B
4.	B	9.	C	14.	B
5.	D	10.	D	15.	C

LAWN DISEASES

How to Control Them

CONTENTS

	Page
Fungus Diseases	
Helminthosporium leafspot and foot rot	1
Brown patch	2
Rust	3
Pythium diseases	3
Dollar spot	4
Stripe smut	4
Powdery mildew	5
Fusarium blight	6
Red thread	6
Copper spot	7
Ophiobolus patch	7
Snow molds: Fusarium patch and Typhula blight	8
Mushrooms and fairy rings	9
Slime molds	9
Other Causes of Poor Turf	10
Undesirable species	10
Undesirable mixtures	10
Insect injury	10
Fertilizer burn	10
Hydrated lime burn	10
Pesticide injury	10
Dog urine injury	10
Improper mowing	10
Improper watering	10
Buried debris	11
Accumulation of runners	11
Compacted soils	11

LAWN DISEASES

How to Control Them

Most of the grasses in lawns grow under artificial conditions and are more subject to attack by disease organisms than they would be in a natural environment. Healthy, vigorously growing, adapted lawn grasses that are properly managed can best survive disease attacks.

The homeowner's best defense against lawn diseases is to follow these basic principles of lawn establishment and maintenance:
- Select grasses adapted to the soil, climatic, and light conditions under which they will be grown.
- Spend the necessary time, effort, and money on caring for the lawn. In addition to disease control, lawn care includes proper fertilizing, watering, mowing, and insect and weeds control.

Proper care does not completely prevent or cure diseases, but it helps to curb them so that chemical controls can be more effective if they become necessary.

Knowing how to diagnose the most common causes of dead or injured grass and knowing the recommended treatments for various unhealthy conditions will help the homeowner to prevent serious lawn damage. Poor turf may be due to disease or to any one or a combination of other causes—undesirable or un adapted species, insect damage, fertilizer and chemical burning, dog urine, improper mowing, improper watering, localized dry spots, and compacted soil.

FUNGUS DISEASES

Fungi cause most of the serious and widespread diseases of lawn grasses. All the diseases discussed in this section are fungus diseases. Most of the fungi that attack lawn grasses occur in the form of microscopically small filaments, or threads. The mass of threads, which sometimes have a cobwebby appearance, are called mycelium. Many fungi reproduce by means of microscopic fruiting structures called spores.

Only those fungi that get their nutrients from a living host are true disease organisms. Such organisms cause Helminthosporium leaf spot, fading-out, brown patch, rust, grease spot, dollar spot, stripe smut, and snow mold.

Mushrooms and slime molds in lawns are examples of fungi that are not true disease organisms. They do not attack lawn grasses directly, but are discussed with disease organisms because they are a common lawn problem.

HELMINTHOSPORIUM LEAFSPOT AND FOOT ROT

This disease, which gets its name from the Helminthosporium fungi that cause it, is one of the most widely distributed and destructive grass diseases. Kentucky bluegrass is one of the species most severely damaged.

The principal fungus causing leafspot in Kentucky bluegrass also causes a foot rot condition known as going-out or melting-out. The disease occurs mainly during cool, moist weather of spring and fall, but it may develop throughout the summer. Pure stands of Kentucky bluegrass favor development of the disease; mixtures of several recommended species usually retard development, because most mixtures contain naturally resistant species.

Symptoms

Damage is most conspicuous in the leaves. However, the fungus responsible for the disease also causes a sheath rot or foot rot. The fungus produces reddish-brown to purplish-black spots on leaves and stems of Kentucky bluegrass. Leaves shrivel and the steams, crowns, rhizomes, and roots discolor and rot. Leaf spots and foot rots produced on other grasses by different species of Helminthosporium resemble those on Kentucky bluegrass. Dead grass in attacked areas often is attributed to drought injury. Weeds and crabgrass usually invade these areas.

Control

In Kentucky bluegrass lawns, you can control the disease by growing less susceptible varieties such as Fylking, Merion, Penn-star, and Windsor. Some leafspot-ting may occur, but these varieties are more resistant than ordinary Kentucky bluegrass and are seldom killed during the destructive foot rot stage.

Follow these management practices to reduce damage: Mow upright-growing grasses to a height of 13A, to 2 inches rather than 1/2 to 1 inch. Apply enough fertilizer to keep grass healthy and thriving. Avoid overstimulation with nitrogen, particularly in the spring. Remove clippings, especially on lawns receiving heavy fertilization.

Fungicides that control *Helminthosporium* leaf spot are listed on page 12.

BROWN PATCH

The fungus responsible for brown patch attacks practically all species of grasses, but it is most serious on bentgrasses, fes-cues, Kentucky bluegrass, ryegrass, centipede grass, and St. Augustinegrass. Brown patch is one of the most prevalent lawn grass diseases in the warm, humid regions of the United States. It occurs during warm, wet weather. Brown patch is most damaging following excessive applications of nitrogen fertilizer. This promotes a lush growth of grass that is readily attacked. The disease spreads by fungus threads, or mycelium. New infections can start from mycelium carried on shoes, mowing equipment, or grass clippings.

Symptoms

Brown patch is characterized by development of irregular circular areas a few inches to several feet in diameter with a brownish discoloration. In bentgrasses a narrow, dark, smoke-colored ring borders the diseased area. This disappears when the weather becomes cool or dry. Sometimes only the leaves are affected and the turf recovers in 2 or 3 weeks. However, if the disease is severe and weather conditions remain favorable for its development, it attacks the crowns and kills the grass. The dead grass generally remains erect and does not lie flat like grass killed by grease spot, a *Pythium* disease. The fungus threads, or mycelium, are frequently observed as filmy, white tufts early in the morning while the grass is still wet with dew. As the leaves dry, the fungus threads shrivel and disappear, and only dead and dying leaves are left. After several weeks, new grass grows back into the affected area.

Control

Management practices that help in control: Avoid excessive applications of nitrogen fertilizer. Water lawns early in the day to give grass leaves time to dry out before night. Remove clippings if excessive.

Brown patch can be controlled if the lawn is watered 48 hours before treating with fungicide and if this is repeated three times at weekly intervals.

RUST

Rust fungi attack many lawn grasses. Rust usually occurs in late summer and remains until frost. Heavy dew favors its development.

Rust damage is more severe on Merion Kentucky bluegrass and zoysia than on other grasses. Meyer and Emerald zoysias are susceptible to rust infection.

Rust has appeared on Merion Kentucky bluegrass from Rhode Island to California and from Canada to Oklahoma. The rust fungus seems to attack Merion wherever it is grown.

Some Kentucky bluegrass varieties resist rust infection entirely. Common Kentucky bluegrass is less susceptible to rust than Merion. However, it is vulnerable to the more destructive *Helminthosporium* leaf spot.

Symptoms

Symptoms are yellow-orange or red-brown powdery pustules that develop on leaves and stems. If a cloth is rubbed across affected leaves, the rust-colored spores adhere to the cloth and produce a yellowish or orange stain.

Control

Lawns containing pure stands of Merion Kentucky bluegrass are especially susceptible to attack by rust fungi. Damage is less severe if Merion Kentucky bluegrass is mixed with common Kentucky bluegrass or with red fescue. Recommended mixtures are 50-percent Merion and 50-percent common Kentucky bluegrass ; 50-percent Merion Kentucky bluegrass and 50-percent red fescue; or 50-percent Merion, 25-percent common Kentucky bluegrass, and 25-percent red fescue.

The Kentucky bluegrass varieties, Fylking, Pennstar, and Kenblue are more rust-resistant than Merion.

Mowing, fertilizing, and watering practices recommended in the summary of management practices (page 16) will help control rust.

Several chemicals (see p. 13) control rust on Merion Kentucky bluegrass and other grasses. Chemicals do not completely eradicate rust or prevent infection of growth that comes out after treatment. Repeated applications may be necessary to keep rust under control, especially on Merion Kentucky bluegrass.

PYTHIUM DISEASES

The two most destructive lawn diseases caused by Pythium fungi are grease spot and cottony blight. Grease spot occurs in many parts of the country on a wide range of grasses; cottony blight occurs mainly on ryegrass in the South.

Pythium diseases occur in humid areas and may be more widespread than is generally realized. The fungi are destructive at 70° F, and above, especially in poorly drained soils. These diseases are most common on newly established turf, but if conditions are favorable they occur on grass regardless of age.

Symptoms

Diseased areas vary from a few inches to several feet in diameter and they sometimes occur in streaks as though the fungus had spread from mowing or from water flow following heavy rains. Injury is most noticeable in early morning as a circular spot or group of spots about 2 inches in diameter surrounded by blackened grass blades that are intertwined with the fungus threads. Diseased leaves become water soaked, mat together, and appear slimy. The darkened grass blades soon wither and become reddish brown, particularly if the weather is sunny and windy. Grass is usually killed in 24 hours and it lies flat on the ground rather than remaining upright like grass affected by the brown patch disease. New grass does not grow back into the diseased area.

Control
The most important management recommendation is to avoid watering methods that keep foliage and ground wet for long periods. Other suggestions: Avoid excessive watering during warm weather. Delay seeding until fall because cool, dry weather generally checks the disease.

Chemicals give best results if used when the disease first appears (see page.12).

DOLLAR SPOT

Dollar spot, also known as small brown patch, occurs on many species of grasses. The disease is particularly destructive in bentgrass-es. It is most prevalent in the humid northern areas of the United States but occurs also in States farther south.

The fungus is most destructive during cool, wet weather. It generally attacks in May and June, stops during July and August, and starts again in September and October. Dollar spot may occur in any turf regardless of management or soil fertility, but damage usually is greatest if there is a deficiency of nitrogen.

Symptoms
The disease is characterized by development of bleached spots the size of a silver dollar. Affected grass is killed, and the turf is left pitted. Sometimes the diseased areas merge and form large, irregular patches. At first, spots of diseased grass are dark and somewhat water soaked; then they turn brown and ultimately bleach nearly white. If the fungus is growing actively, a fine, white, cobwebby mycelium can be seen when dew is still on the grass. Sometimes only the uppermost grass blades are affected and light colored blotches develop on them.

Turf recovers quickly if treated with fungicides in the early stages of a disease attack; if left untreated it may take many weeks for new grass to fill in dead areas.

The best control is to use chemicals listed on page 13.

STRIPE SMUT

Stripe smut fungus attacks several lawn grasses but it is most prevalent and destructive on Merion Kentucky bluegrass, principally in the northern half of the United States.

Smut spores in contaminated soil germinate and produce infection threads that invade grass seedlings and young tillers. Since the fungus grows systematically, infected plants remain diseased until they die.

Symptoms
Narrow gray or black stripes that may be continuous or discontinuous develop lengthwise in leaf blades. The gray stripes are unruptured smut sites called sori. The black streaks result when smut sori rupture and liberate a mass of black, powdery spores. Following rupture of the sori, diseased leaves wither, curl, and shred from the tip downward, and die.

Diseased Kentucky bluegrass plants occur singly, or in spots from a few inches to a foot or more in diameter. Infected plants are often pale green to slightly yellowed. They also are shorter than neighboring healthy plants and may be obscured by them.

Stripe smut is most readily seen on leaves during cool weather in spring and fall. Diseased plants are difficult to find during hot, dry weather because many infected plants die. Smutted plants also are difficult to find shortly after mowing due to their slower growth.

Control

Fungicides are available for treating the disease. Smut damage is less severe if Merion Kentucky bluegrass is mixed with common Kentucky bluegrass, or if smut-tolerant varieties like Fylking, Kenblue, Park, or Pennstar are grown

POWDERY MILDEW

In recent years, powdery mildew has become an increasingly important fungus disease of Mer-ion Kentucky bluegrass and other Kentucky bluegrasses. Powdery mildew also infects red fescue, bermuda, and other grasses used for lawns. The use of high rates of nitrogen fertilizer produces an ideal environment for this mildew fungus.

The disease is generally more damaging to grasses in shaded and protected areas (on north and east sides of buildings), although it also occurs in severe form in fields of Merion during late fall and early spring. Because the fungus significantly reduces the growth of leaves, roots, and rhizomes, it is an important cause of turf deterioration of bluegrass lawns in shaded areas. Many plants may be weakened, die from drought, or be winter-killed because of this deterioration.

Symptoms

Powdery mildew appears first as small superficial patches of white to light-gray fungus growth on leaves and sheaths. These patches enlarge rapidly and become powdery as spores are produced. The older, lower leaves are often completely covered by mildew. The leaf tissue under the mildew becomes yellowed soon after infection and later turns tan or brown and is killed. Severely infected leaves gradually dry up and die.

The fungus survives the winter as a mass of thread-like filaments on the live leaves of Kentucky bluegrass. Numerous spores are produced on these filaments in the spring. Spores are carried by the wind and initiate new infections during cool (optimum 65° F.), humid weather. With favorable temperature and high atmospheric humidity, the host tissue dies and the spores are carried to other grasses in the same or neighboring turf areas to produce new infections and start the cycle once again.

Control

Kentucky bluegrass varieties differ in their susceptibility to powdery mildew. Merion is very susceptible while other varieties exhibit varying degrees of resistance.

To reduce turf shading and improve air circulation be sure to prune or remove trees and shrubs that shade or border turf areas. Keep the lawn vigorous but avoid overstimulation with nitrogen fertilizer. Water during dry periods to maintain adequate moisture in the soil. Where possible, mow at the recommended height and—when the disease is present—collect all clippings.

In the spring or early fall, when powdery mildew becomes evident, one or more applications of a fungicide at 7 to 10 day intervals should control the disease. Suggested fungicides to obtain control are listed in the guide on page 12.

FUSARIUM BLIGHT

Fusarium blight affects Kentucky bluegrass, bentgrass, red fescue, and many other grasses. The fungi that cause Fusarium blight survive the winter months in infected grass roots, crowns, and in thatch covering the lower portion of grass plants. The pathogens are widespread; they occur on blighted turf wherever the above turf grasses are grown.

Bentgrasses are the most susceptible species, followed by Kentucky bluegrass and red fescue. The disease also occurs in Merion and Windsor Kentucky bluegrass, other varieties vary in susceptibility at different temperatures.

The severity of the disease varies directly with light intensity; areas that receive direct sunlight are the most severely infected. Infection of the leaves usually occurs when air temperatures are 70° F. to 90° F. and conditions of high humidity prevail. The disease ceases to be active when temperatures fall below 70° F. and there is an absence of rainfall or humidity.

Symptoms

At first, diseased areas are light green but within 36 to 48 hours the areas fade to tan and then to a light straw color. The diseased areas vary in size from a few inches to 2 or more feet in diameter. Dead areas may be circular, crescent shaped, streaked, or in circles with a patch of green grass in the central portion. The latter forms a distinctive "frog's eye" symptom pattern. Extensive damage occurs when diseased areas are numerous and coalesce.

Individual plants are killed when the crown tissues are destroyed. On individual leaves, the disease is characterized by irregular-shaped, dark-green blotches. These blotches rapidly fade to a light green, then assume a reddish-brown hue, and finally become dull tan.

Control

The fungi that cause Fusarium blight grow in a layer of thatch on the soil surface. To control this disease, remove most of the thatch layer with a rake or lawnmower. A nitrogen imbalance in the soil causes the thatch on which the fungi feed to accumulate more rapidly.

To effectively control Fusarium blight the use of a preventive fungicide spray as well as thatch control is essential. Do not spray when night temperatures fall below 70° F. Spraying should be continued at 7-to-10 day intervals as long as daytime temperatures are 75° F. and above and conditions of high humidity prevail.

Fungicides that will help control Fusarium blight are listed on page 12.

RED THREAD

Red thread especially affects bentgrasses, red fescue, and Kentucky bluegrasses in the Northeastern States and in the Pacific Coast States of Washington and Oregon. In these regions, red thread occurs primarily in the early spring and fall during cool, wet weather. This fungus disease has also been reported on Bermuda-grass lawns in Mississippi during December.

When the grass is growing rapidly, nitrogen fertilization is a rapid and effective means of controlling the disease. However, the fungus again becomes destructive when grass growth slows down. Therefore, fungicidal eradication is necessary for satisfactory disease control.

The pathogen survives unfavorable conditions as fragments of dried fungal tissues and as dormant mycelium in the residues of the diseased plants. These fragments may be carried by the wind or mechanically on mowers or similar machines.

Symptoms

The fungus attacks the leaves and leaf sheaths. These parts later become tan colored as the tissue dries out. The leaves may be completely covered by a pink, gelatinous growth of the fungus. As this growth spreads, it infects plant after plant.

In its final stages, the disease is characterized by reddish fungus threads at the leaf terminals. Diseased areas are usually 2 to 30 inches in diameter and irregular in shape.

Red thread is capable of growing over a wide range of temperatures; growth occurs from slightly above 32° F. to about 86° F. The most favorable temperature range for growth lies between 60° F. and 70° F.

Control

Red thread is serious only when cool temperatures slow grass growth or when the turf is under-fertilized with nitrogen. Fungicides to control red thread are listed on page 12.

COPPER SPOT

Copper spot can cause a serious disease problem on bentgrasses. It is most damaging in the coastal states but is found throughout the United States.

The pathogen overwinters in the debris of the previous season's growth. The disease occurs in warm, wet weather; active growth of the organism begins when air temperatures range from 68° F. to 75° F. When the weather is warm and humid secondary spores are produced and new lesions are formed.

The spores, spread by means of splashing water, germinate rapidly and new leaf infections take place within 24 hours. Outbreaks of copper spot may occur in epidemic proportions within a few days.

Symptoms

From a distance, copper spot looks like salmon-pink or copper-colored turf; the spots range from 1 to 3 inches in diameter. Unlike areas infected by dollar spot, areas affected by copper spot are not definite in outline. Wet weather increases the intensity of coloration.

Control

Copper spot can be controlled by the use of fungicides. Apply preventive fungicidal applications at 10-day intervals when the daytime air temperatures stabilize at 70° F. to 75° F. Make curative applications at 4 to 5-day intervals until recovery is effected.

Fungicides that will control copper spot are listed on page 16.

OPHIOBOLUS PATCH

Ophiobolus patch is the third most important fungus disease in the Pacific Northwest. It occurs west of the Cascades in Oregon, Washington, and British Columbia. The disease is especially common on bentgrass lawns.

The growth of the disease is stimulated by cool, wet weather. However, symptoms become most noticeable during midsummer under drier growing conditions. The disease usually appears as a thinning or drying of the grass in doughtnut-shaped rings or larger areas. Both shoots and roots of the grass are severely attacked. Affected areas do not recover for several months.

Symptoms

The doughtnut-shaped rings range from several inches to several feet in diameter. The injured areas are light brown in color becoming dull gray in winter. The centers of the rings are invaded by weeds and annual bluegrass.

Ophiobolus patch is first seen as depressed circular patches of blighted turfgrass, a few inches in diameter. The affected areas may increase to several feet in diameter and coalesce so that they become large, irregular-shaped patches. The colors range from light straw to bronze. The centers of the patches often fill in with resistant species creating a "frog' eye" symptom pattern.

Control

Ophiobolus patch is difficult to control with fungicides. The use of ammonium sulfate fertilizer as a source of nitrogen has been effective.

Apply ammonium sulfate four times a year in March, May, June, and early September. Apply 7? pounds of the product as it comes from the bag per 1,000 square feet for each application. Turf must be thoroughly watered after each application of fertilizer.

To balance applications of ammonium sulfate apply 0-20-20 (O-P-K) fertilizer twice a year in early spring and early fall. Use 7 pounds of fertilizer per 1,000 square feet for each application. After the disease has disappeared use a 12-4-8 fertilizer for normal lawn fertilization.

SNOW MOLDS: FUSARIUM PATCH AND TYPHULA BLIGHT

These diseases are especially severe on bentgrasses, but they also occur on other lawn grasses. Snow mold, or winter scald, is caused by several different fungi. It is most severe when snow covers grass for long periods. It is particularly difficult to control if the grass is green and growing actively when covered by lasting snow. Fusarium patch, also known as pink snow mold, can occur during the growing season when humidity is high and daily temperatures fall below 65°F. Any condition that keeps the turf excessively wet, such as poor surface drainage, favors these diseases.

Symptoms

Snow mold symptoms appear first as a white cottony growth on the leaves. As the leaves die they turn light brown and cling together. Diseased areas are usually 1 to 12 inches or more in diameter and discolored dirty white, gray, or slightly pink. Fusarium patch is characterized by development of irregular pale yellow areas from several inches to several feet in diameter. Later, affected areas become whitish gray. Sometimes the edge of an affected area has a faint pinkish color.

Typhula blight is particularly active under snow cover and is usually conspicuous at the first spring thaw. At first, the disease appears as light-yellow discolored grass areas 1 or 2 inches in diameter. Leaves of the infected plants change their discolored appearance to a grayish white. As the areas enlarge, a halo of grayish-white mycelial growth up to 1 inch in diameter develops. Affected areas may measure up to 1 or 2 feet, but under optimum conditions the diseased grass may coalesce into larger areas.

Initial disease development does not occur unless there is snow cover on unfrozen ground. When the ground is frozen, parasitic activity of the fungus essentially ceases. The disease is most active with the advent of cool air temperatures and humid conditions in the spring.

Control

Proper management in the fall is especially important because the condition of the turf as it goes into the winter determines whether the snow mold fungus can easily get established. Do not apply high nitrogen fertilizers late in the fall because that might stimulate growth and result in an actively growing turf when snow covers the ground. Keep the lawn cut in the fall to prevent a mat of grass from developing. Apply lime if soil tests indicate a need for it.

For control of snow molds with fungicides, see table on page 17.

MUSHROOMS AND FAIRY RINGS

Many kinds of mushrooms grow in lawns and turf areas. They vary in size, shape, and habit of growth, and in the way they affect the turf. They may grow individually or in clumps. Some grow in a circle and cause a condition known as fairy rings.

Mushrooms

Mushrooms that grow individually or in clumps usually develop from buried organic matter such as pieces of construction lumber, logs, or tree stumps. Mushrooms with this growth habit are usually harmless to grasses but are objectionable because they are un sightly and the fruiting bodies occur repeatedly. They develop following prolonged wet weather, and often disappear as soon as the soil begins to dry or when the grass is mowed.

Eliminate mushrooms that grow from buried lumber, logs, or stumps by digging up the pieces of buried wood. If this is impractical, drench the soil with captan. The simplest way to drench is to punch holes 6 to 8 inches apart and 6 to 8 inches deep in the ground within and surrounding the, infected area. Use an iron rod or pipe for punching the holes, and then pour a solution of captan down the holes.

Fairy Rings

Fairy rings are circles, or arcs, of dark-green grass surrounding areas of light-colored or dead grass. During spring and fall the fruiting bodies (mushrooms) develop in a circle outlining the fairy ring. Unless the fungus is controlled the ring enlarges each year and leaves alternate bands of green and discolored grass.

The fungus that causes fairy rings begins growth at a particular point and continues to grow outward. It may spread from 5 to 24 inches annually; the rate of spread depends on soil conditions, temperature, moisture, and fertility. The fungus is usually several inches below the ground and it forms a dense layer of mycelial threads that break down organic matter at the outer edge of the ring. Grass at the outer edge grows faster than grass outside the ring, and is darker green. Dying or dead grass is inside the zone of stimulated growth. Fairy rings seldom occur in lawns that are adequately fertilized and treated with fungicides for control of other diseases.

For best control, fumigate the affected area with methyl bromide. As an alternate method, punch holes around the outside of the ring and throughout the affected area, then pour a solution of captan into the holes.

SLIME MOLDS

A group of fungi known as slime molds often covers grass with a dusty, bluish-gray, black, or yellow mass. Slime molds are not parasitic on grass, but they are unsightly. They feed on dead organic matter. The most damage they do to grass plants is to shade and discolor the blades. Slime molds occur during wet weather; they disappear rapidly as soon as it becomes dry. The large masses can be readily broken up by sweeping with a broom or by spraying with a strong stream of water. During prolonged damp weather slime molds can be especially annoying and it may be desirable to apply a turf fungicide listed on 13 to affected areas.

OTHER CAUSES OF POOR TURF

UNDESIRABLE SPECIES

Short-lived perennials like red-top and ryegrass or weedy annuals such as annual bluegrass and crabgrass do not make a desirable lawn. Annual species usually die at the end of the growing season, and leave brown or bare areas that may be mistaken for disease injury.

UNDESIRABLE MIXTURES

Bermudagrasses and zoysia-grasses turn straw colored or brown following a killing frost. When these species are grown in a sod composed mainly of cool-season grasses, a mottled brown and green lawn often results because of the differences in sensitivity to cold. This effect may resemble disease injury.

INSECT INJURY

Lawn grasses are often damaged by insect pests. For information concerning lawn insects and their control, see your county agent or write to the U.S. Department of Agriculture, Washington, D.C. 20250.

FERTILIZER BURN

Concentrated inorganic fertilizers, if applied too heavily, burn grass in 2 or 3 days. Burned areas may occur in spots or streaks or the entire lawn may be damaged. To prevent injury, apply the fertilizer evenly in recommended amounts when the grass is dry,
then water immediately. If burning occurs, water generously to wash off excess fertilizer and reduce injury.

HYDRATED LIME BURN

Hydrated lime burns grass if it is applied unevenly and in large amounts. Ground agricultural limestone is safer and is usually recommended for lawns.

PESTICIDE INJURY

Some of the chemicals used for disease, insect, and weed control are potent and may injure grass if improperly applied. Chemical formulations vary with manufacturers. Follow directions and observe all precautions on the label.

DOG URINE INJURY

This kind of injury is frequently mistaken for disease damage. Affected spots are usually round or slightly irregular and variable in size. The grass within the spot turns brown or straw colored and usually dies.

IMPROPER MOWING

Cutting grass too closely or too frequently may result in a condition that looks like disease. Cut Kentucky bluegrass, red fescue, and other grasses with upright growth habit to a height of 13%, to 2 inches. Do not lower the height of cutting in midseason; it may result in serious injury. Mow the grass before it gets too talk; not more than one-half of the leaf surfaces should be removed at one time. The frequency of mowing will depend on quantity of fertilizer and water applied, weather conditions, and other factors that influence plant growth. Clippings need not be removed unless growth is excessive.

IMPROPER WATERING

Frequent light watering induces shallow rooting in grasses. Shallowrooted grasses are readily injured during periods of severe drought. Frequent evening watering favors disease development because it keeps grass leaves moist for long periods.

Do not water grass until it begins to wilt, and then apply enough water to soak the soil to a depth of 6 inches or more. It is more economical to water the lawn only when water is needed and it is better for the grass.

BURIED DEBRIS

A thin layer of soil over rocks or debris such as lumber, stumps, plaster, and cement dries rapidly and may not retain enough moisture to keep grass green. Correct this condition by removing the cause.

ACCUMULATION OF RUNNERS

Another type of dry spot results when an accumulation of runners (thatch) in bermuda-grass, bentgrass, and zoysiagrass becomes impervious and does not let water into the soil. Mowing following vigorous hand raking corrects this condition.

COMPACTED SOILS

Saturated soils pack easily and bake hard when dry, especially where traffic is heavy. The soil may become packed so hard that water will not penetrate the surface. Grass then thins out and bare spots result. To correct this condition, loosen or perforate the soil with a tined fork or aerifying implement and, if necessary, fertilize and reseed the lawn.

COMPONENTS OF RECOMMENDED FUNGICIDES

Acti-dione TGF: ® 3- [2-(3,5-dimethy1-2-oxocyclohexyl) 2 - hydroxyethyl] glutarimide (cycloheximide)

Acti-dione-thiram: cyloheximide plus bis(dimethylthiocarbamoyl) disulfide
Captan: *N-* [(trichloromethyl) thio] - 4-cyclohexene -1,2-dicar-boximide

Cleary 3336: ® diethyl [(1, 2-phenylene) bis (iminocarbonothioyl)] bis [carbamate] (thiophanate)

Daconil 2787: ® tetrachloroiso-phthalonitrile (chlorothalonil)

Dexon: ® sodium *p*-(dimethylamino) benzenediazosulfonate

Dowfume MC-2: ® methyl bromide with 2% chloropicrin
Dyrene: ® 2, 4-dichloro-6-(*o*-chioroanilino) -*s*-triazine

Fore ® coordination product of zinc ion and manganous ethylenebis [dithiocarbamate]
Fungo 50: ® dimethyl [(1,2-phenylene) bis (iminocarbonothioyl) bis [carbamate] (thiophanate-methyl)

Koban: ® 5-ethoxy-3-(trichloro-methyl)-1,2,4-thiadiazole

Mertect 140-F: ® 2- (4-thiazolyl) benzimidazole (thiabendazole)

Tersan 1991: ® methyl 1-(butylcarbamoyl) - 2 - benzimidazolecarbamate (benomyl)

Tersan LSR: ® manganous ethylenebis [dithiocarbamate] (maneb)

Tersan SP: ® 1,4-dichloro-2,5-dimethoxybenzene (chloroneb)
Zineb: zinc ethylenebis [dithiocarbamate]
® denotes a trademark or proprietary product

GUIDE FOR SELECTING FUNGICIDES

Disease and Causal Organism	Fungicides [1]	Application Per 1,000 sq ft		Directions [2]
		Ounces of Formulation	Tablespoons	
Brown Patch *Rhizoctonia solani*	Cleary's 3336® WP 50% Daconil 2787® WP 75% Dyrene® WP 50% Fore® WP 80% Fungo 50® WP 50% Mertect 140–F® liquid Tersan 1991® WP 50% Tersan LSR® WP 80%	2 4 4–6 4 2 2 2 6	11 22 19–28 14 11 4 11 4–5	Disease can appear from June to August. Treat your lawn every 5–10 days until the disease has been controlled.
Copper Spot *Glococercospora sorghi*	See Dollar Spot (Sclerotinia)			
Dollar Spot *Sclerotinia homeocarpa*	Acti-dione-Thiram® WP Cleary's 3336® WP 50% Daconil 2787® WP 75% Dyrene® WP 50% Tersan 1991® WP 50% Fore® WP 80% Fungo 50® WP 50% Mertect 140–F® liquid	2–4 2 2–4 4–6 2 6–8 1 2	11–22 11 11–22 19–28 11 14–21 6 4	Disease can appear from June to October. Treat your lawn at 7–14 day intervals until the disease has been controlled.
Fairy Rings Mushrooms *Psalliota campestris* *Marasmius* *Lepiota*	Captan WP 50% Dowfume MC-2	4–5	15–20	Disease can appear throughout the growing season. Pour double or triple strength concentrate of captan into 1-inch holes punched 4–6 inches deep and 6–8 inches apart both inside and outside the affected area. Alternative method: Fumigate infected area with Dowfume MC-2® (1 lb 100 sq ft) and reseed or resod. Recommended largely for golf courses, parks and other large turf areas.
Fusarium Blight *Fusarium roseum*	Cleary's 3336® WP 50% Fungo 50® WP 50% Tersan 1991® WP 50%	2–4 4–8 2	11–22 19–38 33	Treat at first appearance of disease and repeat 10–14 days later. Water thoroughly to wet into soil.
Grease Spot and Cottony Blight *Pythium*	Tersan SP® WP 65% Dexon® WP 70% Fore® WP 80% Koban® WP 65% Zineb WP 75%	4 2 8 4 2	5–6 14 28 17 13–27	Disease can appear from July to September and in fall and winter during warm humid periods in the South. Treat your lawn every 5–14 days until the disease has been controlled.
Helminthosporium diseases Leafspot (Blight, Going-out, Melting-out) *Helminthosporium* spp.	Acti-dione-Thiram® WP Captan WP 50% Cleary's 3336® WP 50% Daconil 2787® WP 75% Dyrene® WP 50% Fore® WP 80% Tersan LSR® WP 80% Zineb WP 75%	4 4–6 2 4 4–6 4 3–4 2	22 15–23 11 22 19–28 14 4–5 13–27	Disease can appear from April to August depending on kind of grass and species of fungus. Treat your lawn every 7–14 days three times consecutively or until the disease has been controlled.
Ophiobolus Patch *Ophiobolus graminis*	See page — for control.			
Powdery Mildew *Erysiphe graminis*	Acti-dione Thiram® Acti-dione TGF® WP Tersan 1991® WP 50%	4 1–2 2	22 6 11	July–September 7–10 days 7–14 days
Red Thread *Corticum fuciforme*	Acti-dione-Thiram® WP Cleary's 3336® WP 50% Fore® WP 80% Fungo 50® WP 50% Tersan LSR® WP 80%	4 2 4–6 2 6	22 11 14–21 11 4–5	May, June, and August, every 10–14 days.

GUIDE FOR SELECTING FUNGICIDES—continued

Disease and Causal Organism	Fungicides[1]	Application Per 1,000 sq ft		Directions[2]
		Ounces of Formulation	Table-spoons	
Rust *Puccinia*	Acti-dione-Thiram® WP	4	22	Disease can appear from June to September. Treat your lawn every 7–14 days until rust disappears.
	Daconil 2787® WP 75%	4	22	
	Dyrene® WP 50%	4–6	19–28	
	Fore® WP 80%	4	14	
	Tersan LSR® WP 80%	3–4	4–5	
	Zineb WP 75%	2	13–27	
Slime Molds *Physarum cinercum*	Fore® WP 80%	6–8	21–28	Disease can appear throughout the growing season and can be controlled without fungicides. See page —.
	Zineb WP 75%	2	13–27	
Snow Molds Fusarium Patch *Fusarium nivale*	Tersan 1991® WP 50%	2	11	Disease can appear from fall to spring. Treat your law at intervals of 2–6 weeks as needed.
	Mertect 140-F® liquid	2	2	
	Fore® WP 80%	6–8	21–28	
	Fungo 50® WP 50%	2	11	
Typhula Blight *Typhula itoana*	Tersan SP® WP 65%	6–8	5–6	Disease can appear from fall to spring. Tret your lawn at intervals of 2–6 weeks as needed.
	Dyrene WP 50%	2–3	19–28	
Stripe Smut *Ustilago striiformis*	Fungo 50® WP 50%	4–8	19–38	One application in October or early spring before grass growth begins. Water thoroughly to wet into soil.
	Tersan 1991® WP 50%	6	33	

CAUTION: Do not graze treated areas or feed clippings to livestock.

[1] See page 17 for components of registered fungicides.

[2] The directions given in the above table may not be complete enough. Be sure to read and follow the manufacturer's directions the label for all fungicide applications.

MANAGEMENT PRACTICES THAT HELP PREVENT LAWN DISEASES

These practices are general guides to be used according to one's judgment. Their importance depends on the kind and seriousness of the disease threat. Not all of them are practicable under all conditions.

- Select grass species best adapted to the soil, climatic, and light Conditions under which they will be grown.
- Plant mixtures of recommended grasses. Species vary in their susceptibility to different disease organisms, and in a mixture one or more of the grasses usually will survive a severe disease attack.
- Do not clip upright-growing grasses such as Kentucky bluegrass and red fescue too closely-1 ¾ to 2 inches is the best height. Creeping grasses such as bent-grass and zoysia may be clipped at ½ inch or less.
- Mow the grass before it gets too tall; not more than one-half of the leaf surface should be removed at one time.
- Mow the lawn frequently enough in the fall to prevent the accumulation of a thick mat of grass before snow comes.
- Apply enough fertilizer to keep grass vigorously growing, but• avoid over stimulating the grass with nitrogen. Apply lime if soil tests indicate a need for it.
- Clippings need not be removed except on heavily fertilized lawns or during periods when the grass is growing rapidly. Clippings provide nutrients for fungi and help to maintain humidity long after the sun has dried off surrounding uncovered areas.
- Water early enough in the day to allow grass leaves time to dry out before night. Avoid frequent, light watering, especially during warm weather.
- Do not water grass until it begins to wilt, then soak the soil to a depth of 6 inches or more. Provide good surface drainage.

USE OF PESTICIDES

This publication is intended for nationwide distribution. Pesticides are registered by the Environmental Protection Agency (EPA) for countrywide use unless otherwise indicated on the label.

The use of pesticides is governed by the provisions of the Federal Insecticide, Fungicide, and Rodenticide Act, as amended. This Act is administered by EPA. According to the provisions of the Act, "It shall be unlawful for any person to use any registered pesticide in a manner inconsistent with its labeling." (Section 12 (a) (2) (G))

EPA has interpreted this Section of the Act to require that the intended use of the pesticide must be on the label of the pesticide being used or covered by a Pesticide Enforcement. Policy Statement (PEPS) issued by EPA.

The optimum use of pesticides, both as to rate and frequency, may vary in different sections of the country. Users of this publication may also wish to consult their Cooperative Extension Service, State Agricultural Experiment Stations, or County Extension Agents for information applicable to their localities.

The pesticides mentioned in this publication are available in several different formulations that contain varying amounts of active ingredient. Because of this difference, the rates given in this publication refer to the amount of active ingredient, unless otherwise indicated. Users are reminded to convert the rate in the publication to the strength of the pesticide actually being used. For example, 1 pound of active ingredient equals 2 pounds of a 50 percent formulation.

The user is cautioned to read and follow all directions and precautions given on the label of the pesticide formulation being used.

Federal and State regulations require registration numbers on all pesticide containers. Use only pesticides that carry one of these registration numbers.

USDA publications that contain suggestions for the use of pesticides are normally revised at 2-year intervals. If your copy is more than 2 years old, contact your Cooperative Extension Service to determine the latest pesticide recommendations.

The pesticides mentioned in this publication were federally registered for the use indicated as of this publication. The user is cautioned to determine the directions on the label or labeling prior to use of the pesticide.

CONTENTS

Introduction 2

New Lawn Establishment 3
Site considerations 3
Planting 6
Postplanting care 10

Routine Lawn Maintenance 11
Mowing 11
Fertilizing 12
Watering 17
Rolling 18
Topdressing 18
Thatch 18
Lawn maintenance calendar 20

Lawn Pests 24
Weeds 24
Diseases 28
Insects 34

Special Lawn Problems 36
Improving a poor lawn 36
Renovating a poor lawn 36
Lawns in the shade 37
Steep slopes 37
Turfgrasses and substitutes to avoid 37
Moss 38
Moles, skunks, and other animals 38

Appendix 39
Calculations for home lawn practices 39
Directions for soil sampling 40

INTRODUCTION

Lawns play a significant role in the residential landscape. Of the 30 million acres of land in New York State, approximately 1.2 million acres are maintained under turfgrass conditions. About three-quarters of this amount is devoted to the residential lawn.

Lawns can provide many benefits if properly established and maintained. Turfgrass enhances our environment by filtering out atmospheric pollutants; cooling the air as it gives off water, an important process in highly urbanized areas; improving the structure of soils by adding organic matter; eliminating soil erosion; and reducing noise pollution when used in conjunction with physical barriers.

Lawns provide an attractive, inexpensive ground cover especially in the harsh conditions of full sun. In addition, a well maintained landscape greatly increases the value of property. Turfgrass is the only suitable living surface that can be used repeatedly for recreational purposes. Many individuals take great pride in the appearance of their lawns and derive enjoyment in caring for them.

The information needed to establish and maintain an acceptable lawn is presented in this publication and is divided into four major sections: "New Lawn Establishment," "Routine Lawn Maintenance," "Lawn Pests," and "Special Lawn Problems." If you are planning to establish a lawn, you should read the entire bulletin. If you have a special concern, review the information in the most appropriate section.

NEW LAWN ESTABLISHMENT

Site Considerations

Survey the conditions on your property to determine if turfgrass is the most suitable ground cover. Not all residential sites have the most favorable conditions for growing an acceptable lawn. Heavily shaded areas and severely sloped areas are not ideal locations for lawns. Such areas are difficult to establish and maintain and have proved to be very costly.

Site Preparation

Taking the time to carefully prepare your new area will help ensure a successful lawn. Many future lawn problems can be avoided by following the simple procedures outlined.

Control Perennial Grassy Weeds

Certain weeds are impossible to control without killing the lawn. It is important to remove these weeds before establishment. The most troublesome weeds of this type are quackgrass, yellow nutsedge, and creeping bentgrass as well as other coarse pasture-type grasses. A nonselective herbicide should be used in controlling these weeds

However, if the best planting time arrives by the time you begin to work, go ahead with the planting.

Drainage

Unless excess water drains rapidly through the soil, the turfgrass will have a poor root system and weak growth. If your soil stays wet after a heavy rain, you cannot grow a satisfactory lawn until you provide supplemental drainage.

Grading

For a new home, the house foundation and the curb or sidewalk level are the fixed grade points. An older property has more places that cannot be changed. The problem in grading is to arrange the soil between these fixed points in gradual, pleasant slopes to direct water away from the house and off the property.

Avoid sudden steep slopes because they are hard to establish and difficult to maintain. Where much soil must be changed, move the topsoil into a pile and rearrange the subsoil to the desired grade or slope. Then spread the topsoil evenly over the subsoil. In grading, be sure to allow for the gradual settling of loose soil. A 6-inch layer of loose soil settles to about 5 inches. It is better to prepare the seedbed several weeks before the planting time, to allow the loose soil to settle enough to make the final grading easy. Also, you can destroy any weeds that come up.

Soil

Topsoil

If you are building a new home, be sure to see that the topsoil is scraped into a pile and saved for even distribution after the builder has finished and the rough grading has been done. This important point is often overlooked, and only subsoil remains. If you do not have all or most of the original topsoil, plan to add at least 4 to 6 inches of good topsoil, even though it is expensive. This is the surest, and often the most economical, way to produce a good lawn.

Acquiring a good topsoil is often difficult; therefore, you should seek advice from your Cooperative Extension agent. Bring in a representative sample of the soils you are considering buying for an evaluation of soil pH, nutrient level, and physical condition. In many cases the top 6 inches of a farm pasture or cropland soil is very desirable for lawn use. One word of caution: Find out if any herbicides have been used on this land because some are harmful to turfgrass. Do not accept river bottom silt, soil dug from a hill with a power shovel, or factory waste, regardless of how "rich" any of this material looks. If you live near a large city or in some other area where good topsoil is not available, work with what you have.

Even poor soils, if well drained, often can produce a fairly good lawn with proper soil preparation, adequate fertilization, and the right kind of turfgrass seed at the proper season.

Then, if the lawn can be maintained for a few years with adequate water and fertilizer added, the turfgrass will produce enough organic matter to improve the soil gradually. One must be patient when trying to improve poor soils; it may take several years to produce an acceptable lawn.

Soil texture and organic matter

A very sandy soil is too "light or open" in texture. It is like a mass of tiny stones, with too few smaller bits of soil between the sand grains to hold water and fertilizer materials. Turfgrass does not do its best when water and nutrients are lacking. To improve a very sandy soil, work about 1–2 inches of organic matter into the surface 4–6 inches of soil. Another method involves thoroughly mixing 1 inch of heavier soil with the top 4 inches of sand. A sandy soil is improved more if you add both organic matter and heavier soil than if you add either material alone.

A clay soil is a "heavy or dense soil." It is slippery and sticky when wet and shrinks and cracks open as it dries. Turfgrass cannot do its best in heavy clay, for there is not enough air in the soil for good root growth. Heavy traffic from people walking or playing packs a clay soil even more tightly. Work organic matter into a heavy clay soil to improve it. Do not work sand into a clay soil; it will pack harder than before and become much like concrete.

If your soil needs organic matter, any one of several materials will do a good job. *Avoid* using wood chips, shavings, or sawdust since they can "steal" nitrogen, which is vital to the turf, from the soil. For each 1,000 square feet of new lawn, use 4 large (6 cubic-foot) bales of peat or from 2 to 3 cubic yards of well-rotted manure or cultivated peat or 3 to 4 cubic yards of spent mushroom soil. Smaller amounts of organic matter are of little value. Sewage sludge is sometimes available from your local sewage treatment plant. It can be used fairly successfully if it does not contain excessive amounts of heavy metals from industrial wastes.

Cover crops and green-manure crops are not practical for lawns, because the amount of organic matter they add is relatively small and is not worth the cost, effort, and inconvenience.

Lime or sulfur

Some soils are too acid or too alkaline to grow good turfgrass. The best time to correct the soil pH is before planting. First, determine if your soil is too acid or alkaline by

Table 1. Amount of ground limestone needed to raise soil pH in upper 4″–6″ of soil

Raising pH to 6.5*

Original pH	Pounds of limestone/1,000 sq ft of area		
	Sandy	Loamy	Clayey
5.5	45	60	100
5.0	70	90	150
4.5	80	100	180
4.0	100	160	200

*These rates cannot be used on established turfgrass. See lawn maintenance section for rates on established turfgrass.

having the soil tested. The results of the soil test are reported in terms of pH units.[1] The ordinary range for New York soils is from 4.5 (acid) to pH 7.8 (alkaline). It is desirable to have your soil in the pH range from 6.0 to 7.0. Most Cooperative Extension offices can test the soil pH for a nominal fee. Table 1 contains specific ground limestone recommendations when the soil pH and texture are known.

When the pH of the soil is above 7.5, elemental sulfur should be used to lower the pH. Purchase a pelleted elemental sulfur product, which can be easily applied with a drop or centrifugal spreader. Apply sulfur and mix it thoroughly into the upper 4–6 inches at the rate recommended in table 2.

Fertilization

Seed sown on most soils that have not been fertilized either fails or produces a thin, weedy turf. Sod also establishes faster when properly fertilized. Have the soil tested for the level of nutrients. The results will give you a recommendation of how much and the type of fertilizer to apply. If you are not able to have a soil test taken, apply 20 pounds of 5-10-5, 5-10-10, or equivalent[2] with either a drop or a centrifugal spreader.

Final Preparation

Finish all the drainage, rough grading, topsoil additions, and final grading. You should then have a smooth, even expanse of soil without humps or hollows and with no trash or large stones.

Spread whatever organic matter, fertilizer, lime, or sulfur and mix all thoroughly into the top 4–6 inches of soil. Even distribution is important. Spread organic materials with a shovel or fork. Apply fertilizer, lime, or sulfur with a fertilizer spreader. Tilling machines with revolving metal blades are good for soil mixing. Perhaps you can rent or borrow one. Lacking this, turn the soil several times with a spading fork or tractor drawn tool.

It may be more convenient to rake the fertilizer into the surface of the loose seedbed than to mix it deeply. This practice will not harm the seed or sod, and the turfgrass will grow as well.

Rake the seedbed again to produce a smooth surface. If you have a roller, make one trip over each part of the seedbed. This firms the seedbed and shows up small humps and hollows to be corrected. Rake the seedbed once more to ready it for planting. Do not rake the soil so much that the surface is powdery. A mixture of soil granules and small clods is better.

Table 2. Amount of elemental sulfur needed to lower soil pH in upper 4"–6" of soil

Lowering pH to 6.5*	Pounds of elemental sulfur/1,000 sq ft of area		
Original pH		Sandy	Clay
7.5		10–15	20–25
8.0		25–35	35–50
8.5		35–40	40–50

*These rates cannot be used on established turfgrass. See lawn maintenance section for rates on established turfgrass.

---

1. In the pH scale, a value of 7.0 indicates a neutral soil, neither acid nor alkaline. Values less than 7.0 (as pH 6.5) indicate acidity (the higher the number, the more alkaline the soil).

2. Other fertilizers serve as well; see table 4 for rates of other grades of fertilizer.

Planting

Once the site is prepared as described, you are ready for planting. You must decide whether to seed or sod your new lawn. The choice is based on several factors such as cost, time of year, and type of turfgrass desired. Sodding is considerably more expensive than seeding. However, with proper irrigation, sodding can be done almost any time of the year when the soil is not frozen. Therefore, if you must establish your lawn during the early to midsummer period, sodding is your only option. Sod is usually only available as a blend of several improved Kentucky bluegrasses, which may not be suitable for all sites. This is especially true for areas that are droughty and will not be irrigated or fertilized too heavily. You can have a "quality sod" lawn from seed within 2 years if properly maintained.

Seeding

Proper time

Establishing a new lawn from seed is the least expensive and the most widely followed method today. However, it is most important to seed at the proper time. For upstate New York it is best to seed between August 15 and September 15. In southeastern New York, seeding should be done from August 15 to October 1.

Other times

Successful seedings can also be made during the late fall and winter months (assuming no snow), when turfgrass is in a dormant condition, and in the spring. The late fall period varies year to year, but generally begins in November after the last mowing. The seed planted during this period will not germinate until next spring. Dormant seeding of this type should not be done on areas prone to erosion, such as steep slopes. Under most conditions, it is not advisable to spring seed *unless* both irrigation and a preemergence crabgrass herbicide (see reference 9) are applied.

The two times to avoid seeding are October and during June, July, and early August. October seedings generally fail since the very young seedlings are not deeply rooted and are easily killed during the winter and early spring. Seedings made in the summer seldom survive because of a lack of water, reduced vigor of the turfgrass plant, and the competition from fast growing weeds.

Remember the *best* time to seed is late summer to early fall and spring. *Never* seed during October or during June, July, or early August.

Kinds of turfgrass for lawns

A common and most serious error in lawn establishment is choosing the wrong kind of turfgrass seed. If you have already decided to use a mixture of seeds and just want brief recommendations on how to choose a mixture, turn to page 7. However, more study about specific types of grasses and their uses is well worth the effort.

There is no perfect turfgrass for northern lawns; but of the dozens that have been tried, three are far better and more durable than the others. The three basic lawn grasses are Kentucky bluegrass, improved perennial ryegrasses, and the fine fescues (including red, creeping, chewings, and hard fescue). Rough bluegrass can be used but only in moist shade.

Kentucky bluegrass is the basic grass for sunny places in good soil and has long been considered the backbone of mixtures for sunny lawns. It responds well to good care and fertilizer and forms a dense sod. Of importance to the homeowner is its ability to spread and fill in bare spots during establishment and injury. Kentucky bluegrass generally goes dormant and turns brown during hot dry summers when irrigation is not provided, but usually recovers quickly when temperatures cool and rains return.

Several diseases severely injure common-type Kentucky bluegrass, and for this reason two or more disease resistant varieties should be used. Select appropriate varieties from the current issue of *Home Lawns: Grass Varieties and Pest Control Guide*.

Fine fescues are the best grasses for less fertile, sandy, and droughty soils, either in sun or shade. They form a fine textured attractive sod. The leaves are pine needlelike and hard to cut with a dull mower. Fine fescues are somewhat less tolerant of heat than Kentucky bluegrass and may brown off more quickly during hot dry summers. Their ability to recover under such conditions is inferior to Kentucky bluegrass but adequate for all of New York. Red fescue or creeping red fescue, as it is often called, is the most commonly used fine fescue. Improved varieties are available (see reference 9) and preferred to common red fescue. One or more improved varieties of hard and chewings fescues are available and can be substituted, at least in part, for creeping red fescue. Fine fescues blend well with Kentucky bluegrass, but may dominate under low maintenance or dry shady conditions.

Improved perennial ryegrasses, sometimes called turf type ryegrass, are relatively new, but are rapidly gaining acceptance as desirable lawn grasses. They are best adapted to the moderate levels of fertility, moisture, and sunlight conditions, as are many of the Kentucky bluegrasses. They are the fastest to establish from seed, with fine fescue second and Kentucky bluegrass the slowest. Unlike common perennial ryegrass, turf types, are dark green, fine textured, and have good winter hardiness. They require about the same care as many of the Kentucky bluegrasses. Perennial ryegrasses also require a sharp mower for a clean cut. They are best used in mixtures with Kentucky bluegrass, but can be part of a three-way mixture including fine fescue. Wear tolerance of the improved perennial ryegrass is greater than for either Kentucky bluegrass or the fine fescues. The improved varieties (see reference 9) are suitable for southeastern New York conditions. However, the perennial ryegrasses are less well adapted to upstate New York winter conditions and can be killed. This is one reason why perennial ryegrass should not make up more than 20 percent of the mixture.

Rough bluegrass or trivialis bluegrass (*Poa trivialis*) is a special purpose turfgrass for moist shade only. It seldom lasts long in dry sunny areas; seed sown there is wasted. Even in moist shade the bright green, soft leaves never make a really tough sod.

Two unacceptable grasses are creeping bentgrass and Colonial bentgrass. Creeping bentgrass can be used to create a beautiful lawn, but requires far more care than most people can give. It is generally considered suitable for use on golf courses only. Close and frequent mowing, regular watering and fertilization, and constant protection against diseases are required for its success. In the past, some seed mixtures have contained creeping bentgrass. Lawns seeded to these mixtures now contain large patches or areas of fluffy matted turf. Even when not seeded, creeping bentgrass may enter voluntarily into any lawn and should be considered a weed. It can generally be removed by digging it out or by using a nonselective herbicide.

Colonial bentgrass has been used in small percentages as a lawn grass component. It is adapted to poorer soils than Kentucky bluegrass, but is short-lived and makes no real contribution to the mixture.

Redtop, Canada bluegrass, annual ryegrass, and common perennial ryegrass are sometimes included in less expensive lawn mixtures. Most are fast growing and result in a quick temporary flush of green. Redtop and Canada bluegrass are adapted to wetter acid soils and may be justified for rough lawn mixtures that are to receive minimum care. The common ryegrasses are suitable for use in sloping areas because of their ability to establish quickly and minimize washing or erosion. Not more than 10 percent redtop or 20 percent ryegrasses should make up any such mixture.

Timothy, orchardgrass, and meadow or tall fescue are all coarse-textured pasture or hay-type grasses. They have no place in a lawn mixture because they produce unattractive, coarse, clumpy, or stubble-like growth. They are occasionally added to lawn grass mixtures. Read the label and do not purchase any lawn mixture containing these grasses.

White clover is used in some lawn-seed mixtures. The advantages of clover are that it provides some fertilizer nitrogen (taken from the air) for the lawn grasses, remains greener than most grasses during hot dry periods, and may survive after mismanagement and neglect have killed the good lawn grasses. Clover is coarse textured and forms patches that give the lawn a spotty appearance. It is soft and slippery, attracts bees, and is the cause of "grass stain" on clothing; it does not compete with weeds as does good turfgrass. In winter the clover patches are bare and are more likely to winter kill than lawn grasses. Thus, some people like clover in the lawn, whereas others consider it a weed. If clover is to be used in a lawn mixture, several cultural practices must be followed to ensure its survival. First, do not use herbicides that control clover (see reference 9). Second, avoid the use of high nitrogen fertilizers since clover produces most of its own nitrogen. Third, clover grows best at a neutral pH of 7 or above. Therefore, acid soils must be limed to benefit both the clover and the turfgrass.

Seeding blends or mixtures

Although a single species, such as Kentucky bluegrass, can be used to establish a lawn, a mixture of species is preferred. Since all turf grasses are not equally susceptible to disease, insects, and environmental hazards, a mixture has a much greater chance of success. If one species is injured or eliminated by disease or other hazards, the others may be able to fill in the voids. Species also vary in such factors as speed of establishment, recuperative potential after injury, fertility requirements, and tolerance to close mowing. The mixture chosen should have at least two of the basic species, which are Kentucky bluegrass, fine fescues, and improved turf type perennial ryegrass. If for aesthetic or other reasons you still prefer a single species lawn and are willing to chance the risks, always include at least three recommended varieties of that species.

Choosing a ready-made seed mixture

The most important information printed on a seed package is the content label. Required by law, it lists individual species in the mixture. For each grass the percentage present is given along with germination percentages, weed seeds, and other facts. To judge the quality of a seed mixture, add the percentages of Kentucky bluegrass, fine fescues, and improved perennial ryegrasses. If the total of these basic lawn grasses is 80% or more and does not contain the objectionable grasses listed on this page, the mixture is suitable to buy.

For most sunny lawns with a normal moisture supply, Kentucky bluegrass should make up at least 55% of the mixture. For dry soils, either in sun or shade, fine fescues should total at least 65% in the mixture.

SPECIES	SHADY SITES*	SUNNY SITES†
	(% by weight)	
Kentucky bluegrass	10%	55%†
Fine fescue	65%	25%
Improved perennial ryegrass	15%	20%
Total lb of mixture/1000 sq ft	5–6 lb	3½–4 lb

*Rough bluegrass can be substituted in moist shade
†The remaining species of any mixture should not include bentgrass, tall fescue, and other pasture-type grasses.

If you buy a mixture of the quality suggested, it is unlikely that you will get seed that is of inferior quality so far as germination percentages, weed seed content, and inert matter are concerned.

Remember to look for at least 80% total basic lawn grasses, including at least 55% Kentucky bluegrass or 65% fine fescue, depending on your own lawn situation. If you cannot obtain this desired mixture, you may need to buy the components separately and then make your own seed mixture.

After the seed is sown, rake the soil lightly. Use just the tips of the rake teeth and cover the seed about 1/8 inch deep. Seed covered too deeply will be lost; so omit this raking unless you can do it carefully. Go over the area lightly with a roller to firm the soil about the seeds. If you cannot roll the seeding, no harm will be done; the seed will merely germinate more slowly.

Sowing seed

Seed can be sown immediately after fertilization; no delay or waiting period is necessary. Sow seed evenly, or there will be an uneven pattern of grass and bare ground. A mechanical drop or centrifugal type spreader does the best job of seeding (or fertilizing or liming), but hand seeding is satisfactory if it is done carefully. To seed by hand, first divide your seed into two equal parts. If this is your first attempt to sow seed, mix each half of the seed with some sand or fine topsoil to give you more material with which to work. When there is no wind, scatter one half evenly and carefully while walking back and forth in parallel lines. Scatter the other half in the same manner while walking in lines at right angles to the first (fig. 1).

Mulching

A straw mulch is not necessary for most new seedings, but is helpful for warm-weather seedings, on sandy soils, or on steep slopes. Shake out the straw thoroughly, spreading it uniformly to a depth of about 1 inch. When you have finished, you should still be able to see about half the soil surface through the straw. The mulch slows up surface drying and breaks the force of rains and watering. On steep slopes, anchor the straw in place with wooden stakes and heavy twine. Tack the twine to stakes driven flush into the ground on 3-foot centers. Hay is not a satisfactory substitute for straw because it will very likely contain an abundance of seeds of hay-type grasses and weeds.

Sodding

A poor weedy lawn can be removed with a sod cutter and replaced with dense, green, weed free sod in one day. Although such a practice is possible, and even feasible in certain situations, sodding generally requires the same preliminary procedures as for seeding. A sodded lawn can be installed anytime during the growing season. The extra cost of the sod and the labor of installation provide turf quality that would take at least a full year to develop from seed. Sodding may be the only answer for steep slopes or spots where traffic ruins young seedlings.

Nursery-grown sod with blends of improved Kentucky bluegrass is available in most suburban areas. This makes an attractive lawn in sunny situations, but a fine fescue mixture is a better choice for dry or shaded areas.

Large areas are best sodded by landscape contractors because the labor and machinery requirements are more than the average person can supply. Small areas and patches can be sodded by an energetic amateur.

To install sod, prepare the soil just as though seed were to be planted. The soil should be moderately moist when the sod is laid. After all is ready, purchase the sod. Large lots of sod can be obtained for direct delivery to the job. Small lots of sod for patching are available from garden supply firms. Do not accept sod that is dried or wilted. For best results the sod should be laid soon, no more than 36 hours, after it is cut.

Nursery grown sod is about 1-inch thick with little or no soil attached and of uniform width. Before laying the sod, lightly water the soil. This improves the ability of the sod to survive and knit in faster. Lay the sod strips on a prepared soil, tightly together, edge to edge, and with staggered joints like bricks in a wall. Fill all cracks with screened soil.

Soak the newly laid sod thoroughly. As soon as it is dry enough to walk on, lightly roll or tamp the sod to give a good contact with the soil beneath. Water often enough (every 2 or 3 days) in the early part of the day to keep the soil moist until the sod is securely rooted, usually within 2 weeks. Avoid overwatering.

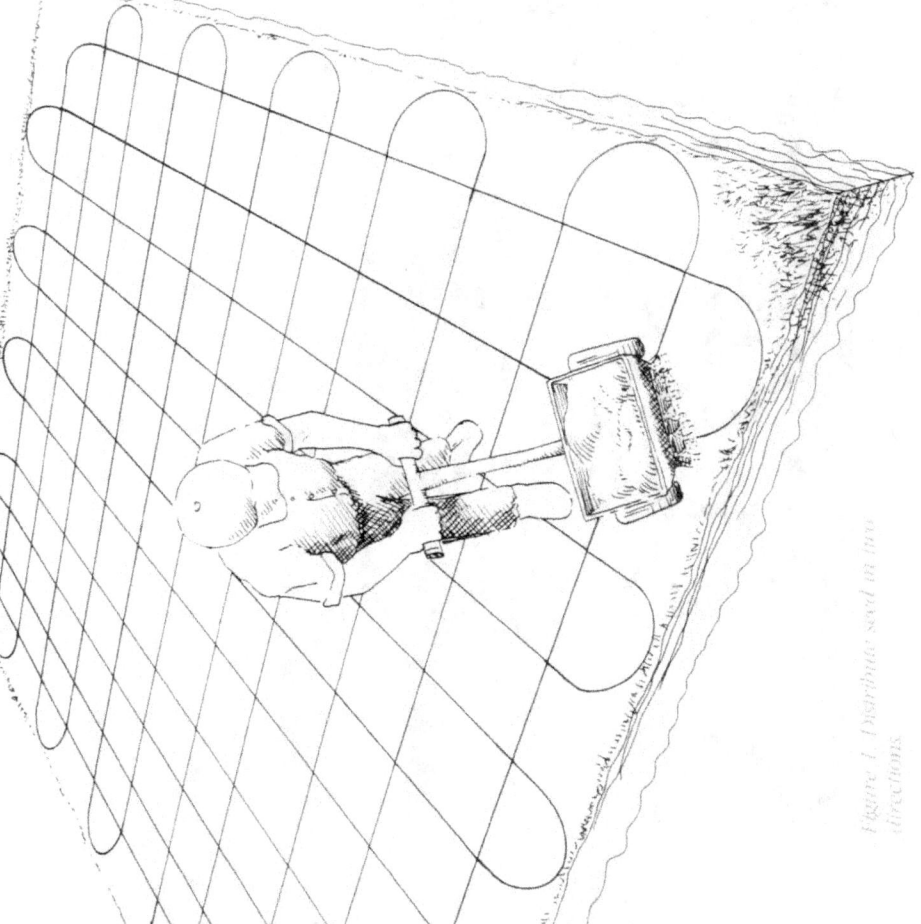

Figure 1. Distribute seed in two directions.

Postplanting Care

Watering Your New Lawn

Seed must be wet before it will germinate and grow. Dry seed in dry soil will not germinate until conditions are favorable. Birds may feed on the seed, but the amount of seed they eat is seldom important. Rain usually falls often enough for good growth, but results are quicker and more certain with artificial watering. The first sprinkling must be thorough but gentle; avoid washing the seed or soil away. Keep the seedbed moist until the grass is well started, or the entire planting may be lost. Watering may be as frequent as once or twice daily, especially for the first several weeks. Water more deeply once the grass comes up. Keep the soil moist but not soaking wet.

If there is little or no ryegrass in your seed mixture, seedlings may not appear for 10 days or more after the soil is thoroughly wet. *Do not be alarmed.* A poorer mixture will produce a quicker cover, but this is mostly show. After the second or third mowing, little or no watering should be required unless there is a week or more without rain. On sodded lawns, daily watering may be required to keep the sod moist until the sod has securely rooted. This generally occurs within 2 to 3 weeks.

Removing Mulch and Twine

If properly applied the mulching material seldom needs to be removed. Remove mulch only when the young turfgrass plants are being smothered. Twine used for securing mulch to the ground should be taken up before the first mowing to avoid jamming the mower.

First Mowing

For the first mowing, set the mower to cut at least 2 inches high. Mow as soon as the turfgrass is tall enough to reach the mower blades. Be sure the mower is sharp and the grass is dry. If the soil is too moist, seedlings will be pulled up. Mow often enough so as not to leave matted clippings to smother the new turfgrass. Keep matted clippings and fallen leaves off the new seeding by careful sweeping with a rake.

Fertilizing

To help ensure a dense weed-free stand of turfgrass, fertilize 3 to 4 weeks after the seeds have germinated or following sodding. Use a complete fertilizer with a ratio of 2-1-1 or 4-1-3 at the rate of 1 pound of nitrogen per 1,000 square feet (see table 4 for the correct amount of fertilizer). Lightly water in the fertilizer after application to avoid possible fertilizer burn of the turfgrass plants.

ROUTINE LAWN MAINTENANCE

Every lawn, good or bad, needs to be mowed regularly and fertilized occasionally. In many areas, liming is equally important. Watering may or may not be desirable on your particular lawn. These four operations, with particular emphasis on fertilization and mowing, are all that need concern you except for special circumstances.

Mowing

Close mowing ruins many lawns. The rule should be mow high and often. Set your mower to cut at least 1 1/2 inches high for spring and fall and slightly higher for summer or leave at 1 1/2 inches throughout the year. Your lawn will look neat at this height, and you will still be leaving enough top growth to produce food for a deep root system and a solid dense turf. Mow throughout the season whenever there is 1/2 inch or more of growth to be cut. Keep on mowing as long as the grass continues to grow in the fall. Mow often enough for the clippings to disappear by the next day. Always leave the clippings where they fall, for they return nutrients to the soil. You can reduce your fertilizer needs by 25 percent if clippings are returned to the lawn. This saves you both money and the time needed to remove clippings. If, by chance, you delay mowing so long that bunches of clippings remain the day after cutting, rake up these clippings or spread them so that they will not smother the grass.

make the mower safer.

Choosing a Mower

Two types of lawn mowers are widely available. The older reel type mower has revolving knives that cut the grass blades against a stationary bed knife in a scissors type action. This mower shears the grass blades cleanly when it is properly adjusted and leaves no brown or ragged tips. A reel type mower is best adapted to smooth areas that are mowed regularly.

Rotary mowers depend upon the high-speed whipping action of a sharpened blade whirling in the air. They handle taller grass on irregular areas and are useful on areas not mowed regularly. Unless the blade is very sharp, a rotary mower tears the leaf tips; the lawn as a result appears scorched or singed gray the day after mowing.

The rotary mower can be a dangerous tool. Many operators have been injured by the whirling blades and bystanders by thrown stones or other debris. Only an adult should operate a rotary mower. Do not remove any of the mower's guards that have been installed for safety reasons. Some of the safety features may seem unimportant, but remember they were included to

Rotary Type of Mower

In the past several years a new type of rotary mower has appeared on the market, namely the mulching mower. This mower was developed to cut the turfgrass clippings finer than the conventional rotary mower does. This enables most of the clippings to work their way into the turfgrass canopy. Thus, mulching mowers can further eliminate the need for removing clippings since they cannot be seen after mowing. If you have or are considering the use of a mulching mower, review these helpful tips:

- The grass must be relatively dry before mowing to help prevent machine clogging and the formation of large clumps of clippings.
- You need to mow more often in the spring and fall because of the faster grass growth rate. Again this can help prevent the mower from clogging and the clippings from clumping. You may need to switch to conventional mowers during these periods.

Just because a power mower is easy to run, do not use it when it is dull or out of adjustment. Do not ruin your light machine in work too heavy for it.

Reel type mower

Adjusting the Mower Cutting Height

Both reel-type and rotary mowers can be adjusted for height of cut. This important adjustment is easy to make. The height of cut of most rotary mowers is set by adjusting the height of the wheels. Height adjustment is slightly complicated for reel-type mowers. In either case, follow the instruction manual for proper adjustment.

Fertilizing

Adequate turfgrass nutrition is crucial to the establishment and development of a healthy vigorous lawn. Such a lawn is less likely to be invaded by weeds or troubled by most insect and disease pests. Because the soil generally cannot supply all the needed nutrients, routine applications of a complete fertilizer are necessary.

A complete fertilizer contains nitrogen, phosphorus, and potassium. These nutrients are required in larger amounts by turfgrass than are other minor nutrients usually found in adequate supply in the soil. Nitrogen is required in the largest amount. It is responsible for overall growth and color, and the effect of its application is most readily seen. Phosphorus is critical at the time of lawn establishment to encourage root growth and development. Potassium is associated with the overall growth of the turf and is required in the second largest amount. Tolerance to extremes in temperature, moisture, and wear is enhanced by sufficient amounts of potassium.

The law requires that every package of fertilizer be labeled to show the guaranteed minimum percentages (or grade) of the three important fertilizer nutrients. For example, a fertilizer with the analysis of 10-6-4 contains at least 10% total nitrogen, 6% phosphoric acid, and 4% potash. Many grades of complete fertilizers are available. You can also purchase fertilizers containing one or two nutrients. For example, superphosphate 0-20-0 contains only phosphorus, and potassium nitrate 13-0-44 contains both nitrogen and potassium.

Properties of Fertilizers

Nitrogen is the plant nutrient required in the largest amount by turfgrass. The nitrogen found in a bag of fertilizer in many cases is a mixture of several types, that is, water soluble and water insoluble (slow release).

Nitrogen sources can be classified into two groups with the following properties:

Water soluble sources—
- are very readily available to the turfgrass plant, response after application being rapid;
- are subject to leaching;
- can burn turf if applied at high rates and not watered in;
- are less expensive;
- should be applied at lower rates more often;
- have the potential for lowering soil pH;
- have a good cool weather response.

Slow release sources—
- are more slowly available to the turfgrass plant (release is dependent on temperature and moisture);
- provide a more constant supply of nitrogen;
- have less potential for leaching;
- have less potential for burning;
- are generally more expensive;
- can be applied at slightly higher rates less often;
- have a moderate to poor cool weather response.

Examples of several types of fertilizer, their analysis, and properties are outlined in table 3.

There are different types of phosphorus and potassium, but their properties are similar, and the consumer is not faced with the choice of purchasing different types.

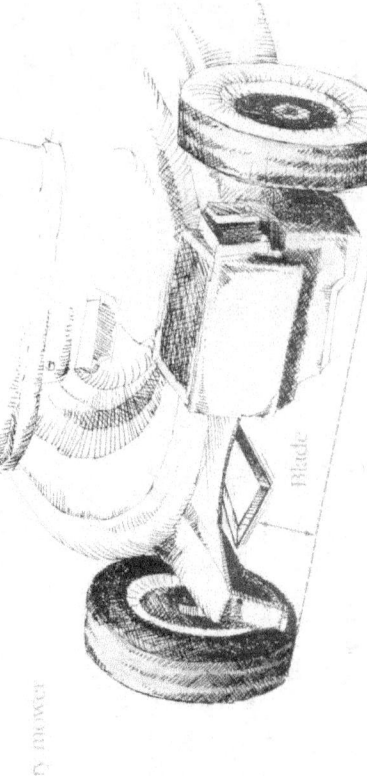

Figure 3. Types of mowers

Table 3. Properties of fertilizers used on turfgrass

Nitrogen carrier	Type	Nutrient content (%) N	P$_2$O$_5$	K$_2$O	Soil acidifying effect	Water solubility	Potential for burn
Ammonium nitrate	Syn. inorganic	33	0	0	Moderate	High	Very high
Ammonium sulfate	Syn. inorganic	21	0	0	Great	High	High
Urea	Syn. organic	45	0	0	Moderate	High	High
Monoammonium phosphate	Syn. inorganic	11	48	0	Slight	Moderate	Low
Diammonium phosphate	Syn. inorganic	20	50	0	Moderate	Moderate	Moderate
IBDU (isobutylidine diurea)	Syn. organic	31	0	0	Undetermined	Very low	Low
Sulfur coated urea (SCU)	Syn. organic	32	0	0	Undetermined	Very low	Low
Ureaformaldehyde	Syn. organic	38	0	0	Undetermined	Very low	Low
Milorganite	Nat. organic	6	4	0	Undetermined	Very low	Low
Methylene urea	Syn. organic	38	0	0	Undetermined	Very low	Low
Superphosphate	Inorganic	0	20	0	Low	Low	Low
Treble super phosphate	Inorganic	0	45	0	Low	Low	Low
Muriate of potash (KCl)	Inorganic	0	0	60	Low	Moderate	Moderate
Sulfate of potash (K$_2$SO$_4$)	Inorganic	0	0	50	Low	Moderate	Low
Potassium nitrate	Inorganic	13	0	44	None	Moderate	Very high

Table 4. Maximum amount of fertilizer to use for each application

If the first figure (% nitrogen) of the analysis is:	For 1,000 square feet of area	
	of established lawn (to apply 1 lb nitrogen)	of new seedbed or lawn to be renovated (to apply 2 lb nitrogen)
	pounds	pounds
4	25	50
5	20	40
6	17	33
7	14	28
8	12½	25
9	11	22
10	10	20
20	5	10
25	4	8

Fertilizing Established Turf

Test your soil

Soil testing is the only way to determine how much phosphorus, potassium, and lime or sulfur your lawn may need for optimum growth. The soil in your lawn should be tested every 2 to 3 years. Be sure to sample the soil well in advance of when you plan to apply fertilizer. If a fall application is planned, submit a sample in early summer. Remember not to take a soil sample 3 to 4 weeks after fertilizer or lime has been applied. See the soil sampling section in the Appendix for specific instructions. The soil test will help you select a fertilizer best suited for your individual soil condition.

Frequency

Frequency of fertilization depends upon your circumstances and aesthetic standards. The amount of a nitrogen fertilizer that most lawns require depends upon many factors such as the predominant species of turfgrass, soil type, desired turfgrass quality, and climatic factors. Most New York lawns need between 2 to 5 pounds of actual nitrogen per 1,000 square feet during the growing season. On Long Island where the ground water is becoming increasingly contaminated with nitrates, only 1 to 3 pounds of nitrogen should be used. This is especially true on sandy soils that are highly irrigated.

Lawns that contain mostly fine fescues should need only 1 to 2 pounds of nitrogen per 1,000 square feet during the year. Kentucky bluegrass lawns that are frequently irrigated may need up to 5 pounds of nitrogen. In general, lawns on sandy soils that are routinely irrigated and (or) receive heavy traffic require more nitrogen and potassium.

Rate

Lawn fertilizer manufacturers have made the application of fertilizers more convenient and easier by providing information directly on the fertilizer bag. The bag lists the total amount of fertilizer, the fertilizer analysis, the area to be covered at a given rate, and the setting for various fertilizer spreaders. When this information is not available, you need to determine the proper rate for a single application. Consider only the first figure in the fertilizer analysis. In a 10-6-4, the 10 represents the nitrogen content percentage. Do not apply more than 1 pound of nitrogen per 1,000 square feet per single application. On Long Island, reduce this rate to 1/2 pound of nitrogen per 1,000 square feet, except when all the nitrogen is in a slow-release form. To determine the amount of fertilizer needed, see table 4. Use the first figure of the fertilizer analysis. If you had a 10-6-4 fertilizer and planned to apply 1 pound of nitrogen, you would use 10 pounds per 1,000 square feet.

Timing

The best time to fertilize lawns is when the turfgrass needs the nutrients most. For established lawns in the Northeast this generally occurs in spring and again in the late summer to early fall. Temperatures during these periods usually run from 70°–80° F during the day to 40°–65° F during the night; such temperatures have been found to be most conducive for turfgrass growth. Other factors should be considered when determining how much and how often to apply fertilizers: the total amount of fertilizer to be applied annually, type of fertilizer, soil type, and irrigation practices. Generally, more fertilizer is needed when water soluble fertilizers are used on sandy soils that are highly irrigated.

The number of fertilizer applications needed is based in part on the total pounds of nitrogen to be applied annually. The maximum rate of application of nitrogen is 1 pound per 1,000 square feet per single application. Therefore, if you plan to apply 3 pounds of nitrogen per 1,000 square feet per year, a minimum of three applications must be made.

If you plan to fertilize your lawn only once per year, then a later summer or early fall treatment is best. For more than one fertilizer application per year, refer to table 5 for suggested times of application.

Since seasonal weather conditions vary from year to year, use the following guide for interpreting the seasons described in table 5:

EARLY SPRING
the period when the lawn has just started to green up and grow, but before the big "spring flush" of growth

LATE SPRING
the period just after the "spring flush," but while temperatures are still very mild (i.e., 60°–70° F day, 40°–60° F night)

EARLY SUMMER
usually occurs late May to early June when day temperatures are consistently in mid 70s to lower 80s.

LATE SUMMER OR EARLY FALL
after summer heat spell, usually in late August or early September when temperatures start to moderate and nights are cool.

DORMANT OR LATE FALL
the period just after last mowing until winter snow cover.

There are several times during the year when fertilizing should be avoided. In most cases a heavy early to mid spring application of a fertilizer (especially nitrogen) can lead to certain disease problems and make your turfgrass shallow rooted. Both results can lead to serious trouble for your lawn during the summer. If an early spring application is desirable, apply about one half the recommended rate of fertilizer. Do not fertilize heavily during the summer; then at least part or all of

Table 5. Suggested timing of fertilizer application based on the number of yearly applications

Number of yearly applications	Early spring	Late spring	Early summer	Late summer or early fall	Late fall or dormant*
1				I	
2	II		II	I	II
3	II	II	III	I	II
4		III	IV	I	II
5	III	IV	V	I	II

NOTE: When there are two or more of the same numeral on a line, apply at only one of the times.
*Avoid late fall (dormant) fertilizer application on Long Island if water soluble fertilizers are used.

For example, if you are applying 3 lb of nitrogen per year, you have three choices for times of application:

1. (late summer or early fall) + (late fall or dormant) + (early summer)

   OR

2. (late summer or early fall) + (early spring) + (early summer)

   OR

3. (late summer or early fall) + (late spring) + (early summer)

the fertilizer should be a slow release form. Be sure to use half the recommended rate at this time. Another time not to overfertilize is midfall. Then heavy fertilization can lead to winter disease problems and a greater chance of damage.

How to Apply

It is very important to apply fertilizers evenly. Careless distribution causes uneven growth and color. Heavy concentrations of fertilizer result in burned spots in the turf. A mechanical spreader is best for this work. You can apply a natural organic fertilizer at almost any season without danger of burning your grass. Inorganic fertilizers can be used during the growing season, but take these precautions against burning; be especially careful about even distribution, spread fertilizer only when the grass is completely dry, and immediately wash the fertilizer off the grass blades to the ground.

Dry fertilizers can be applied with either a gravity drop type spreader or a centrifugal spreader. Use a drop-type spreader when applying fertilizer herbicide products (i.e., a feed and weed product) to minimize the chance of herbicide injury to trees, shrubs, and vegetable gardens. Also, a drop type spreader is good for applying ground limestone.

Centrifugal spreaders generally cover a larger area with each pass and cut down the time it takes to fertilize your lawn. Fertilizer particles are more susceptible to wind blowing by this method, a uniform application being made more difficult. Centrifugal spreaders can be used to apply granular lime and sulfur materials as well.

When using either spreader, make at least two passes over your lawn. Apply half the amount of fertilizer in one direction and make the second application at a right angle to the first pass. This will help eliminate the streaks that develop from an uneven fertilizer application. See figure 1.

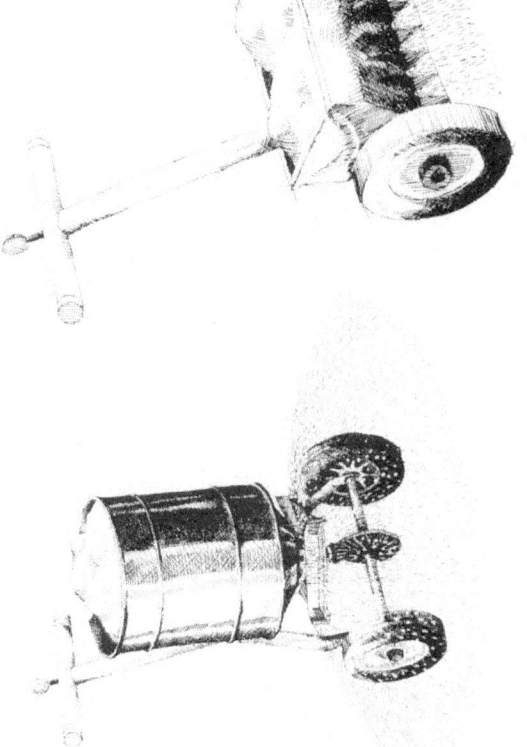

Figure 1. Types of fertilizer spreaders

Rotary

Drop type

Lime or Sulfur

Soil pH modification

For the best turfgrass growth the soil should be kept at a pH of 6.0–7.0. In some regions of New York, soils naturally have an acceptable pH and may never need lime or sulfur. In other regions the pH may be higher than 7.5 (too alkaline) or lower than 6.0 (too acid). The only way to be sure of the soil's pH is to have it tested. Your local county Cooperative Extension agent can assist you with this pH test.

To raise the soil pH

When you know the soil pH, refer to table 1. On established lawns, apply half the recommended rate.

Liming can be done in either spring or fall. Do not apply lime during the summer or within 2 weeks after applying fertilizer. Hydrated lime should not be used because it is caustic and difficult to handle. See table 6 for a description of several liming materials and suggested rates of application.

When a large amount of lime is to be applied to established turfgrass, that is, more than 50 pounds per 1,000 square feet, a split application is recommended. Apply half the rate in the spring and the other half in the fall. Apply water to remove lime from the shoots and to move it into the soil.

To lower the soil pH

When the pH is greater than 7.5, acidifying materials must be applied. Elemental sulfur is the preferred material to lower soil pH. For ease of application, use a pelleted form of sulfur, which can be applied with a centrifugal spreader. Do not apply more than 5 pounds of elemental sulfur per 1,000 square feet per application to established lawns. Be sure to water in sulfur to avoid burning. Only apply sulfur during spring and fall. Table 2 lists the rate of sulfur to be used when sulfur is to be incorporated into the soil during lawn establishment.

Avoid the use of ferrous sulfate and aluminum sulfate for soil acidification. Remember that the use of certain fertilizers, for example, ammonium sulfate and urea, can lower the pH over a period of time.

Watering

Most lawns, if not irrigated, turn brown in midsummer, but recover quickly when cool damp weather arrives. If your lawn does not survive an ordinary drought without watering, it probably needs renovating. You can avoid numerous problems and save time and effort if you can learn to accept an occasional brown turf in dry summers.

You can improve the appearance of your lawn by proper watering, but you can also ruin it if you are careless. A few waterings should keep your lawn fairly green during the summer. Water when the soil begins to dry out but before the grass wilts and turns brown. To test if your lawn needs watering, dig into the soil to a depth of 3 to 4 inches. If the soil is dry, soak it to a depth of 5 to 6 inches, which equals about 1 to 2 inches in a can or rain gauge. If the grass has a purplish cast and if footprints remain after you walk across the lawn, then the turfgrass is wilting and in need of water. It is best to water in midmorning, if possible; but excellent results can be achieved at other times of the day.

Avoid frequent light sprinklings because they benefit shallow-rooted annual grasses and weeds, while the deeper-rooted turfgrasses suffer from inadequate moisture. Eventually desirable deep-rooted turfgrasses will be taken over by undesirable shallow-rooted annual grasses and weeds.

Table 6. Liming materials and their characteristics

Material	Composition	Rate of reaction	Method of application	Comments
Ground limestone	Granular ground limestone	Slow and gradual	Drop spreader	Water in if lawn appearance is a concern; only a slight chance of leaf burn. Its effect can last up to 2 years.
Pelleted limestone	Pelleted finely ground limestone	Very fast	Centrifugal spreader	Apply 60-70% the ground limestone rate; effect is not long lasting. Yearly applications are necessary.
Slurry limestone	Finely ground limestone in 20-30% water	Very fast	Power sprayer with high power agitation, i.e. pesticide type sprayer	Apply 60-70% the ground limestone rate; effect is not long lasting. Yearly applications may be necessary

Generally, your lawn requires only 1 to 2 inches of rainfall or irrigation per week during June, July, and August. Water only once or twice per week for a long enough period to apply 1 inch of water. To test how long to leave the sprinklers running, put out several small cans, cups, or rain gauges and calculate how long it takes to obtain 1 inch of water in them. Never apply water faster than the soil can absorb it. Clay soils generally absorb water very slowly, whereas sandy soils absorb water more rapidly.

Rolling

As a regular maintenance practice, use a roller at most only once a year. If convenient, roll your lawn in early spring with a roller just heavy enough to press the frost heaved plants back into the soil. Do this before growth starts, when the soil is dry enough to crumble easily in your fingers. Then put the roller away for the season. More rolling will do no good, and on a heavy clay soil it may be harmful. Spring rolling is the least important chore and can be omitted without serious harmful effects.

Topdressing

Golf course managers routinely topdress or spread thin layers of soil or sand over their putting greens. However, this practice is seldom done on home lawns. Topdressing helps smooth out uneven spots in your lawn and helps reduce a thatch problem. Topdressing can be done with screened, weed-free topsoil, compost, or soil from the vegetable garden. Broadcast this weed-free soil over the lawn in either early fall or early spring. Push the topdressing from the high spots to the low spots with the back of a rake, or fasten a rope to a metal door mat and drag it back and forth. Fill deep holes by lifting the sod and filling under it, or fill the deep holes with soil and sprinkle a little seed on the soil. Water the lawn to settle the loose soil and proceed with your regular maintenance program. Do not spread pure peat or humus on your lawn. These materials can do little or no good and may cause future problems

Thatch

There are many misconceptions about thatch, its causes and problems. First, thatch is the accumulation of dead and dying turfgrass plant parts, such as roots and stems. This layer develops above the soil surface and, in many cases, contains turfgrass shoots. Thatch is not the accumulation of clippings as some believe. A layer of thatch less than 1/2 inch thick does little, if any, harm. However, when this layer is in excess of 3/4 inch, the turf is more susceptible to disease and insect problems and has less wear, drought, heat, and cold tolerance. Also, thatchy turf can be difficult to water since thatch can become water repellent when dry. Factors that lead to a thatch buildup are acid soils with a pH less than 6.0, too little or excessive fertilization, poor drainage, compacted soils, droughty conditions, and overwatering.

When excessive thatch develops, several steps should be followed to eliminate the problem. Be sure you have a thatch buildup in the first place. Take several wedge-shaped slices of your lawn, including the surface soil layer, at several locations. Inspect the samples to determine the thickness of the thatch. A layer less than 1/4 inch is considered acceptable. When the layer is between 1/4 and 1/2 inch thick, you may want to slow down further buildup by eliminating the cause(s) of the thatch. A 1/2-inch or thicker layer of thatch requires a slow but careful process of removal.

The only effective method of thatch removal is mechanical dethatching. The repeated use of a dethatching machine can, with time, reduce the thatch layer. Even though it may seem that you have removed a lot of thatch during the

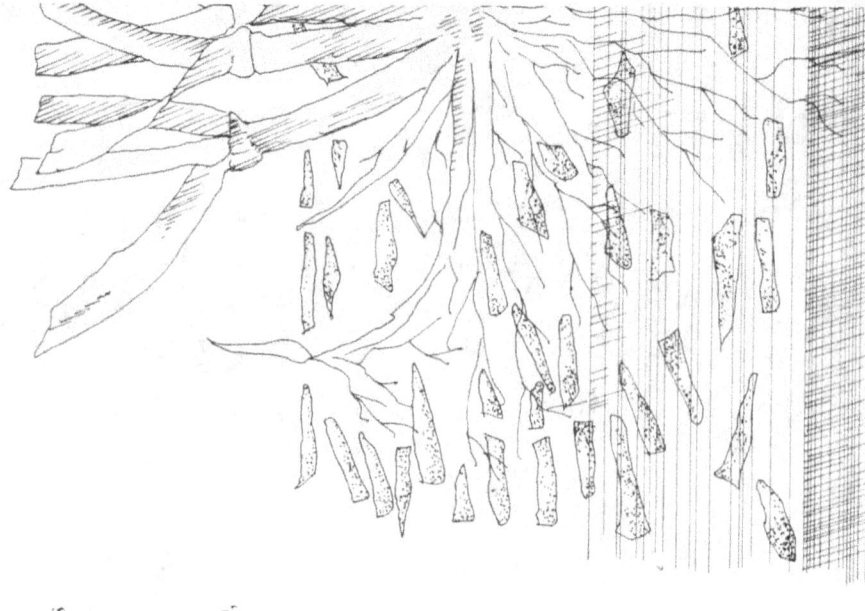

Figure 5. Thatch, mat, and soil layers

dethatching operation, it generally takes several dethatchings to significantly decrease the thatch layer.

The best time to dethatch a lawn is during the spring and early fall when weather favors a fast recovery of the injured turf. Avoid dethatching during the summer.

Biological and other chemical dethatching methods have proved to be ineffective and are not recommended. You may want to try such products on a small scale to see if they are effective on your lawn.

Topdressing is beneficial in reducing thatch. Topdressing as a means of decreasing thatch accumulation may be impractical on large lawn areas; however, you can achieve similar results in the following way: core cultivate your lawn (a core cultivator is sometimes called an aerifier or plugger and can be obtained from some garden centers or equipment rental shops), and lightly break up and work the soil back into the lawn with a metal drag mat or metal rake. In this case soil is added to the turf surface in a similar manner as described for topdressing.

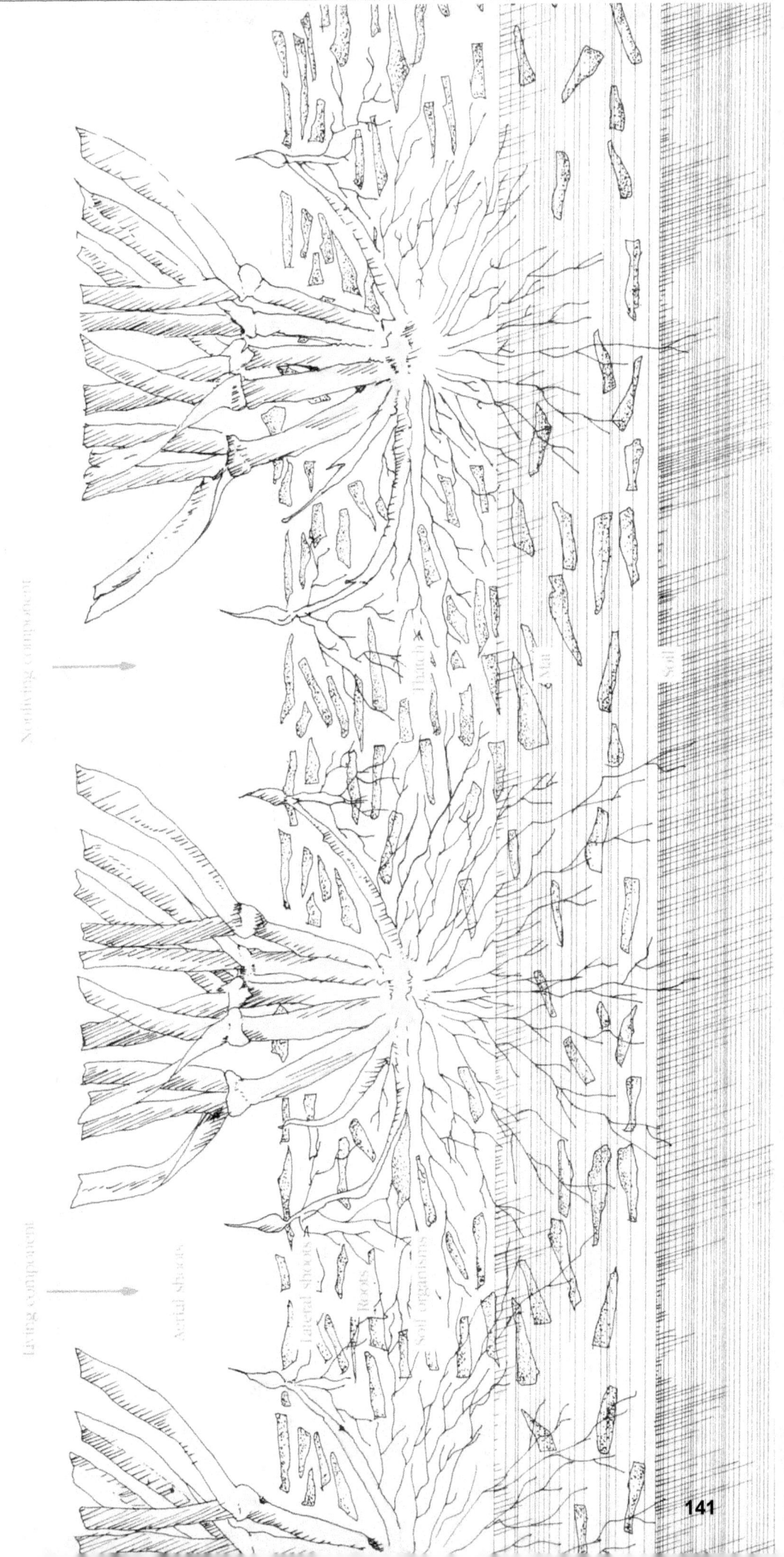

TURFGRASS MANAGEMENT CALENDAR

UPSTATE NEW YORK

	JAN.	FEB.	MARCH	APRIL	MAY	JUNE	JULY	AUG.	SEPT.	OCT.	NOV.	DEC.
Establishment												
Seeding											*	
Sodding						if water available						
Maintenance												
Mowing						as needed						
Watering												
Fertilizing												
Liming/sulfur												
Dethatching												
Renovating												
Pest Control												
Disease occurrence	Snow molds			Leaf spots	Melting out		Pythium blight	Dollar spot	Rust	Leaf spot		
				Stripe smut			Red thread	Fusarium blight	Brown patch	Stripe smut	Snow molds	
Insect occurrence					Grubs	Chinch bug	Sod webworms		Grubs			
Weed control — Broadleaf			Postemergence						Postemergence			
Weed control — Crabgrass			Preemergence			Postemergence						

Possible
Preferred

*This time period is for dormant seeding.

LAWN MAINTENANCE RECORD CHART

Operation	JAN.	FEB.	MARCH	APRIL	MAY	JUNE	JULY	AUG.	SEPT.	OCT.	NOV.	DEC.
Fertilization												
Lime/sulfur												
Mowing												
Watering												
Weed control												
Insect control												
Disease control												
Dethatch												

Specific Note

Fertilizer	Analysis ——— Amount ——— Date ———	Analysis ——— Amount ——— Date ———	Analysis ——— Amount ——— Date ———	Analysis ——— Amount ——— Date ———
Lime/sulfur	Material ——— Amount ——— Date ———	Material ——— Amount ——— Date ———	Material ——— Amount ——— Date ———	Material ——— Amount ——— Date ———
Insect control	Material ——— Amount ——— Date ———	Material ——— Amount ——— Date ———	Material ——— Amount ——— Date ———	Material ——— Amount ——— Date ———
Weed control	Material ——— Amount ——— Date ———	Material ——— Amount ——— Date ———	Material ——— Amount ——— Date ———	Material ——— Amount ——— Date ———
Disease control	Material ——— Amount ——— Date ———	Material ——— Amount ——— Date ———	Material ——— Amount ——— Date ———	Material ——— Amount ——— Date ———

Lawn Maintenance Calendar

The following charts can be used as a guide to annual lawn maintenance practices. Some lawn maintenance operations can be conducted many different times during the year, but in some cases there is a preferred time of implementation.

Climatic factors will greatly influence the occurrence of lawn diseases, insects, and weeds and the growth of the lawn. Therefore, it is impossible to predict the exact length and kind of growing season that will happen in a given year. However, the maintenance calendar can serve as a useful guide.

The Lawn Maintenance Record Chart is included to help you keep track of your lawn maintenance practices. Post the Lawn Maintenance Calendar and the Lawn Maintenance Record Chart in a convenient place.

TURFGRASS MANAGEMENT CALENDAR

SOUTHEASTERN NEW YORK

	JAN.	FEB.	MARCH	APRIL	MAY	JUNE	JULY	AUG.	SEPT.	OCT.	NOV.	DEC.
Establishment												
Seeding											*	
Sodding						if water available						
Maintenance												
Mowing												
Watering												
Fertilizing											**	
Liming/sulfur												
Dethatching												
Renovating												
Pest Control												
Disease occurrence		Snow molds		Leaf spots / Stripe smut	Melting out	Red thread	Pythium blight / Dollar spot / Fusarium blight		Rust / Brown patch	Leaf spots / Stripe smut		Snow molds
Insect occurrence				Grubs		Sod webworms / Chinch bug / Bluegrass billbug	Cutworms		Grubs			
Weed control — Broadleaf				Postemergence		Postemergence			Postemergence			
Weed control — Crabgrass				Preemergence								

Possible

Preferred

*Mid-Nov. through Dec. is the period for dormant seeding.

**Mid-Nov. through Dec. is the period for dormant fertilizing.

LAWN PESTS

Weeds

In your lawn, there is a constant battle between the grasses you want and the weeds you do not want. Lawns get weedy if conditions are more favorable for the weeds than for the grasses. Turfgrass predominates if growing conditions are better for the grass than for the weeds. By altering growing conditions, you can control the kinds of plants in a lawn. When you start a new lawn, try to prevent weeds from getting a foothold. If you remove weeds from an established lawn, stimulate the grass to better growth, or weeds will fill in the bare spaces again. Any sound weed control program is based upon these principles.

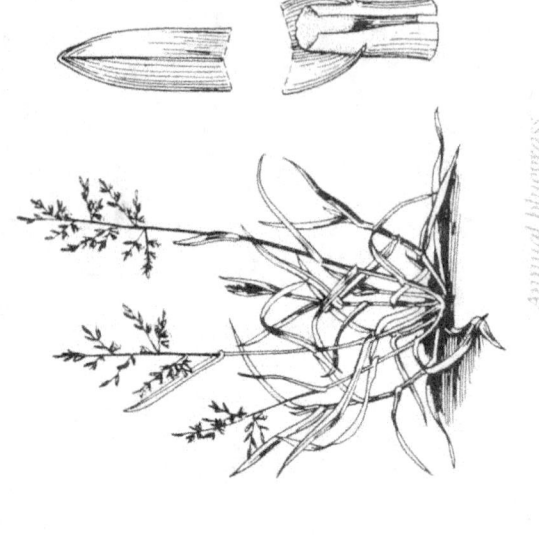

Annual bluegrass

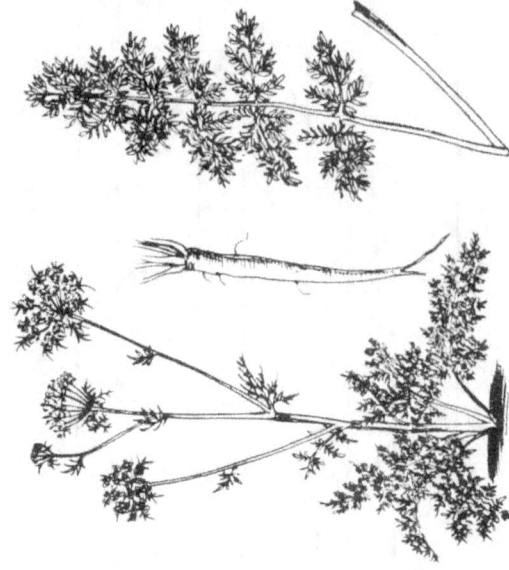

Wild carrot

Identifying Features of Weeds

Weeds differ greatly in their appearance, growth patterns, and reaction to herbicides. Grassy weeds have long narrow leaves with parallel veins and may complete their life cycle in one season. Some annual grassy weeds like crabgrass, goosegrass, and annual bluegrass recur from seed every year. Tall fescue, bentgrass, and quackgrass are grassy weeds that grow vegetatively for many years. Dicots, or nongrassy weeds, have wider net veined leaves and are called broad leaved weeds. Common annual broad leaved weeds are prostrate spurge and common chickweed. Perennial broad leaved weeds include dandelion, plantain, white clover, hawkweed, and ground ivy. Yellow nutsedge and wild onion are narrow leaved, but are not grasses. Consult Cornell Information Bulletin 131, *Weeds in Ornamental Plantings*, or your Cooperative Extension agent for help in identifying weeds.

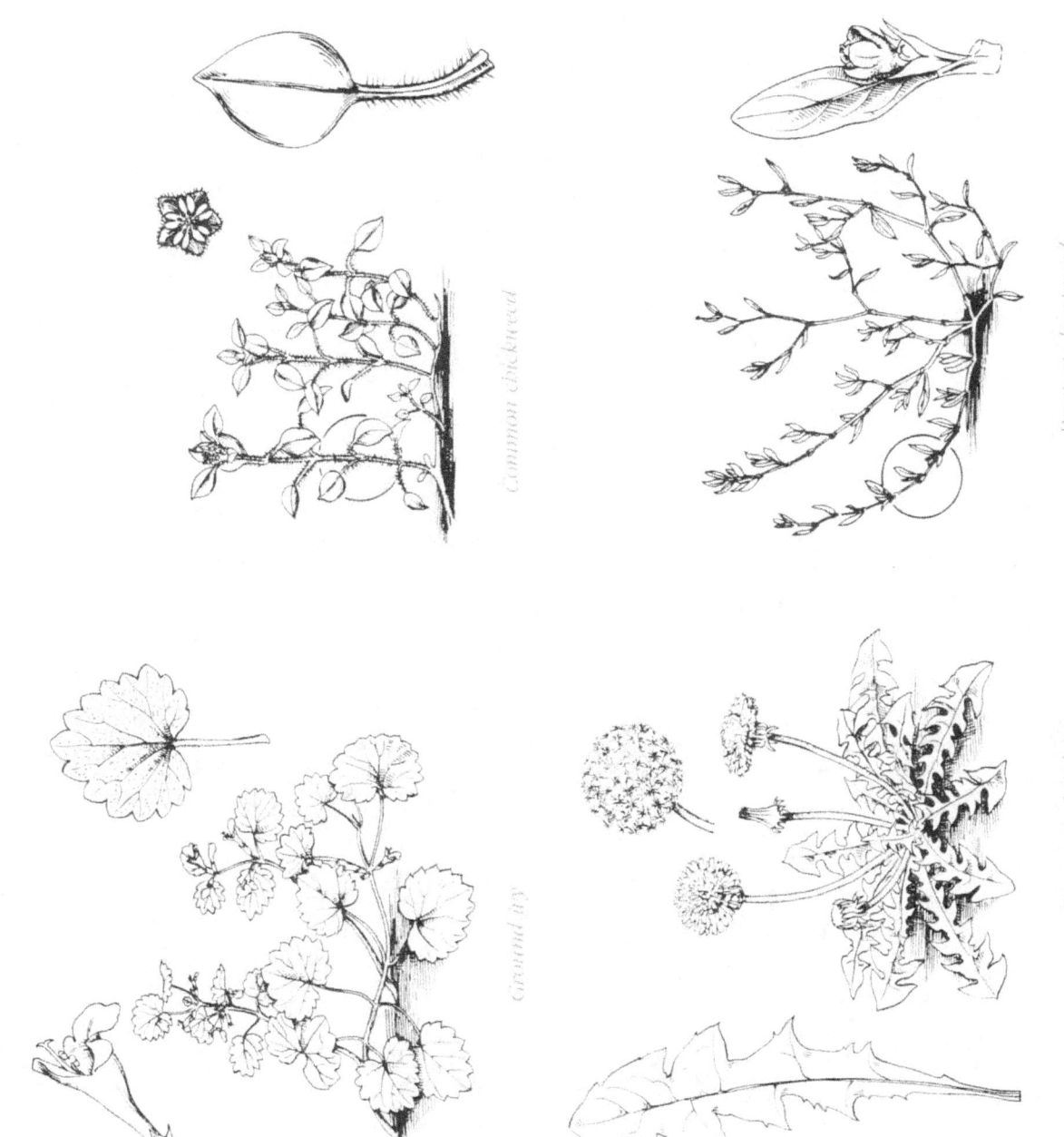

Common chickweed

Prostrate knotweed

Ground ivy

Common dandelion

Preventing Weeds in New Lawns

The greatest source of weed seeds in a new lawn is the soil itself. Almost any soil contains many more weed seeds than are carried in the grass seed. Scraping off the surface of the soil only exposes another layer of weed infested ground and solves nothing. Where crabgrass is not a particular problem, as in upstate areas, good soil preparation gives your new lawn a satisfactory head start on the weeds.

Planting at the proper season with the right grasses and adequate fertilization at seeding time are the most important practices in minimizing weed problems. In southeastern New York and on Long Island, fall planting is almost the only means of preventing crabgrass from taking over the lawn. If you plant in early fall, the grass plants will spread later ally, and the turf will be dense and mature before most troublesome lawn weeds start growth the following spring. Use recommended fertilizer rates to speed the development of the grasses.

Do not try to prevent weed establishment by sowing an extra large amount of grass seed. A dense growth results, but the individual grass plants will be crowded and weak. Then diseases may kill large patches of grass, the lawn being left wide open to weed invasion. To save money and get better results, sow no more seed than is recommended and fertilize it well at seeding time so that each grass plant becomes established quickly.

Spring-seeded lawns have a better chance of development free of crabgrass if the recommended pre-emergence herbicide is used. Even though crabgrass can be controlled in a spring seeding, fall is the preferred planting time.

Weed Control in Established Lawns

If your lawn is weedy, it is likely that you established or maintained it in such a way that the weeds were favored at the expense of the grass. A few kinds of weeds may resist efforts to control them, but most of the common lawn weeds can be greatly reduced by improved lawn care. If your lawn has reasonably good drainage, you can probably produce a striking improvement in the weed situation merely by fertilizing and mowing properly. The broad-leaved weeds such as dandelion and chickweed more troublesome the weeds, the more important it is that proper maintenance practices be followed.

Sometimes weeds persist in spite of good maintenance. Then you have to decide to control them by hand pulling or using herbicides. For small lawn areas or where there are only a few weeds, hand pulling as weeds appear can be good exercise and give good temporary results. Weeds are pulled much more easily right after a heavy rain or watering. Herbicides are chemicals used to control weeds. The use of herbicides to control weeds is more practical for large areas, more difficult to pull weeds, and small patches of persistent weeds. Large areas can be treated with sprays or granules that give good weed control with minimal injury to turfgrass. Single clumps can be spot treated with a small aerosol container, which sprays only a little herbicide over a limited area. In some situations you can brush an herbicide on a limited area. A commercially available wax bar impregnated with an herbicide can be brushed on undesirable foliage.

The best control method for general weed control on an area of any size is an overall treatment with a selective chemical that will kill the weeds and leave the grass unharmed. The broad-leaved weeds such as dandelion and chickweed require different methods of control than do annual grasses such as crabgrass and goosegrass or perennial grasses such as tall fescue and quackgrass. If the weed situation is serious and the turf is poor, you may well consider renovating the lawn.

Chemical Methods for Controlling Weeds

Herbicides

The testing of herbicides has resulted in materials that are effective and less expensive. The list of recommended herbicides changes continually as more effective materials are approved for use and as others become unavailable. Therefore, this bulletin makes no recommendations of specific herbicides and only uses herbicides currently available to illustrate methods of control (see reference 9).

Formulations

The pure chemical compounds are not usually effective or easy to use. They are made more useful by manufacturers by combining them with other materials in a formulation. The chemical can be adsorbed on clay, vermiculite, or other suitable materials and applied as granules. Application of granules to foliage is best done early in the morning when the granules stick to

the dew on the weed leaves. For soil application the granules are applied to dry foliage so that they fall through the leaves to the ground. Moisture is necessary to spread and activate the herbicide and hasten weed seed germination.

For spring application the chemical compound may be a soluble liquid or powder that readily mixes with water. It may be an emulsifiable concentrate that readily disperses in water forming a milky substance. Some chemicals are made into a finely ground powder that is not soluble, but is easily wetted by and dispersed in water; this type of mixture must be agitated for the particles to stay in suspension and be spread evenly.

Time of Application

Preplant treatments are applied before planting when there is little danger to the turfgrass. Soil fumigants are applied to the soil with water to kill underground plant parts, including seeds, roots, and stems.

Preemergence herbicides are applied to the soil surface to prevent weed seedlings from getting started. Once the seedlings have passed a certain stage of development, the treatment may no longer be effective. Applying recommended preemergence herbicides to a lawn when forsythia is in bloom prevents crabgrass seedlings from developing. Too early an application lessens the effect, and too late a treatment may not get the seedling in time and may result in a lawn full of crabgrass.

Postemergence herbicides are applied to foliage of actively growing weeds. The control may be by direct contact on the leaves or by the herbicide moving in the plant.

Check the herbicide label to see what the optimum time is for treatment to secure the best results at the least cost and with the least injury to desirable plants.

Systemic Herbicides

Some chemicals only affect the part of a plant that is directly touched (contact). A systemic herbicide is one that is absorbed by leaves or roots and moves through the plant, affecting areas distant from the point of contact and often the entire plant. Systemic herbicides control growing crabgrass and yellow nutsedge. Systemics must be applied at the proper concentration to be effective. Too high a concentration may injure plant tissue; as a result movement through the plant is prevented. Too low a concentration may not be effective, but repeated applications at low rates may be most effective.

Herbicide Selectivity

Most of the herbicides we use on turf weeds are effective at specific rates on certain weeds with no injury to grass. This differential effect is called selectivity. For example, an herbicide such as 2,4-D sprayed on a lawn eliminates dandelions and plantains, may not be very effective on white clover, and usually does not injure mature turfgrass. Bluegrass seedlings are easily injured until large enough to have been mowed two to three times. Many herbicides may be safe on turfgrass, but are definitely not safe on nongrassy ornamentals, vegetables, and other plants.

Safety

Check the herbicide label for the safest, most effective time to apply herbicides. If used according to directions on the package, herbicides should not be a hazard to people, pets, turfgrass, and other desirable plants in the garden or landscape. Do not use at rates above those recommended. It is best to use phenoxy herbicides, such as 2,4-D, MCPP, and the like, in early spring and late fall when temperatures are lower and there is less foliage of desirable plants exposed. Do not use a sprayer for growth regulator herbicides, such as 2,4-D, on any plants other than grass. Use another sprayer for controlling insects, diseases, and weeds in the garden. Handle all pesticides with care and read the directions on the label for special precautions.

Summary

To minimize weed problems—

- select the recommended grass for your site;
- plant your new lawn in the fall;
- use adequate fertilizer (and lime or sulfur if needed), especially when starting a new lawn;
- mow your lawn at least 1 1/2 inches high to reduce weed competition;
- control diseases and insects that damage turf and allow weed encroachment;
- water the lawn frequently but thoroughly, not too little too often;
- consult the *Home Lawns Grass Varieties and Pest Control Guide* for the list of current weed control measures;
- follow label directions and precautions on specific amounts and timing when using herbicides.

Diseases

Unhealthy and dead grass in a home lawn can be caused by a number of factors. Diseases caused by specific living organisms, usually fungi, are only one of many factors to be considered in maintaining an aesthetically pleasing and durable lawn. Other factors involved in the establishment and maintenance of a good lawn, as discussed earlier in this publication, are prerequisites for growing good turfgrass. No amount of disease control effort can overcome poor growing conditions or improper maintenance practices. Diseases are more likely to occur when lawns have been improperly established or maintained. By altering some management practices, you can appreciably retard disease development. Inadequate soil aeration, overwatering, poor drainage, improper fertilization, and mowing too low may all lead to disease problems.

Turfgrass injuries from other causes are frequently confused with symptoms of turf diseases. Drought injury, for instance, may resemble disease. In many cases drought occurs where thin layers of soil lie over buried debris such as rocks, lumber, plaster, and concrete. The soil dries rapidly in hot summer weather. Dead spots or patches that suddenly appear in a lawn may be caused by fertilizer burn, dog urine, spilled fuel oil, gasoline, oil and grease, exhaust heat from power mowers, or improper use of herbicides and insecticides.

Mowing practices can cause a diseaselike condition as well as influence the actual development of disease. Cutting grass too closely, called scalping, or using a mower with dull blades may result in a condition that looks like disease. Infrequent mowing, which produces excessive clippings in a mat, may encourage disease in the hot, humid environment under the mat. Grass weakened by frequent low mowing often appears off-color and is more susceptible to disease.

Diseases in a home lawn are often difficult to diagnose until the symptoms are obvious and the disease is in an advanced state. Disease symptoms vary in type and degree, depending on the variety of grass in the lawn. Some varieties have resistance to some diseases, but no variety is resistant to all turf grass diseases. For the latest list of disease-resistant varieties, see *Home Lawns: Grass Varieties and Pest Control Guide* (reference 9).

Diseases on susceptible grass varieties can usually be controlled with chemicals called fungicides. These materials are applied with a sprayer or a spreader, or they can be incorporated with a fertilizer. The frequency of fungicide application depends on weather conditions, the disease to be controlled, grass variety, cultural practices, and the degree of perfection desired by the homeowner. Disease control materials are toxic and should be stored, handled, and used with proper precautions.

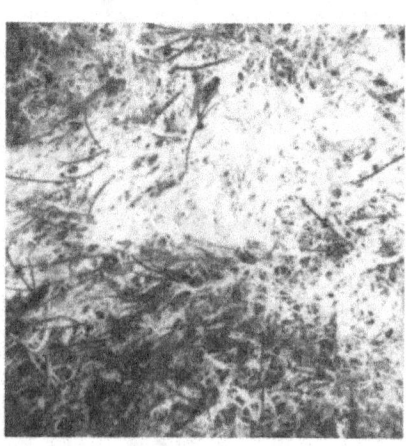

Snow mold

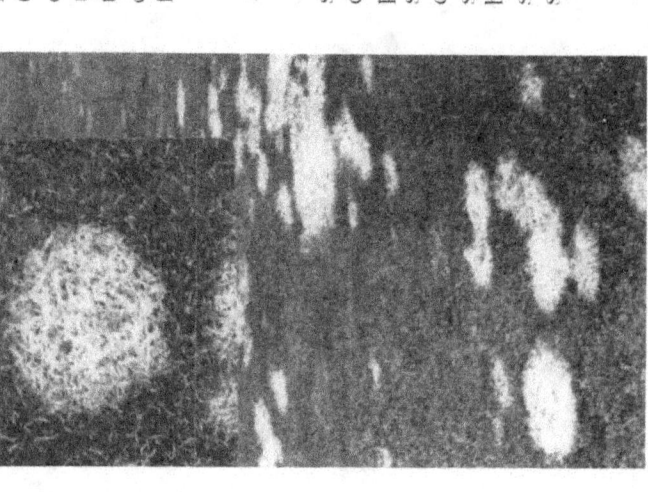

Snow Mold

Snow mold is the first disease to appear on a lawn in late winter or early spring. Snow mold diseases may occur on home lawns when temperatures are in the 32° to 45° F range and very moist conditions prevail. This is frequently the case under a snow cover during a thaw period. Spots of dead grass varying from an inch to several feet in diameter occur. The fungus growing in the spots gives the grass a grayish-white or pinkish appearance.

Snow mold can be lessened by fertilization practices that do not leave the grass in a lush growing stage as winter begins. Continue mowing in late fall so that long grass (which has a tendency to mat down) is not present. Snow mold is usually not a serious problem for the home lawn. Effective chemical controls must be applied before the first lasting snow falls.

Leaf Spot

Leaf spot is one of the most destructive lawn diseases. Leaf spot disease usually attacks lawns during periods of cool, moist weather in spring or fall. The first stage of the disease appears on the leaves as straw-colored spots with reddish brown to black borders. In the second stage (melting-out) the stems, crowns, and roots become

Brown Patch

Brown patch is most likely to occur in summer during periods of hot, humid weather. Lawns of any grass variety may be attacked, and the affected areas appear as brown patches a few inches to several feet in diameter. A severe attack leaves bare spots where the turf is killed. High nitrogen fertilization favors the occurrence of this disease. Watering early in the day to allow the grass to dry before night also helps to prevent this disease.

Pythium Blight or Damping-off

Pythium blight is most troublesome during hot weather on poorly drained areas. The diseased patches often follow shapes of the wettest areas. Plants are killed and feel slimy or greasy in the early morning. The *Pythium* fungus is especially apt to attack young, newly seeded grasses, a disease known as damping off results. This disease is less trouble some if you plant seeds in the fall or early enough in the spring to allow the grass plants to mature before hot weather begins. Avoid overwatering the seedling turf. Standing water and hot weather encourage damping off.

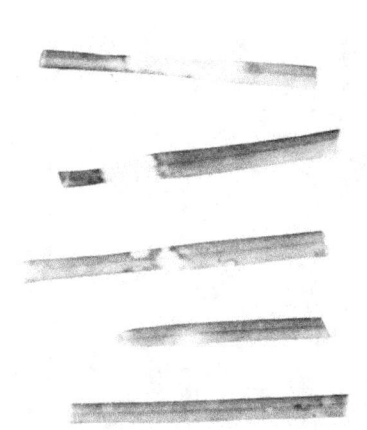

Dollar spot

Leaf spot

Dollar Spot

Dollar spot disease may appear on lawns as straw-colored areas 2 to 6 inches in diameter. These areas may coalesce to form larger dead patches. Close inspection of the leaf blade reveals bleached areas across the width of the leaf and tan borders above and below the lesion. This disease is most prevalent during summer when hot days are followed by cool nights. Dollar spot seldom damages turf permanently, but it may lead to increased weed encroachment. The disease is more active when nitrogen fertilization has been inadequate and the soil is dry.

discolored and rot. It is important to diagnose leaf spot and spray for its control during the first stage of the disease. Extensive damage may result if the disease is permitted to proceed to the second stage. Most varieties of Kentucky bluegrass are resistant to this disease, and many fine fescues are susceptible. Mowing at 1 1/2- to 2 1/2-inch heights and using lower than usual rates of nitrogen fertilizers (in early spring) may decrease the damage from leaf spot. Those lawns that have exhibited severe leaf spot occurrence should not be fertilized until the weather becomes warm and dry in late spring.

Rust

Rust may be found on lawn grasses in late summer or fall. A heavy attack causes the turf to have a reddish brown cast because of pinhead sized pustules on the leaves. The brown, powdery spores can be wiped from the leaf. Rust is frequently a problem on some Kentucky bluegrasses and on all perennial ryegrasses. Fungicides can be applied to eliminate rust soon after it has appeared. Adequate fertilization and good watering help to reduce rust damage to a lawn.

Powdery Mildew

Powdery mildew usually appears during moist weather in summer or in shaded areas of a lawn. The disease can be identified from the white powder that can be wiped from the leaf blades. Powdery mildew usually is not a serious problem, but a mildew fungicide can be used, if desired, to eradicate the disease after it has appeared. Any management practices that reduce shading of the grass and increase the air movement help to reduce mildew disease. Some grass varieties that are particularly shade tolerant and are resistant to this disease have been developed and are recommended.

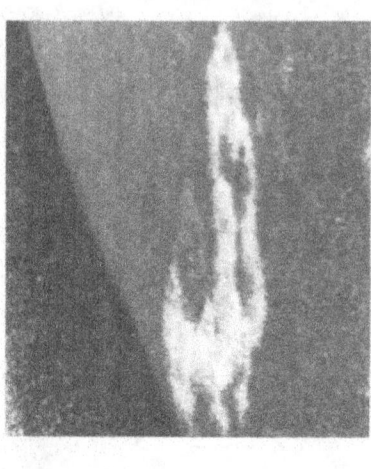

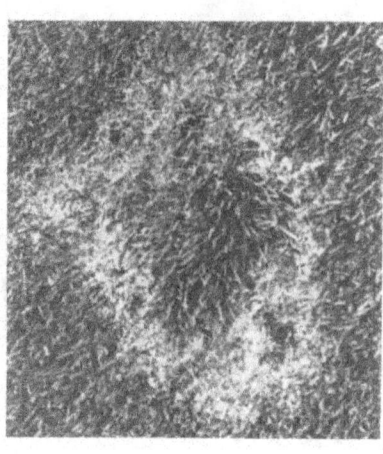

Fusarium blight of Kent bluegrass

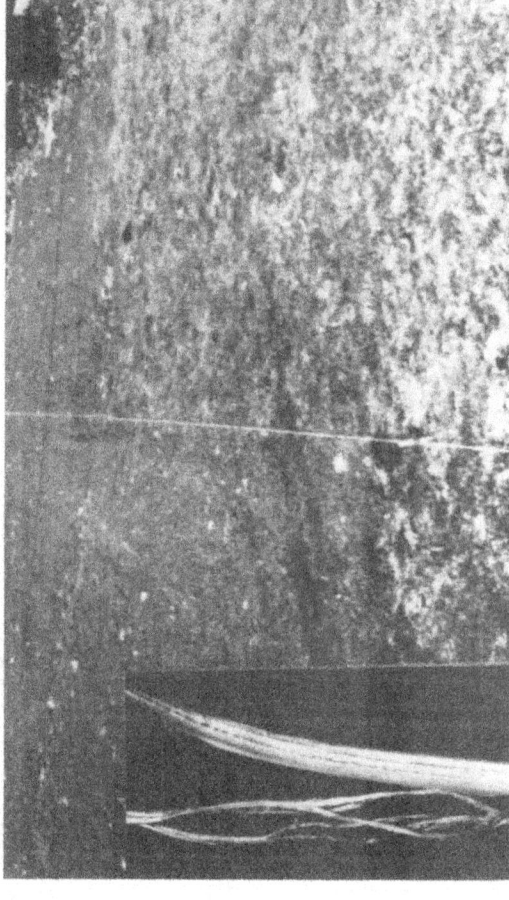

Stripe smut

Stripe Smut

Stripe smut may be a problem on Kentucky bluegrass lawns. The infected grass has the general appearance of poor growth, and close inspection of the leaf blade reveals gray or black longitudinal stripes caused by the fungus growing inside the leaf blade. When the stripes rupture, the black, powdery spores are released, and the leaf dries and dies. A white cloth rubbed over the grass becomes discolored by the black spores. Symptoms are most noticeable in late spring and early fall. Fungicide treatments help to control this disease, but must be applied in the early spring or late fall.

Fusarium Blight

Fusarium blight occurs mainly on Kentucky bluegrasses. It is most prevalent during periods of high temperatures in July and August. Frequently the first symptoms appear on turf along walkways and driveways. Sometimes an island of unaffected grass will remain in the center of the diseased patch, giving its characteristic "frog-eye" appearance. On individual leaves the infected tissue fades to light straw color and is without a distinctive border. In dealing with this disease it is important to keep the grass in a healthy, vigorous condition. Adequate, but not excessive, fertilization and watering practices are important. Any cultural practice that weakens or places a stress on the grass makes it more vulnerable to this disease. Fungicide controls must be applied before the onset of the disease. Effective treatments should be started in early June.

Red thread. D, red threads protruding from tips of diseased grass blades. H, healthy grass blades.

Fairy Ring

Many kinds of fungi growing in a lawn can produce a condition known as a fairy ring. This disease appears in the spring as circular bands of dark green grass. The grass on the inner side of the ring often dies. The rings will enlarge each year and may achieve large diameters. In late summer, mushrooms may develop in some rings. There is no adequate control for this disease. Aeration of the soil in the compacted ring area is advised. Symptoms can be masked by an early spring application of a soluble nitrogen fertilizer, adequate watering, and frequent fertilization.

Red Thread

Red thread or pink patch disease occurs on perennial ryegrasses and fine fescues and somewhat less on Kentucky bluegrasses. The disease affects small patches of grass, which can coalesce to cover large areas when the disease is severe. On humid nights a pink fungal layer may cover leaf blades, or a pink to red fungal strand (red thread) may grow from the end of blighted leaves. The disease is reduced by adequate nitrogen fertilizer and watering. Fungicides may be required for controlling this disease on some grasses.

Disease Control

A satisfactory home lawn often can be maintained with only a little attention to disease control. The amount of effort spent on the control of lawn diseases depends on the excellence of the turf desired and on the seriousness of the disease threat. Cultural practices that encourage a vigorous, hardy turf help minimize both the occurrence of turf diseases and the necessity for control measures. Proper control of a turf disease starts with proper identification of the problem. Early disease diagnosis makes control easier. Table 7 provides a key to help in identifying common lawn diseases. Alternatively, contact your local Cooperative Extension agent for assistance.

Chemical control is justified when diseases become severe and when they reoccur on the lawn each year. Fungicides are often effective in curing a disease soon after the disease is first observed. Curative control is best for controlling leaf spot, dollar spot, brown patch, rust, powdery mildew, and red thread. For other diseases such as snow mold, stripe smut, and fusarium blight, the chemicals must be applied before disease symptoms appear. This approach is called preventive control.

A simplified preventive spray program to control most lawn diseases would include an early spring, late spring, and late fall application of a fungicide. Recommendations for specific problems can be found in *Home Lawns, Grass Varieties and Pest Control Guide* (reference 9). All fungicides are limited in the number of diseases they control; proper selection is, therefore, very important. Once the grasses are dead, chemicals will not bring them back to life. But the fungicides do promote the growth of healthy new grass blades. Where death is extensive, reseed the dead areas and be alert for early symptoms the following year.

Table 7. Key to common diseases of lawn grasses

(Choose between each pair of numbered statements the one that better fits the observed condition. Then proceed to the number referred to and make another choice. Continue until the disease is named.)

0. Young grass seedlings collapse or seed does not germinate .... Damping off; seed rot
0. Disease is present on mature grass stand .... *See* 1
1. Disease occurs in winter or cold weather ... *See* 2
1. Disease occurs in spring, summer, or fall .... *See* 3
2. White to pinkish fungal growth on leaves; later the patches of dead leaves are matted and whitish gray .... Fusarium patch (pink snow mold)
2. White to black halo of fungal growth surrounds young patch; dead leaves are tan and crowns often contain tan, red, brown, or black spherical growths .... Typhula blight (gray snow mold)
3. Diseases often of general occurrence rather than in distinct patches .... *See* 4
3. Diseases occur mostly in distinct patches; patches may coalesce .... *See* 12
4. Leaves with distinctly outlined spots .... *See* 5
4. Leaves without distinct spots, but colored fungal growth visible .... *See* 8
5. Spots mostly found in midleaf .... *See* 6
5. Spots in midleaf or leaf ends blighted ...... *See* 7
6. Straw-colored leaf spots with reddish black borders; predominant in cool, moist weather .... Helminthosporium leaf spot
6. Straw-colored spots with dark brown margins across entire leaf .... Dollar spot
7. Leaf spots variable; leaf ends may be blighted; tiny black spherical fungal growths may be in dead leaf .... Ascochyta, septoria, and other leaf spots
7. As above, but small black spines emerge from blighted leaves .... Anthracnose
8. Fungal growth pink, red, or reddish brown .... *See* 9
8. Fungal growth white, gray, or black .... *See* 10
9. Red to reddish brown pustules on leaf ..... Rust
9. Tiny pink to red fungal threads on ends of dead leaves .... Red thread
10. Gray to black spherical growths on outside of leaf .... Slime mold
10. Fungal growth visible inside leaf or flat on surface .... *See* 11
11. Gray to black stripes between leaf veins; or leaf may be shredded .... Stripe smut
11. White fungal mats over part or all of leaf ... Powdery mildew
12. Small to large patches (6 in. to many feet in diameter) .... *See* 13
12. Mostly small patches (less than 6- to 12-in. diameter) .... *See* 15
13. Circular patch of living grass surrounded by adjacent rings of stimulated and depressed (or dead) grass; mushrooms may occur .... Fairy ring

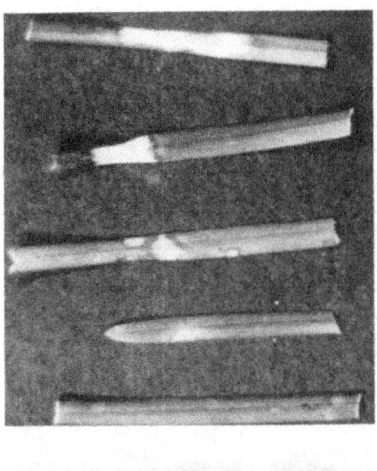

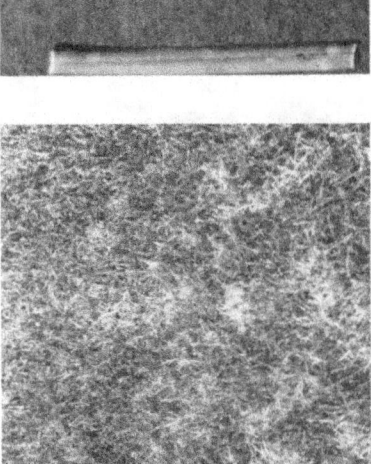

An example of how to use the key given. The disease shown above is dollar spot, and the following are the steps used to determine the disease:

0. Young grass seedlings collapse or seed does not germinate .... Damping off; seed rot
0. Disease is present on mature grass stand ... See 1
1. Disease occurs in winter or cold weather ... See 2
1. Disease occurs in spring, summer, or fall ... See 3
3. Diseases often of general occurrence rather than in distinct patches .... See 4
3. Diseases occur mostly in distinct patches; patches may coalesce .... See 12
12. Small to large patches (6 in. to many feet in diameter) .... See 13
12. Mostly small patches (less than 6 to 12 in. diameter) .... See 15
15. Fungal growth or bordered leaf lesions on grass around patches .... See 16
15. Indistinctly bordered lesions or no lesions on grass around patches .... See 17
16. Tiny pink to red fungal threads or mats on dead leaves .... Red thread
16. Straw colored spots with dark brown margins across entire leaf .... Dollar spot

13. Irregularly shaped patches without a ring of stimulated grass .... See 14
14. Dying grass surrounded by gray ring in morning; hot, humid weather .... Brown patch
14. Patches in thinned turf; helminthosporium leaf spot and rotted stems present .... Melting out
15. Fungal growth or bordered leaf lesions on grass around patches .... See 16
15. Indistinctly bordered lesions or no lesions on grass around patches .... See 17
16. Tiny pink to red fungal threads or mats on dead leaves .... Red thread
16. Straw colored spots with dark brown margins across entire leaf .... Dollar spot
17. Circular, crescent, or doughnut shaped dead patches in full sun; irregularly shaped leaf lesions are straw colored and without distinct borders .... Fusarium blight
17. Small patches of blackened, greasy-feeling leaves intertwined by cottony fungal growth in early morning; reddish brown patches of matted leaves later in day; patches coalesce to form streaks in low areas; hot, humid weather .... Pythium blight

NOTE: Damage due to insects feeding on grass plants may resemble disease damage. Frequently, the responsible insects or wormlike grubs can be found by careful examination of the thatch and upper soil layer in damaged areas.

Insects

Certain scarab grubs and other turf pests are serious in many areas of New York State. The Japanese beetle has spread to most city and suburban lawns throughout the state except in the northern-most counties. The oriental beetle is as destructive as the Japanese beetle in southeastern New York. The European chafer is gradually spreading and is now serious throughout most of the state. Other grubs, such as Asiatic garden beetle and masked chafer, are often troublesome in the southeastern part of the state. Chinch bugs and sod webworms were previously regarded as turfgrass pests of southeastern New York, but are now serious pests of many areas of upstate New York. The bluegrass billbug is a lawn pest that may be found anywhere in New York.

Insect damaged lawns may yellow, look thinned out or ragged, and become brown when irregular patches of grass are killed. In areas where grubs are known to be present, you should look for them and protect lawn areas before serious damage occurs. You can be sure it is insect damage only if you find the insects.

Bluegrass billbug larvae, the destructive stage

apart the sod over a piece of cardboard and examine the soil carefully. If there are five or more grubs under any square foot, treat the soil immediately. Remember that during midsummer there are no grubs, because the insects are in the adult stage. One indication of a potential grub problem is the obvious heavy flight of adult beetles.

Mid-July through August is the most effective treatment period on annual grub problem areas. It is much easier to control grubs during this period because they are small. During very late fall, winter, and early spring, grubs are much deeper down in the soil and cannot be controlled easily. Make sure the soil is moist before treatment to encourage grub feeding near the soil surface. It is not necessary to know which species of beetle grub is present to apply effective control measures at this time. All species of grubs can be treated in April.

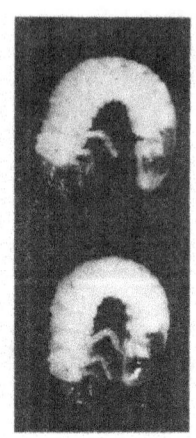

Mature scarab grub, the most destructive stage

Grubs

Scarab larvae chew off grass roots. Seriously grub-damaged turf can easily be pulled because of the lack of roots. In September and October and again in April to early June, the grubs can be found easily and quickly under the loose sod. Grubs are white, wormlike insects with brown heads and three pairs of legs near the head end. They are C shaped and may be from 1/2 to 1 inch long, but are smallest in late summer when still young. Grub injury is most often worst in sunny areas. Symptoms appear as wilted turf occurring after the ground dries out in late spring or early fall. In an area where you suspect grub damage, dig a square foot sample of sod to a depth of 3 inches. Pick

Turf easily lifted as a result of scarab grub feeding

Bluegrass Billbug

Bluegrass billbug adults (weevils) are black, about 5/16 inch long, and have a prominent snout. Billbugs can be seen walking over driveways and sidewalks adjacent to lawns during warm sunny days of early spring and summer. This provides a warning of possible lawn destruction later. If one or two adult weevils are observed within a minute's search, treatment should be applied immediately to kill the adults before further egg laying occurs. Adults feed on the grass stems near the base of the plant, but cause only minor damage. Eggs and larvae are present in the same areas. Destruction of lawns occurs when the larger grubs feed on the crowns of the grass plants and cause weakening and death of large patches of grass during late June into August. The brown-headed, white legless grubs

An adult scarab, the Japanese beetle

Sod webworm moth; stays most weekly seen

are about 1/4 inch long when mature and can be found within an inch or two of the soil surface. The presence of frass, which resembles fine sawdust, around the crowns is characteristic of their activity. Treatments should be made to arrest further lawn damage, although treatment at this time is not so effective as killing the adults.

Chinch Bugs, Sod Webworms, and Cutworms

Chinch bugs, sod webworms, and cutworms feed on the leaves and stems of the grass, not on the roots as do the grubs. They do not occur in the soil but above or on the soil surface. Treatments for these insects may be required even though grub control methods have been used. Applications for these pests must be made to the grass rather than to the soil.

Chinch bugs cause yellowing and subsequent browning of the grass, usually in gradually enlarging patches. Damage is most likely to be seen during June to August. Chinch bugs are active earlier in the year and should be controlled when first seen. Populations build up in thick turf, particularly in bentgrass. Adult chinch bugs are very small, about 1/5 inch long, and black. Young nymphs are red or brown and black, measuring 1/8 inch in length. By examining the grass closely at ground level, you can find the tiny bugs. There are two methods to test for chinch bugs: (1) Select a sunny spot along the border of the yellowed or suspected area of your lawn. Cut out both ends of a large tin can and push one end of the can about 2 inches into the sod. Then fill the can with water nearly to the top. If chinch bugs are present, they will float to the surface of the water in about 5 minutes. (2) Place a 1-foot square piece of white cloth over the suspected area of the lawn and thoroughly flood the sod beneath it. If chinch bugs are present, they will crawl up on the cloth in about 5 minutes. If several are found, treatment is necessary.

Sod webworms, feed on blades, stems, and crowns

Moths of sod webworms may be seen during cloudy days and at dusk of hot summer days. As you walk across the lawn, the moths fly ahead of you a short distance in a zig zag pattern before alighting. They drop their eggs over the lawn during their nightly flights. As eggs hatch, young worms feed on grass blades; but as they grow larger, they feed on blades, stems, and even the crowns of grasses. Worms feed only at night and rest in silk lined tunnels during the day. Small yellow spots of damaged grass coalesce with other spots; eventually, large areas of grass may turn brown and die. Cutworms also feed during the night and cause similar yellow spots, which may coalesce to form large patches of dead grass. If large numbers of webworm moths are seen flying over the lawn during the evening, insecticides should be applied within a week or two at the most. If yellowing of grass occurs and worms and green masses of fecal pellets are found in silken tunnels on the ground or in the thatch, either webworms or cutworms may be present, and treatment should be started immediately.

Ants, Earthworms, and Other Insects

Neither ants nor earthworms are damaging to the grass itself, but may spoil the appearance of a good lawn by the mounds of earth thrown up as they tunnel into the soil. Wasps or hornets also may nest in lawns, especially on lighter or sandy soils. They cause little damage to the grass, but may be objectionable because of the danger of stinging. For specific control methods see *Home Lawns: Grass Varieties and Pest Control Guide*.

Hairy chinch bug adult and nymphs

SPECIAL LAWN PROBLEMS

Improving a Poor Lawn

An old, established lawn that has been neglected for years is sometimes easy to repair. First, control weeds that are competing with the turfgrass for nutrients and water. Refer to the weed section for further details. Second, make sure the pH is in the proper range. Third, fertilize at least three times during the first season. In many cases proper fertilization will dramatically improve the quality of a poor lawn. Fourth, water to avoid drought stress. Fifth, mow at the proper height and frequency. Most older lawns often need no more than these simple, inexpensive steps to provide a beautiful lawn within a few years.

At the other extreme is the lawn that contains only scattered patches of turfgrass with many bare and (or) weed areas. This may have been caused by poor drainage, poor soil, the wrong kind of turfgrass for your site, improper maintenance practices, crabgrass and other weed infestation, insect and disease damage, and other problems.

Renovating a Poor Lawn

If your lawn contains at least 50 percent of desirable turfgrass in a fairly uniform stand, a thorough renovation may save it. However, if more than 50 percent of the lawn contains undesirable turfgrasses or is in weeds, especially weeds like quackgrass, yellow nutsedge, bentgrass, or annual bluegrass, consider starting all over and reestablishing the lawn. Remember you must include a nonselective herbicide treatment to control all undesirable weeds and any remaining turfgrass.

Lawn renovation should *only* be done in late summer to early fall, usually from August 15 to September 1. Plan ahead by taking a soil sample in June and have it tested for pH and nutrient content. The results may help explain the cause(s) of your poor lawn and help eliminate similar problems in the future.

The first step in lawn renovation is to remove undesirable weeds. Annual grassy weeds such as crabgrass and goosegrass will die after the first frost and, therefore, may not be worth controlling. The two types of weeds that need to be controlled are broadleaved and perennial grassy weeds. Refer to the weed control section for further details.

You must wait at least 2 weeks after applying a nonselective herbicide before proceeding any further. This allows the herbicide to totally kill the weeds and also reduces the chance of injuring the turfgrass seedlings. At this time, you can rake the bare areas to remove any debris and loosen the soil. A power dethatching machine can also be used for this purpose.

One of the most important and overlooked steps in lawn renovation is applying enough fertilizer. It is essential to apply 2 pounds of actual nitrogen per 1,000 square feet in establishing a new lawn. Use a complete fertilizer with a ratio of 1:1:1 or similar ratio. Refer to table 4 for the specific amount of fertilizer required. If the soil test results indicated the pH was below 6.0 or above 7.5, apply ground limestone or elemental sulfur at the amount recommended.

Your lawn is now ready for seeding or sodding. If the bare spots are small and evenly distributed throughout the lawn, broadcast the seed over the entire area.

However, if the bare spots are confined to large patches, only seed those areas. The seed must have good contact with the soil to germinate and grow. A slicer seeder machine is well suited for this purpose. Lawns that contain a lot of thatch are difficult to reseed. Therefore, the thatch should be removed before seeding.

If possible, carefully rake the seed into the surface 1/8 inch of soil and lightly roll the entire area to help ensure good seed soil contact. As with any seeding it is important to properly water, mow, and fertilize. Follow the methods outlined in the postplanting section for these operations.

Lawns in the Shade

Shaded lawns are troublesome because of reduced light and competition with trees for water and nutrients. Even the most shade-tolerant grasses never make as good a sod in the shade as grasses growing in the sun.

Sometimes shade alone is the chief difficulty such as on sites near buildings or under deep-rooted, high-branched trees. In many cases good soil preparation plus a shade-tolerant turfgrass mixture makes for an acceptable lawn. It has been found that fine fescues are the best grasses to use if the soil is dry, or rough bluegrasses if the soil is moist. Under trees with about 60 percent shade where some sunlight streams through, several shade-tolerant Kentucky bluegrasses do well. Refer to *Home Lawns: Grass Varieties and Pest Control Guide* (reference 9) for specific varieties.

Under dense, shallow-rooted trees, the turfgrass has a much harder time, because trees cut off the light and rob the soil of water and fertilizer. Of the common trees, Norway maple is the worst offender. In such situations even your best efforts to establish a lawn may fail. Give your new lawn every advantage. This means special care in all details of planting. Fertilize lightly spring and fall and mow at 2 inches or higher. Also do not overwater. In many cases, deep feeding and watering of trees can help improve your lawn.

If your best efforts fail and you still want a lawn, try ryegrass. Use perennial ryegrass at the rate of 6 to 8 pounds per 1,000 square feet instead of the other grasses. Mow it high, water whenever the soil is dry, and fertilize each spring and fall. Whenever dead patches appear, loosen the soil and sow more seed.

If you are unable to grow a lawn, you must look for a lawn substitute or ground covers suitable for your area. If these also fail, consider flagstone, brick, or gravel.

Steep Slopes

Avoid steep slopes whenever possible. They tend to be dry, and lawns are difficult to establish and maintain. If you have a steep slope and decide to use turfgrass, be sure to round off the crest of the slope to avoid scalping.

Whenever possible, sod a steep slope. You avoid the chance of a heavy rainfall washing away all the topsoil. Also, sodding generally ensures that the slope will become established. On very steep slopes, each piece of sod may need to be fastened with a peg and twine. Follow the sodding procedure described previously.

To plant a slope with seed, be careful not to skip any of the important points described for seeding. Pay special attention to seedbed preparation and fertilizing and be sure to plant in early fall. A straw mulch, burlap, or cheesecloth covering is essential during the first few weeks of establishment. Give turf on steep slopes the same care as other lawn areas and remember to fertilize, mow, and water properly.

Ground covers such as crown vetch may be used as substitutes for turf on steep slopes. Consult your local Cooperative Extension agent for assistance in selecting a suitable substitute for turfgrass on steep slopes.

Turfgrasses and Substitutes to Avoid

For lawn use in New York State, avoid the following plants: Mondo, Dichondra, pearlwort, St. Augustinegrass, Bahiagrass, and Bermudagrass.

In midsummer, a good sod of zoysias (*Zoisia japonica* and *Z. matrella*) is superior to that of unirrigated cool season grasses. It is more durable to summer traffic; is more tolerant of low fertility, heat, drought, close cutting, and summer therefore, improve the drainage before you take other measures. In some cases lime may be needed (test the soil), but lime without fertilizer is seldom helpful. Rake off the moss with an iron rake and follow the renovation program suggested earlier. Carry on with routine proper maintenance practices, and the moss problem will gradually disappear.

Several chemicals have been found to control moss, but it is important to correct the cause of the problem. Use these materials at recommended rates (see table 8) when all other methods fail. Under certain circumstances repeat treatment may be necessary.

Moles, Skunks, and Other Animals

Moles raise ridges in the lawn as they burrow through the soil in search of grubs and earthworms to eat. Grubproofing your lawn will decrease mole troubles. If moles persist, try a mole trap.

Skunks may dig holes in your lawn in search of grubs and earthworms. Their activities often indicate the need for grubproofing. Once the grubs are killed, the skunks usually go elsewhere. Refer to the insect section for further details on grub control.

weed invasion; and requires a bit less mowing. These advantages are especially noteworthy in Meyer zoysia, a selection of *Z. japonica*. Accompanying disadvantages are that the zoysias turn straw brown in autumn and remain so until mid to late spring. They are not resistant to traffic or weed invasion when dormant, must be started from plugs or sprigs of sod, and are not tolerant of shady conditions. It takes several years of patience to produce a solid sod of zoysia, which has not been consistently winter-hardy in New York State. In addition, a severe outbreak of chinch bug can totally destroy a zoysia lawn in one season.

Hobbyists may find trial plantings of zoysia interesting. This may be especially true on Long Island or in similar situations where turf is desired and used only in summer. Zoysia is unlikely to satisfy the desire for a troublefree carefree lawn in New York.

Moss

Moss is an indication that growing conditions are not ideal for turfgrass and often occurs under shaded conditions. Moss does not "crowd" the grasses; it merely occupies spaces where grass has not survived. Improving the conditions for the lawn, in many cases, drives out the moss. Sometimes poor drainage is the reason for moss to prevail;

Table 8. Materials and rates used to control moss

Material	Amount/1,000 sq ft
Copper sulfate*	2–3 oz
Superphosphate	2–3 lb
Ferrous sulfate*	1–3 oz

*Mix in 2–3 gal water, then apply.

APPENDIX

Calculations for Home Lawn Practices

You must be able to determine the area of your lawn if proper applications of fertilizer, lime or sulfur, and pesticides are to be made. Follow the given formulas to determine the area of your lawn.

Area of a Square or Rectangle

Area = L × W
L = length
W = width

Area = 60' × 20' = 1,200 square feet

Area of a Circle

Area = ΠR^2
Π = 3.14
R = radius

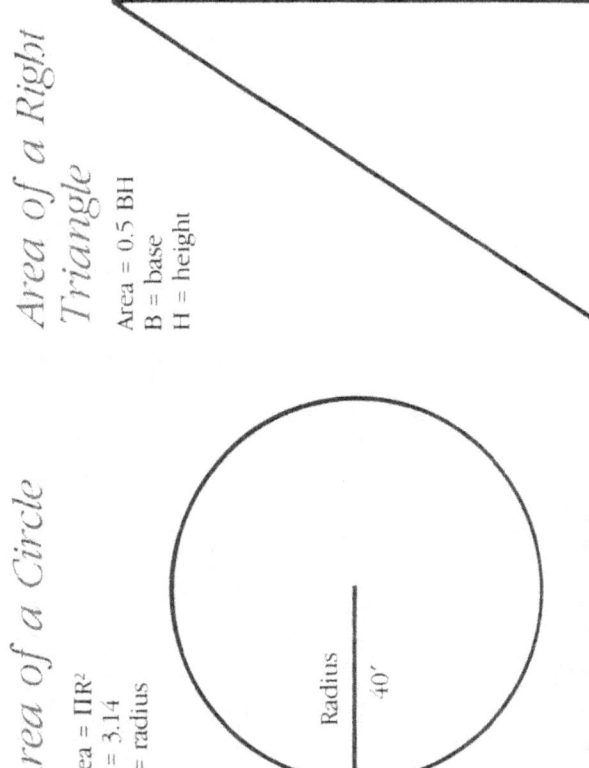

Area = 3.14 × 40' × 40'
Area = 5,024 square feet

Area = $0.8 D^2$
D = diameter

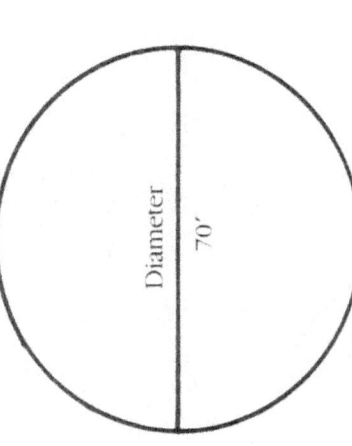

Area = 0.8 × 70' × 70'
Area = 3,920 square feet

Area of a Right Triangle

Area = 0.5 BH
B = base
H = height

Area = 0.5 × 50' × 110'
Area = 2,750 square feet

Area of Irregular Shape

When the lawn area is irregularly shaped, fit the area to standard geometric shapes, determine the area of all components, and add to obtain the total area.

In this example the upper section can be divided into two right triangles and the lower section into two circles. Find the individual areas of 1, 2, 3, and 4; then add all areas to determine the total.

If you know the dimensions of your property, subtract the area of the house, garage, driveway, and plantings to approximate the lawn area.

The amount of fertilizer needed to cover your lawn is determined by the total lawn area and the fertilizer rate and analysis. Review the following example:

Your established lawn is 5,000 square feet; an application of 1 pound of nitrogen per 1,000 square feet is to be applied, and you have selected a fertilizer with the analysis 25-5-10. Refer to table 4 on page 14 to find the amount of fertilizer to apply to provide 1 pound of nitrogen per 1,000 square feet. You will find that 4 pounds of 25-5-10 will be needed to provide 1 pound of nitrogen per 1,000 square feet.

4 lb 25-5-10 × .25 = 1 lb total nitrogen
4 lb 25-5-10 × .05 = 0.2 lb phosphate
4 lb 25-5-10 × .10 = 0.4 lb potash

To cover the entire lawn area of 5,000 square feet, you will need 20 pounds of this particular fertilizer, i.e., 4 pounds/1,000 square feet times 5,000 square feet equals 20 pounds of 25-5-10 for 5,000 square feet.

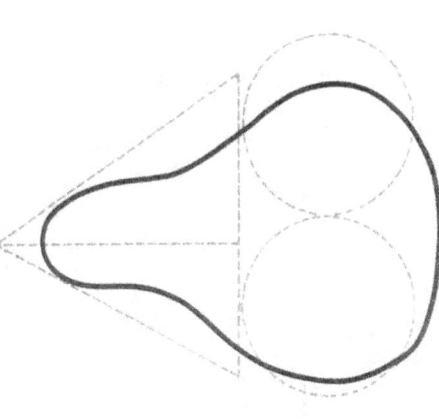

Timing

The best time to sample the soil is before a lawn is established. Proper soil amendments can then be purchased and incorporated into the seedbed before seeding or sodding.

It is advisable to have your soil tested every other year unless there has been a history of soil-related problems. Samples can be taken any time during the year when the soil is not frozen. Always sample the soil at the same time each year so that comparisons can be made. The two preferred times to sample the soil are early spring, so that results can be received well in advance to plan for the upcoming growing season, and fall, to plan for the next year's growing season.

Do not take a soil sample from an area that has had lime or fertilizer applied recently, within 3–4 weeks.

Directions for Sampling Soils

Routine soil sampling is the best way to determine the soil nutrient levels and the pH level. This is the only way to know the proper fertilizer type and rate to apply to maintain a healthy, vigorous lawn.